Memoirs of a Belfast Boy

To Tom

Liam Kelly

Big Liam

Liam Kelly
07849551515

Liam Kelly Publishing, Belfast, County Antrim, North of Ireland.

———

First published 2024 (The Hole Shebang Press)

© Liam Kelly 2024 All rights reserved. The material in this publication is protected by copyright law. Except as may be permitted by law, no part of the material may be reproduced (including by storage in a retrieval system) or transmitted in any form or by any means; adapted rented or lent without the written permission of the copyright owner.

ISBN: 9798321133613

Acknowledgements

Kind acknowledgements are extended by the author to the following people: Pamela Brown, mentor extraordinaire with Prison Arts Foundation (PAF). Fred Caulfield, Executive Director, and the wider PAF support staff including Jason Thompson for his 'global' edits. Kieran Murray, Murray & Co. jewellers, 29 Talbot Street BT1 2LD for his sponsorship and faith in the author. Patrick Devlin for the front cover image. JPW for cover design. Caoimhne McGarry my formidable typist and not forgetting my draft proof team of proofreaders, from the 'Nextdoor' App: Anne Cobbe, Margaret M, Hilary T. Last but by no means least, Denise, my dearly departed wife who is profoundly missed by me and our two wonderful sprogs, Lia-Maire and Chei Kelly.

This book is based on facts, kinda, sorta. Names, characters, businesses, and products are very much alive in the author's imagination and not presented in a fictitious manner. Any resemblance to actual persons, living or dead, or actual events is purely one hundred percent correct, if you know what I mean.

"Say nathin till ya see yer solicitor"—a Belfast Bo

In the Beginning…

It was the early 1970s, and no one was ever guaranteed a full night's sleep. Not where I grew up. One thing was definitely guaranteed, and that was to be woken by the sound of the foghorn honking its message out down at Belfast docks, telling all the dock workers to get up for work. 6am on the dot. Two long toots, and at 6:45am one more long blast, a last-minute call, reminding the dockers that work started at seven. I clearly recall hearing that horn, HONNNK HONNNNK, communicating to all and sundry, dock worker or not, that it was 6am.

I'd rolled over to doze off again, when I heard noises on the hall landing. I tippy-toed out of the bedroom to look, and saw that the bathroom light was on. I pushed the door open, and my oldest brother, John, stood there, fixing his monkey hat. He had a big thick woolly scarf on, and a pair of black woolly gloves tucked under his arm.

'Where ya goin?' I asked.

'Ssshhh. Get back ta bed. An' keep yer fuckin voice down.'

'But where are ya goin?'

He put his finger up to his lips, shushing me, and shook his other fist.

'Fuck up, ya'll waken Ma.'

He grabbed me by the ear, and pulled me downstairs into the living room, where he gently closed the door.

'I'm doin a milk run,' he said.

'With who?'

'With the fuckin milkman, ya dozy cunt,' he gave a wee snigger and shook his head.

'Can I come?' I whispered.

'No fuckin way, you're only eight. An' ya have ta be in secondary school, before the milkman lets ya help him.'

'Come on, come on. I won't get in the way.'

'No way, definitely nat. Ya start school at nine. We wouldn't be back till half-eight, an' if Ma catches us, we're fuckin dead.'

'Look, Ma's gonna be in the livin room, fixin the girls' hair for school, so I can sneak back in. As long as ya keep dick fer me.'

'Fer fuck's sake, come on, ya can carry the crates,' he said.

Although I was 8 and my brother was 13, I was the same size as him, only broader. I had two big rosy red cheeks that Da always said, 'Looked like a well-skelped arse.' Whatever that meant.

'An' wrap up well,' said John, 'cos it's fuckin freezin out there.'

'Yo, it's fuckin freezin in here,' I exhaled a large cloud of vapour from my mouth.

Our house had no central heating, just a two-bar electric fire in the living room, and that was all we had to heat a four-bedroom house.

'Put yer school uniform on nigh, as we're gettin picked up in five minutes at the corner.'

I shot upstairs and got dressed and was back down in no time at all. My brother handed me a jam sandwich.

"Here, get this down yer neck. An' fer fuck's sake, don't bang the door on the way out.'

I was sucking on the last bit of jammy crust when my brother stuck his head in the door, 'Come on, he's here.'

We ran to the corner and jumped into the milk lorry.

'Jesus, it's fuckin freezin, this mornin. An' who's this?' the driver said, as he looked me up and down.

'He's my kid brother, an' he wanted ta give me a hand.'

'No probs,' the driver said. 'We've a runner the day,' he laughed.

I didn't know what a runner was, and tossed it about a bit in my head.

The driver handed John a sheet of paper, which he looked at intensely, and shouted, 'Right, onion head, let's go.'

We got out of the lovely warm cab, which was great, except for the strong diesel smell, and we hopped on to the open back part of the van, with all the milk crates loaded up. My brother was like a machine, swapping over crates and making up orders for people, crate after crate he sorted out, bottles of milk, orange juice and blocks of butter. He stacked them all up, three to four crates high.

'Houl on tight,' John yelled, as he stood up and grabbed hold of the iron bar that ran across the back of the cab.

I jumped up and copied him. The driver took off and the freezing cold air bit into my hands and face. I could hardly keep my eyes open, it was so cold but I felt exhilarated. We came to a stop and my brother and me jumped off the back and lifted three crates, and the driver took off to the next street. John lifted a crate and told me to lift the other two. I tagged along after John, as he clinked away, swapping empties for full ones. Once his crate was full of empties, he took a full crate and gave me the empty one. Before I knew it, we had done the entire street, one end to the other. We got back onto the lorry and took off again, manoeuvring around the burnt-out cars that were used as roadblocks, which were still smouldering from the riot the previous night.

The iron bar I was holding onto froze my hands, numbing them. The icy cold air blew into the backs of my eyeballs so much that they were closed most of the time. We bumped and navigated our way through the narrow streets, and before we knew it, the two hours flew in. The driver pulled up at the bottom of the New Lodge, on North Queen Street.

'Hey, bro,' John shouted at me, as he climbed up into the cab to get his wages, 'grab a couple ah bottles ah orange juice.'

'Brilliant,' I screamed.

Suki milkman orange was a real treat.

I grabbed a couple of bottles and jumped down onto the road. I remember holding firmly onto the bottles, so that I didn't drop them.

Then everything went black.

The next thing I recall is waking up, to the sound of a girl shouting:

'He's awake! Oh my God! He's awake!'

My Granny Kelly came running over and kissed me on the forehead. I looked up at her and saw tears streaming down her face.

'It's a miracle,' she gasped. 'It's a miracle!'

A doctor came flying over to the bedside and started pulling tubes and wires out of me.

'Don't crowd him,' he shouted. 'Step back. Give him some space. Let him breathe.'

A few minutes later a wee woman with a load of curly black hair, two young girls and an older boy came over to the bed.

'Well,' the woman said, 'how are ya feelin?'

I stared up at her with a puzzled look on my face, 'Who are ya?'

'I'm yer mother,' she said.

She reached her hand out and touched mine. I pulled away and put my hand under the bedcovers. The two young girls started crying, and the wee woman comforted them.

The young boy said, 'Bro, do ya know me? I'm yer brother, John.'

I started to cry, and the doctor said, 'Everyone clear the room for now. We have to do more tests.'

Later that day, my Ma and Granny Kelly came into the hospital to see me. Ma explained what had happened: I'd been in a coma for over three months. When I jumped off the milk float, I'd been hit by an oncoming car, which fractured my skull, damaged my ribs and my leg was broken. On top of all that, I badly damaged several of my fingers when I skidded across the road. The medical professionals had to keep me in an induced coma on a life-support machine.

They kept me in the hospital for another three months and I couldn't remember anything before the accident. I'd completely lost my memory, all of my memories, and didn't recognise anyone, except for my Granny Kelly. As far as I was concerned, those strange people who were gawping at me on the day I came out of the coma made me feel unsettled and nervous. Nevertheless, I was sent home with a family that I'd no recollection of in any shape, fashion or form.

Once at home, all day long, people stuck their heads in the door asking: 'D'ya remember me? What about me?'

I was looking frantically at all these strange people who meant nothing to me. And I was home for about a week or so when a man arrived. He was only 5 foot tall, with a thick mop of wavy hair. He ran to me and hugged me.

'Son. My son, I've missed ya so much.'

And the wee woman came in crying. 'This is yer Daddy,' she said, expecting me to recognize him.

'I dunno ya, an' I dunno ya,' I pointed at the man and then the woman, and screamed at them, 'I fuckin dunno anybody here. I wanna go back ta the hospital.'

'Okay, we know ya can't remember anythin, so we'll stop pesterin ya.'

I was soon updated and informed that Da had been interned in 1971, and was due to get out of jail in 1975, with a 4-month spell outside in 1974.

Internment was introduced to the North of Ireland in 1971 by the British government. A person only had to be suspected of being in a paramilitary organisation and they were imprisoned without judge and jury, and held at the authorities' discretion in Long Kesh H-Blocks. Internment was the arrest and imprisonment of anyone considered a member of the IRA (Irish Republican Army). It was brought into legislation by the Stormont Unionist government, determined to break the back of the IRA but the policy backfired, and turned out to be a trigger for one of the largest recruitment drives that the IRA had ever seen.

After the accident, I was slow at speaking and had to concentrate hard at times, before I could say anything. Half my head was shaven, and I had a tube that came out the back of my neck, at the base of my skull, to help drain the fluid away. It was called a 'shunt'. There was a wee balloon inserted that could be inflated or deflated to help with swelling, or something like that, according to the experts. My head was still pretty much swollen from the accident and my brain would swell up, causing my body to go into seizures and fits.

I could hear voices from the kitchen.

'Frankenstein, he looks like Frankenstein.'

My Ma screamed, 'I don't wanna hear that kinda talk in this fuckin house. God forgive me. D'all of yis hear me? My son's home, an' I still can't believe it.'

And I knew she was crying sore.

I was told by the many consultants that I would always have a hairline fracture on my skull, and I would have to be careful in the future not to bang my head.

The house was busy: people coming and going non-stop, with three brothers and three sisters and another sister on the way.

It was a nuthouse, people fighting, doors banging, and a constant stream of nosey fuckers, who wanted to see the freak show. That was me.

One day, my brother Kieran, a year younger than me, thought my head looked like a big fat Easter egg. He hit me on the back of the head with a wooden spoon and shouted, 'Egg head!', thinking it would be funny but as soon as he hit me, I went into a seizure, followed by a fit of shaking.

Ma came running in. 'What happened?' She shouted, while tending to me. 'Well? What happened?'

Everyone just stood there and said nothing.

'Right, that's fuckin it. He's goin up ta live with 'is Aunt Sally in Glengormley.'

Sally was Ma's sister, who was married to an American Air Force pilot she had met during the blitz. His name was Jackie, and they had a daughter, whose name was Jeraldine but everyone called her Jay. They owned an off-licence on the Ballysillan Road and spoke very politely. Compared to the rest of my family, they were very well-to-do. They also had a son who lived in London, so Sally was overjoyed about having a boy live with her again.

There was only a year or so between Jay and me, so we were good company for each other. They lived in a three-bedroom bungalow, which was beautiful. They even had a bidet that I washed my feet in one time, before I took a bath, as no one had told me what it was used for. They had perfect lawns at the front and rear of their house. A driveway *and* a garage. Sally and her family treated me as if I were their own. They bought me whatever I needed, and we became very close. They had a greenhouse, and grew their own tomatoes. I absolutely loved it there.

A year and a half later, Sally told me that her sister, my Ma wanted me home, as Da was getting out of the

Maze prison for good this time. Sally broke her heart over the next few weeks, until it was time for me to leave Glengormley, and return to Belfast.

The day arrived and I was brought back home.

'I don't wanna stay here,' I cried, while hanging on to Sally.

'I'm yer mother, nat Sally. Sally was only takin care ah ya till ya recovered,' Ma said.

'I don't care,' I cried.

'I want ya back home. This is yer home, son, and this is where yu're gonna stay. Yu'll be startin school soon, at the Christian Brothers in Pim Street, where Kieran goes.'

My Granny Kelly came flying in, shouting: 'Is he home yet, is he home yet?' She looked at me and said, 'Oh my God, yu're taller than all ah us, ya big galoot, but yu're still my wee angel.' And she kissed me on the forehead.

I was very embarrassed about getting a big smacker off my Granny in front of everyone.

'If ya need anythin, just call over ta me an' I'll get it sorted. An' I mean anythin.' Granny said.

Granny Kelly, Ma and Aunt Sally went into the kitchen for a cup of tea. I could hear Sally begging and pleading to keep me but my Ma and my Granny Kelly were having none of it.

Lots of people were calling and leaving tins of biscuits and chocolates and stuff. Someone had baked a massive chocolate cake and brought it around to our house. And we were all over it like a rash. We looked like we worked in a coal mine, we were covered in chocolate cream and icing. We had a party every day for a week, and there were still loads of food left.

I felt self-conscious in this environment, where I didn't particularly feel a bond yet with anyone, and not least because I was a good 10 inches taller than Ma. I remember the doctor saying that 8 years of age was the biggest developmental time for learning in the brain but with head trauma, they found that growth was the biggest development and the brain lacked cognitive and learning skills.

In a few days, Da came home from the Kesh, and we had a celebration, loads of people from the neighbourhood kept calling, drinking, singing, and dancing. My Ma was so happy, because her whole family were back together again, and it took a few days for the excitement to die down.

At 5am one morning, me and my siblings were pulled out of bed by our parents. There were loads of people out on the street, shouting and roaring. Some of them rattled metal bin lids on the ground.

The British Army kicked our front door in, and I was quickly at the bottom of the stairs, with my sisters just behind me. Two soldiers had my Da pinned on the ground, one stood with a foot on the back of his neck, and the other had a foot on his lower back. My Ma was pinned to the wall, and got knocked to the ground by a soldier, as he barked, 'Get down! Get down!'

By now, all of us children were downstairs, and I was holding everyone back. When my Ma saw us, she tried to crawl over beside us.

The soldier who had knocked her down shouted, 'Don't fucking move, you Fenian cunt,' and kicked her.

We all started crying and Da let out a yell but he had succumbed to the brute force of the two British soldiers and Ma begging to get over to protect her brood. The scene went into slow motion: the spit coming from the soldier's mouth, as he shouted at my Ma, while my sisters squealed at the top of their voices. This act of pure hatred towards my family felt barbaric to me. I could hear the Peelers outside, laughing during this attack, as if it were funny.

I stared into the eyes of these bully-boy beasts, as they turned a 10½ year-old boy into a monster. Not only did any scrap of remorse and empathy within me die that day, I felt filled with sadness, as if part of me died in front of my new-found family.

Those soldiers were like dogs; when one dog has another by the throat, exhibiting total dominance, while the other dog shows complete submission. That was how the scene looked to me: utterly cruel and unjust. It was as if a white-hot branding iron burned and stamped an image into my mind that will haunt me for eternity.

They arrested Da and took him away and then they pulled our house apart but found nothing. They left our home wrecked, with all the floorboards pulled up, and everything scattered all over the place.

Ma huddled us all into the living room and made a big pot of tea and a whole loaf of toast. We stampeded towards the kitchen, like a herd of wild buffalo, pulling each other back, everyone trying to clamber over everyone else. I had two of my siblings on top of me but there was no way I was going down; one was on my back, the other, around my waist. We were all laughing and shouting, as we got to the kitchen door, and when we saw a tin of biscuits coming out, that gave each of us the final burst of energy to try to get there first. We were like piranhas: plates stripped clean as bones. I had a big fat toasted heel in my hand, and everyone was trying to grab it. It was chaos, total chaos. I dunked the last big fat slice of toast into my tea and slurped it down.

Sixteen hands delved into the biscuit tin and the biscuits were gone in seconds, even the custard creams that nobody liked. A second tin hit the table but Ma dished them out, since the girls got very little from the first tin, because they were a lot smaller than the boys and just not as quick.

We headed back into the living room after the feeding frenzy and started knocking the crap out of each other. An hour or so passed then my Da came in through the door. He had been badly beaten and had black eyes, a busted nose, and was covered in blood. He threw his arms around my Ma, cradling the back of her neck with his hand, and patting her with the other, to console her.

'Kids, up ta bed. I need ta talk ta yer Ma in private.'

We could hardly sleep, as ones were out still rattling their bin lids, while the raids continued. A riot of noise: people blowing whistles and shouting to one another; the heavy whirring noises of the Saracen engines, first roaring, then screeching to a halt; the troops shouting in their thick English accents, as they smashed down doors.

We were all glued to the bedroom windows, watching everything: cars on fire and the flames licking ten feet into the air, casting massive shadows of people that looked twenty foot tall. My eyes and face felt the heat from the glass, as the fires roared outside.

Crack, crack, crack, then some shouting and *crack, crack* again, as people opened fire. The onslaught due to their civil liberties being trampled into the ground. Now men were being pulled out of their houses, they were half-naked and being dragged away by the Peelers, while their wives and children looked on, shocked and helpless.

Da shouted, 'Stay away from the windies an' get down.'

Everyone did what they were told, except me, of course. I was fixated, as I watched everything unfold. One of our neighbours, Dolly Paterson, looked up to the bedroom window and shouted, 'Get down, son, get down.'

Crack, crack, a shot echoed, Dolly ducked down, covered her head with her hands and ran up the street. I could see tracers coming from the high-rise flats, almost like wee laser beams, as someone opened up with a machine gun: a quick burst *dat dat dat* followed by *dat, dat, dat, dat, dat.* This was a ferocious fight, and I don't know how long it went on for, because I woke up in bed the next morning.

Later that morning, I went downstairs for breakfast. Ma and Da were sitting at the kitchen table. My Da told me to sit down and he made me a cup of tea. He grabbed a big crusty bloomer and cut off some big thick slices, buttered them and topped them with cooked ham. He cut some cheese off a huge block that was on a plate that he had taken out of the fridge.

'Are ya okay, son?' He asked and stared directly into my eyes. 'I know that this is an awful lot fer ya ta take in right nigh, but we're yer family, an' we love ya dearly.'

I looked at him and then at Ma and said, 'I know, I'm okay.'

I mauled the crusty sandwich in seconds. I chugged down the big mug of tea, I looked at Ma and Da and they were just staring at me devour my food like a starving animal. The two of them burst out laughing.

'Well, Donna,' my Da said, 'I don't think it's affected 'is appetite.' And the two of them continued laughing.

I stood up. 'Please, may I be excused from the table?'

Ma and Da looked at me puzzled.

'Son, yer nat up in yer Aunt Sally's nigh,' Ma said. 'Ya don't need ta be excused from the table.'

I opened the front door, and it was like scanning a war zone after a long-drawn-out battle. Bricks and broken glass everywhere, cars burnt out, some still on fire, the black carcass of a bus strewn across the road and kids were hitting it with sticks and their hands and faces were as black as the ash that they rolled about in. Then reality hit, and it was like a freight train, and I wanted to go back up to my Aunt Sally's, where there were no old derelict buildings, no army troops kicking in our door, no reek of burnt rubber and bonfires. It was bowling green lawns with flower beds, lovely fresh air rushing off the side of the Cave Hill, picnics in the garden. Instead, I felt trapped in this concrete jungle of hand-me-downs and brutality.

I walked up the New Lodge and saw a large crowd gathered outside the wee nursery school. There was lots of shouting and jeering. I pushed my way through the crowd to see what was going on. A man had been stripped to his waist and tied to the nursery railings.

'Ya dirty bastard!' a woman yelled and poured what looked like hot black paint over him.

The man yelled out in pain. People hurled bricks at him, as they booed and jeered.

'Child abuser,' a woman shouted.

An old woman came towards me, holding a stick, and said 'Bate that monster. If I was twenty years younger, I know what I'd give him. Here, son...' and she pushed the stick into my hand.

I went over and cracked the man over the head with the big heavy stick. The crowd of women cheered, so I cracked him a few more times around the head and torso.

'That's it, kill the bastard,' someone shouted.

By now the man was barely conscious, as I got tore into him, beating him fiercely. The crowd was ecstatic, and you could feel them feed off the cruelty that I inflicted, which put me on a high. There was a young girl, about fifteen years old, who must have been his victim, stood in front of the tarred man. She spat on him, ripped open the pillow, and stuck handfuls of feathers all over the hot tar. I remember feeling nothing for this man, as I beat him. The louder he screamed, the harder I hit. The crowd were on their tiptoes, screaming in victory, as if they had won something.

I went home after that, and we were all sitting eating our dinner. I felt proud of myself, as if I had achieved something. Da came over and patted me on the back.

'Donna, I think he's gonna be okay.' Da said.

Word had gone around like wildfire about the beating that I had given the fella.

'Aye, he's big enough an' ugly enough ta look after himself.' Da spoke as if he were proud of me.

Even though I was only ten years old, I was about five eight in height and built like a brick shithouse.

'Y'know, son, we were worried that ya just wouldn't be able ta adjust ta the madness down here. But ya'll do okay.' Da said.

'I know, Billy,' said Ma, 'but the doctors said he shouldn't get banged on the head, as it could be dangerous.'

'Donna, relax, if anythin is gonna be dangerous, it's him. Look at the size ah him. He's like Man Mountain Dean.'

The next few days were pretty quiet as people licked their wounds from the onslaught of the British Army and Peelers. I was just out taking a walk down Harding Street, where my Da grew up. It was just one street over from where we lived now, life was like that. You lived, loved and died in the same house, in the same street as your parents did. There was no getting out of the madness, hour after hour, day after day.

'Yo.' A man shouted. 'Over here.' He was standing on a pile of rubble. 'Wawawawhat y'at?' he asked.

'I'm just takin a dander,' I said, with a laugh.

'Dadadadadander,' he said.

'What's yer name?' I asked.

'Tatatatommy.'

I burst out laughing. 'Ya sound like a machine gun. So, Tommy Gun's yer new nickname, mate!'

He laughed and said, 'Wawawa.'

'I'm Liam,' I interrupted, and we both laughed. 'How oul are ya?' I asked.

He was only small, about 5 foot 2 and very lean.

'Fafafa.'
'Fifty,' I said.
'Fafafafa.'
'Forty,' I said.
By now, he was stamping his feet in anger.
'Fafatafifteen,' he said.
We were in stitches laughing.
'Wawawawa.'
I interrupted again, 'Ten.'
'Fuck yu're a big un. I'm gonna call ya bababa…'
'Ba-ba-black sheep,' I said.
'Nananah, Big L, cause ya look like ya could carry half-a-stone ah spuds in yer cacacap.'

He banged himself on the back of the head to spit out the words.

'Two broken souls, we are,' I said, smiling.

We ended up back at his house, round the Barrick, which was part of the New Lodge housing estate. Two more of his friends called and we got introduced. They passed around bottles of cider and started sniffing glue. They offered me some and showed me what to do.

'Oh, here's a bag. They're nice an' rustly,' one of the guys said.

I got stuck in, after a big swig of *Olde English* Cider. Hours passed, as I had no track of time when tripping. It was dark when I left, and I walked into a full-scale riot.

I got showered by a hail of bricks. I dove into a hallway for cover: petrol bombs were raining down and people were shouting, 'Murderin bastards,' as the police with their riot shields advanced about 10 feet or so away from me.

I managed to get behind the angry mob, who were running about gathering up bricks, bottles, rubble, anything that could be used as a weapon.

Crack, crack, someone opened up with a firearm and everyone hit the deck, and crawled about for a minute or so, and then we all jumped straight back up again.

Someone handed me a petrol bomb. I ran right up to the police line and hurled it over the riot shields. *Boomph boomph,* as they fired at me. The crowd cheered and shouted, 'Burn the bastards!'

I took another petrol bomb and charged the line, hurling it over the shields again. The crowd went ballistic, as I ran back, evading the bullets.

I was still high as a kite and felt no sense of fear whatsoever, not to mention the danger of getting shot.

The crowd then charged the police line, and they backed off eventually.

About an hour or so later, when the effects of the glue wore off, I decided to head home.

I saw a bit of commotion at the back of Alexander Flats, a 12-storey high-rise. The bin yard was enclosed and serviced the bin-chutes from each floor. The bins were 8 feet high and about 6 foot wide. The closed bin yard had become a pop-up petrol bomb factory. Let's be honest, we invented the pop-up industry. I saw men go in and someone stood outside, to keep watch. As I passed, he started talking to me, saying, 'Yu're the fucker who bate yer man at the nursery.'

'Aye, that was me.' I said, smugly.

He gave a wee whistle and one of the large doors opened. A hand beckoned me in. Another man had laid six crates of empty milk bottles out in a row. Someone else went along with a bag of sugar and a funnel, pouring about half-an-inch into each one.

'What's the sugar fer?' I asked.

'Once it melts, the petrol sticks ta yer skin, so it's harder ta put out and hurts like fuck,' the man said.

Another man was going along, with a wider funnel, three-quarter filling the bottles with petrol.

The man mentioned something that had happened earlier that day and he said we would have a 9pm rendezvous the following night. I went home feeling exhausted and strung out from the glue come-down.

BANG Goes the Fire

I eventually drifted off to sleep, and morning came soon enough. I charged downstairs to get my breakfast.

'Fer fuck's sake son, go easy, Da said. 'Yer Ma's still asleep. Ya sounded like a herd ah fuckin elephants comin down there.'

He made the tea, lifted the pot from the stove, and poured me a mug. He gave me four slices of Belfast bap, four slices of bacon and two sausages. He then fried an egg and flipped it over in the pan.

'Eggs over easy comin up,' he said.

Da put the eggs on to my bap. The butter was rock hard, as it was freezing cold in the kitchen, so I sliced it like cheese and put it onto the bap and transferred the egg and bacon on top to soften the butter. A few blobs of HP sauce and it was good to go. I was nearly licking the butter off my elbows, as it oozed out everywhere. I ate the food and sipped my tea, thinking about the sausage sandwich to come.

'Watch em wee pink things. Ya don't wanna bite em, cos they're yer fingers,' Da joked. 'I'm goin down ta Rab Maguire's in a wee while fer a haircut. Ya can come along, as ya look as though yu've escaped from an asylum.'

'Okay, Da. No bother.'

'In fact, we'll go nigh,' Da said. 'So, we can get back, before the rest ah the tribe get up.'

So, we dandered the fifteen-minute walk to Castle Street, and went into Rab's barber shop.

'Well, Scalper, how are ya?' Rab asked.

'Aye, I'm doin well.'

'An' what about the good lady? How's she?' Rab asked.

'Aye, she's well an' all.'

'Good, good. What can we do ya fer the day?'

'The usual fer me, an' a short back an' sandpaper fer him, or just do whatever ya can ta make him look even a wee bit normal.'

'An' who's this, Scalper?'

'That's my son, Liam.'

'Well, it's nice ta meet ya. I'm Rab. An' how oul are ya?'

'Ten,' I said,

'What did ya say?'

'I said, I'm ten.'

Rab looked up at me, and then over at my Da and turned back to me again.

'What the fuck are ya feedin him?'

'Oh, the usual,' Da said. 'Only, we feed him with a shovel. Or is it a catapult? I can't remember, but I've already lost a finger.'

He lifted his hand up and bent his finger down, as though it were missing.

The two of them laughed.

'Here, Scalper, what's the name ah the boy I shaved, an' he gurned that much yu'd ta take him next door an' buy him a bike.' Rab said.

'Martin. Twenty-five quid that cost me. It was the dearest haircut in history.'

'Here, Scalper, Geordie Best wouldn't pay that much fer an oul haircut. I tell that story ta all my customers. It always gets a good laugh goin.'

Going into Rab's was an experience you enjoyed, lots of banter, great craic, and he knew everybody, especially all the old hands, who had been about forever. He was very well-respected in both north and west Belfast.

'How many kids d'ya have nigh?' Rab asked Da.

'Eight.'

'Jesus, Scalper, have ya nat gat a TV!'

'Aye, we do, but we never get a chance ta watch it, cos ah all the kids.'

The two of them laughed.

'Here, Scalper, did y'ever see that wee fucker ya 'it with that hatchet?'

'Nah, nah, definitely nat. Never saw him again. Funny that, isn't it? Neither has anyone else.'

As their eyes met, they burst out laughing.

'Aye,' Da said, 'yu're a barrel ah laughs. Sure, yu'd be quare craic at a wake.'

Rab looked at me. 'That's why yer Da's called Scalper, as he's a force ta be reckoned with, I kid ya nat. Hey, whaddya think ah that? Rab asked me.

'I'm sayin fuck all, till I see my solicitor,' I blurted out.

The entire barber shop roared laughing.

'Scalper, he's definitely one ah yurs. A chip aff the oul block, I see.'

'Okay, calm down,' Da said to Rab, 'an' go easy with them there scissors. We don't want any accidents. An' watch my fuckin ears, as y'already have a bucket fulla em out the back, that ya bring home fer the dogs.' He sniggered to himself.

Rab looked over at me, 'Jesus, Scalper he's like a big fuckin navvy. Here, son, have ya laid many railway tracks lately?'

'What's a navvy?' I asked.

'They were immigrants, who built America in the early nineteen-hundreds, an' they were the size ah barn doors.'

I sat looking at all the boxing memorabilia that was plastered over the walls: Rinty Monaghan, Cassius Clay, Sugar Ray, Frazier, Foreman, Bugner and Marvellous Marvin Haggler. The walls were covered with posters and pennants everywhere. There wasn't space to stick a postage stamp on the wall, without it overlapping onto something. It looked like an old barber shop that had been there for a lifetime, with its bright red cracked leather barber chairs, which looked tired. They creaked, as Rab pumped on the pedal to raise them, as required.

'Right, Scalper, that's ya done,' Rab took the protective apron off his shoulder and brushed the hairs off the back of Da's neck.

Da looked in the mirror at his new haircut and got out of the chair.

'Aye, Scalper, yer an oil paintin. Right, son, come on,' Rab beckoned me to sit down. 'Oh, I see I don't have ta readjust the chair. Just remember, son, if ya break it, ya own it.'

Everyone laughed.

The chair creaked really loudly as I sat down, and Rab began to shave my hair off. He had the shears to the side of my head and when I looked at him in the mirror I noticed that the tears were running down his face. Unbeknownst to me Da had said to Rab, 'do you know when you blow up a ballon, and you pinch the bottom of it, and you hear that high pitch screech, well, he hears that in his head twenty-four seven…'

'Isn't that right son,' Da shouted to me.

I nodded in agreement, 'aye, Da.' because I couldn't hear over the buzzing noise coming from the shears.

Every time a jibe could be made, it was made, and when I asked why my parents would say that it was to harden me to the outside world.

'Right, Scalper, that's thirty bob. The two ah yis are good ta go,' he said, about ten minutes later.

Da paid his dues. 'Right, bumpy nut, let's go.'

He handed me my coat.

'Thanks, Rab,' Da said and waved, as we left the barber's.

'O'Hara's first an' then home,' he said to me.

We walked into the bakery and the girl spoke immediately, 'Hello, Billy, what can I get ya the day?'

My Da looked around, 'Six coconut fingers, a big yella scone an' a fresh cream custard flan. Whaddya want son?'

I ran my eyes up and down the counter.

'Please, may I have a snowball?' I said excitedly,

'Sorry,' Da said, 'he thinks he's Lord Muck.'

The girl giggled and handed me a snowball which I sank my teeth into immediately. My Da looked at me and shook his head in disbelief as I got stuck in.

'Ta hell with poverty,' my Da said. 'Stick a Paris bun in a bag an' all. Donna loves em buttered with a wee cuppa tea. An' would ya give us one ah the German biscuits an' a cream caramel? That's fer me.'

Talk about feeling special, Da buying me a snowball! He was penny-wise and I was floating on cloud nine. We arrived back home to a hive of hungry people, and they were buzzing about like flies, as if they'd never seen food before. They were clambering over each other, trying to get into the kitchen to see what delights there were.

'Stap!' Da shouted. 'Everyone, inta the livin room.'

By the looks on their faces, as they dragged their feet into the living room, it was as if someone had died.

'Just lemme get everything sorted first,' said Da.

He made everyone tea and sliced the scone and buttered it. He opened the hatch between the kitchen and living room. It was a wee two-door serving hatch above the table that allowed food to be passed from the table into the living room. When the hatch flew open, there was a clambering of feet to get to the food first. It was like feeding time at the zoo. The girls were small, so they could snatch and grab from the serving hatch. We boys clustered around the table and shoved each other, to get the best pick of the crop, as we munched, snatched and grabbed what we could to have our fill. Soon, we were all fed and watered and were told to go out and play.

'Cos I'm gonna make yer Ma a nice wee cuppa tea, an' give her breakfast in bed,' said Da. 'Nigh don't be slammin the door on the way out.'

BANG. The door slammed, as we raced and charged out, as though there were a fire.

After half-an-hour, me and my brother, Kieran, went back inside.

'I'm goin ta work soon,' Ma said, 'So you two can watch the house, an' no fuckin about. Are yis even listenin?'

'Aye, Ma, I am,' said Kieran.

Ma worked as a school dinner lady in the Star of the Sea primary school. Monday through to Friday, she would leave the house at 11am and return at 2pm.

Since I had returned home from my Aunt Sally's, it was my brother Kieran's job to look after me, until Ma got home, even though he was just nine years old, a year younger than me. Until I found my bearings, of course.

So, something happened on this particular day in question, something that we both deny and claim was the other's idea, even now, forty years later.

The idea was to heat a thick sewing needle up on the electric fire. First, I took a needle out of the pack I found in the kitchen drawer. I then went into the garden shed and found an old pair of rusty pliers.

'Yes!' I screamed. 'These'll do nicely.'

I ran into the living room, stuttering with excitement.

'Kieran! Kieran!' I yelled.

'Calm down, bro, calm down,' Kieran said and waved his hands, to usher me onto a seat. 'Ma left me in charge, so yu've ta do what I tell ya.'

'Nah, I'm the oldest, so *I'm* in charge,' I shouted back.

'Okay, okay,' he said, 'we're both in charge, how does that sound?'

'Aye, that sounds better,' I said. 'So, we're both mindin the house, then.'

'Okay, Liam, you can be in charge ah the house, an' I can be in charge ah you, an' that way, we can both be in charge.'

We turned on the electric fire, as it was cold, and we stared mesmerised at the electric bar burning so bright and hot you could barely look at it without squinting. I pulled the pliers and the needle out of my pocket and knelt down in front of the fire. Kieran hunched over, leaning on my shoulder.

'What're ya doin? What're ya doin?'

'Jesus, bro, will ya give us some room?' I shrugged him off. 'Just stand behind me.'

'I wanna see, I wanna see.'

'Fer fuck's sake, will ya calm yer knickers?'

My eyes were fixated on the super bright glowing bar. I raised my hand over my eyes, as the heat was so intense.

'What're ya gonna do? What're ya gonna do?' Kieran blurted out excitedly.

'I'm gonna heat this here needle up, till it's the same colour as the fire.' I turned to look at him, raised my eyebrows and smiled.

'No fuckin way,' he said.

'Relax, I know what I'm doin.'

And I showed Kieran the rusty old pliers. I'd no sooner said this when the needle touched the red-hot electric bar.

BANG. The electricity shot through me like a bolt of lightning. Not only was I blinded by the bluey-white flash but Kieran and I were both catapulted back about eight feet, hitting the wall just above the sofa and knocking Ma's favourite picture off the wall and smashing the glass.

'Holy fuck, bro,' I said, shaking, while Kieran yelped like a pup.

'Ma's gonna kill us.'

'Us?' I said. 'Sure, Ma put you in charge.'

'Okay, okay. I won't tell, if ya don't tell.'

The picture was a print of a beautiful Asian woman with an emerald tunic, gold buttons and a pink satin scarf. We took the picture frame out to the bin and carefully picked out all the shards of glass, without damaging the picture. We scrutinized the picture as it leaned against the back door and the light came in, highlighting all the gold paint.

'Nat a mark, phew,' I said and wiped imaginary sweat off my forehead.

Kieran already had his head in a cupboard under the kitchen sink. He was looking for Ma's cleaning basket. He pulled out a soft polishing cloth and dusted over the picture.

'Houl on, houl on,' I said.

I reached into the cupboard and pulled out a can of *Mr.* Sheen furniture polish. I sprayed the picture and frame. Kieran then buffed with the dusting cloth.

'Jesus fuckin Christ,' the two of us said, at exactly the same time, 'it looks as if the glass is still there.' And we burst out laughing.

We carefully carried the prized picture back into the living room and hung it above the sofa. We then turned to check the electric fire and could both see that the needle had gone right through the heating bars and was sticking out the other end.

'Right, Kieran, you switch it aff at the plug an' I'll pull it out with the pliers.'

'What?' Kieran screamed. 'Are ya fuckin mad? Yu'll blow yerself up again.'

'Nah, turn it aff at the plug an' I'll take it out with the pliers.'

As I did so, the bar snapped, as if it were made of glass but the needle came out okay.

'Da's gonna murder us,' Kieran squeaked nervously.

'In the name ah good fuck, be quiet. We'll just put on our coats an' climb over the back wall. We won't come home, till way later on, when everybody's in. Then we'll just deny everythin. Ma'll be home soon, so she'll probably just go straight ta bed, cos her and Da start work the night at seven o'clock in the Felons, so she'll be busted.'

No beatings and no punishments and we lived to fight another day, as Da would say and the broken bar on the heater was never mentioned.

It is worth noting that ten years passed and Denise, now my wife, and I were down in Ma's for Christmas dinner, when Ma looked up at her favourite picture.

'Is there glass in that, or what?' Ma said.

Kieran and I burst out laughing and Denise shook her head, because I had already told her the story about what we had done, years previous.

'Yis two dirty fuckin hallions!' Ma yelled.

'Shut up, Ma an' give us a hug,' I said and threw my arms around her.

'Jesus, son, get aff me. Yu're like a big fuckin bear.'

Ma, Am I a Giant?

There was always an urgency about everything with me: first to get fed, first to get out, as if it meant something, like winning a game.

One Saturday afternoon, the girls had their skipping ropes out, with one tied round a lamppost, to create a swing. Their four wee dolls had been sat in an old pram, to get the best view of proceedings, all crammed in together.

We boys had our football, marbles and "chasies" and we were all quite content with ourselves, as we beat the crap out of each other, arguing over goals, or one thing or another, but as soon as Ma's arse hit her chair, we were like flies around shite.

'Mammy, Mammy, Mammy,' all looking for some kind of acknowledgement or affection.

'Right,' Ma spoke to my sisters. 'Girls, get on the sofa. There's a Doris Day film startin soon, it's *By the Light of the Silvery Moon*.'

The girls all screamed, and sat comfortably on the sofa, fluffing up the pillows and loving life.

'Nat that oul shite,' the boys all said together.

'But after that, there's a James Cagney film on, called *Angels with Dirty Faces*. It's nat on till after three, so here's 50p between yis for Thompson's shop, but don't go any further than that an' I'll call yis when it's ready ta start.'

We went to Maggie Doc's instead, as all her sweets were in big glass jars, and there were millions of them. We had to cross a road to get there but it was well worth it. We got 50p worth of Midget Gems: a big white bag, full to the neck, to share between us.

We ran back home and sat outside our front door and split them into four piles, which we shoved into our pockets.

We watched the Peelers drag two men out of Artillery Flats. They screamed, as they were beaten with batons and dragged around by the hair.

Our sweets were now safe, so we went down to get a closer look. A large crowd had gathered at Artillery House, which was one of the few high-rises that didn't have an army post on top of it and had sixteen floors, four more than all the rest.

A woman, Sarah Webb, pushed us into a shop, as the crowd swelled.

'Go out the back door, up the steps an' straight home, an' tell yer Da what's happenin.'

Mr Thompson, the shop owner, handed us all a 10p mix-up and pointed to the back door. We ran out and up the steps and straight home.

'Da, Da,' we shouted, and Ma came out.

'There's somethin happenin at Artillery Flats.'

'Okay, okay, he knows. He's away ta a meetin already, if anyone asks.'

The tension was building all day and eventually erupted around seven that evening. We were ushered upstairs.

'Stay away from the windies, okay?' Ma shouted.

At 8:30pm I sneaked downstairs. I could hear Ma and Da talking in the living room. I peeked through a tiny opening in the door and saw my Da sitting with all the usual suspects that he knocked about with. They were all talking softly but I could still recognise their voices.

I quickly and quietly opened the back door then closed it quietly behind me. I climbed over the back wall and ran up to the grotto. I knelt down, letting on to pray in front of the shrine, while watching the bin-chutes. As soon as the big bin chute doors opened, I ran down. The Peelers had scooped Fat Dennis and Seany Rice earlier.

'So, we're gonna have ta move some stuff about,' said the quartermaster. 'We need ta create a diversion, so we're gonna have ta concentrate on the top ah the New Lodge fer a few hours. So, we'll have ta move all these petrol bombs up through the hole in the wall and up Dawson Street. There's an entry up there that we can use.'

As we opened the bin-chute doors, a crowd had gathered at the grotto, ostensibly praying. One by one, they all came down and lifted a crate of petrol bombs and then started running.

'Ya can't see what's in front ah ya, when yu're liftin em,' I said, 'so, if three ah yis lift two crates and run side-by-side, at least yu'll be able ta see what's exactly in front ah yis.'

I was worried about the kerbs and the bricks and the rubble. I could see that the quartermaster was well impressed, as he put the plan into action; and, before long, the cargo was shifted.

We all stood in the entry; crates piled everywhere. One man just walked out onto the Antrim Road, pulled out a gun from underneath his jacket, and stopped a double-decker bus. He told everyone to get off, driver and all. The man manoeuvred the bus to block both sides of the Antrim Road and we smashed the windows and lobbed about a dozen petrol bombs into it. It was soon ablaze and soon after the Peelers arrived, riot shields at the ready.

Two six-wheelers trundled up to the bus and tried to push it to the side, to clear the road. We lit them up with a crate of petrol bombs. You could smell the burning rubber everywhere. About two hundred rioters had gathered and they hurled bricks and petrol bombs and whatever they could find at the police line. Everyone shouted and cheered, as they went to war. It was ferocious and fierce and carried on, until about twelve or one in the morning, before dying out like the flames of the bus, which was now only smouldering.

I don't know the ins and outs about the two men the police had arrested that day, or what they had been moving but I had a fair idea. The two men were committee members of The Felons and that was likely the reason why Da had been at the meeting earlier.

I arrived home and climbed over the back wall, in the hope of sneaking back in again. But Ma stood at the back door.

'Where ta fuck have ya bin? Ya look like JJ McKenna.' (He was the local singing coal man). 'Did I nat tell ya ta stay upstairs? Look, look, look at the state ah ya: yer face is pitch black.'

'I rubbed ashes on it, so the Peelers wouldn't see me.'

'See you, see you. Look at the fuckin size of ya. Ya could see ya from the fuckin moon.' She yelled, crying as she went. 'Yu've changed, yu've fuckin changed. See since that accident, yer whole personality has changed. I dunno what I'm gonna do with ya. I can't put my finger on it. Ya don't listen, ya don't do what yu're told, yu've no respect,' and she sobbed into her hands. 'Get up em fuckin stairs, an' get inta that fuckin bath, an' try an' wash some of that badness outta ya.'

I walked up the stairs and I could hear her crying her heart out in the kitchen. I slowly and sadly dragged my feet up the rest of stairs and got in the bath and gave myself a good scrub and went to bed.

The following evening, I called for Tommy Gun, and we went around to the garages. There were four garages that were disused and abandoned and had a few burnt-out cars in them. We climbed up onto the roof of a car and then manoeuvred onto the garage roof and jumped over onto the old graveyard wall. There was a three-foot gap between the garage wall and the graveyard wall, and in this gap was barbed wire, loads of it, you could see the odd shoe, where someone had fallen in. and their laces got caught on the barbed wire and God only knows what they were like, never mind their shoes.

We dropped down the graveyard wall and onto the grass. There were already three or four fellas there, drinking and sniffing glue. One of the guys handed me a bottle.

'Here, take a slug,' the guy said.

I took the bottle from him and took a long swig.

'Woooow,' I said as it burned my throat, and everyone laughed.

'That's Scotch Mac, so it is.'

'Scotch Mac? What's that?'

'It's whiskey an' wine an' it kinda grows on ya.'

'Here ya go,' he said and handed me a bag.

'These are the best bags, they're nice and rustly,' he said, as he held it open and poured in a big dollop of *Evo Stick*.

'C'mere an' watch me,' he said, and he showed me what to do.

I took a few sniffs and instantly got a buzz.

'Whooa,' I said, 'that's madness in a bag.'

'Aye, we take it ta kill the pain,' he said and lifted his shirt to show me the bruises all over his torso. 'The fuckin Peelers gat me the other night an' kicked the bollocks clean outta me.' He then dropped his bags, and his legs were just as bad. 'Dirty rotten bastards,' he said, and carried on sniffing. He stopped a few minutes later and introduced himself, 'Hello, I'm Muchacho,' he slurred out.

'Muchacho? Ya sound like a Mexican.'

'Fuck, ya should see my brother, Chico, he's got a big handlebar moustache an' all.'

Muchacho had tanned skin and dark greasy hair and looked as though he had just walked off a movie set. A western movie, that is.

Two or three hours seemed to pass in the blink of an eye, and I headed home. For a few weeks, I went to the graveyard every night, and we had to dig out one of the crypts so we could sniff our glue out of the rain, and sometimes even light a fire to keep warm.

September soon approached and it was time for me to start school. Even though I was ten years of age, I had to start off in primary one, as I couldn't even do simple sums. My brother, Kieran, who was a year younger than me, was in primary six but I was confined to the kiddies playground, even though I was as tall as my teacher. When lunchtime came, Kieran and I headed home, as it was only a few minutes away. We had boiled eggs, mashed up in a cup, with loads of butter and salt on them. He had two eggs and I had six, which had to be put into two cups. There were two Belfast baps sliced and heavily buttered on a plate and we got stuck in. We had two big mugs of tea, set down in front of us and we dunked the heels of the baps into them, and we were done in no time at all.

We all went into the living room to watch *Champion the Wonder Horse*.

Ma came in with a coconut finger for each of us, which we quickly snatched out of her hands.

'Ma, can I ask ya somethin?' I asked.

'Aye, son, go ahead.'

'Ma, am I a giant?'

My brother Kieran nearly choked.

Ma looked at me in disbelief, 'What did ya say, son?

'Am I a giant Ma? Cos I can barely fit inta the wee *toddie* chairs in school an' my knees go up over the table.'

Ma nearly wet herself laughing.

'No son,' she said, 'yu're just big boned.'

'Big boned,' Kieran screamed, as he rolled about the sofa laughing. 'That's a cracker! Am I a giant?'

'Fuck up,' I yelled, 'or I'll wring yer scrawny wee neck.'

'Now, now,' Ma scolded, 'behave, you two, an' scoot back ta school. An', son, if anyone asks if yu're a giant, ya just tell em yer big boned.'

My brother and I ran back to school, mainly me chasing him, as he was teasing me, because of what I'd just asked Ma. I swung my fists furiously at him but he just ducked and dived out of the way. We reached the school and went our separate ways.

I went into the classroom and sat down. Everyone was chatting and messing about, waiting for the teacher.

One boy spoke to me, asking, 'Are ya a giant?'

He laughed, and I jumped up and grabbed him by the throat and pushed him against the blackboard. I lifted him up with one hand, shaking him like a rag doll.

'Nah, I'm nat a giant, I'm just big boned,' I shouted.

The teacher came in at that very moment.

'Put him down,' she said loudly.

I let go, and the boy fell onto the floor. He was crying. The teacher went over to him and stood him up.

'There, there,' she said, 'sure, you're okay, you're okay.'

The boy stopped crying and the teacher gave him the once over, just to make sure he was okay.

'Put your two hands above your head, and touch your nose with your left hand. Now watch my finger, follow it with your eyes. What's this all about?' she scolded me.

I told her what he had said, and then what Ma had told me, and the teacher addressed the class.

'Liam is different from all of you. He's a special case, and I don't want to hear any more silly talk about giants or monsters. Is that clear, everyone?'

'Yes, Miss,' the class said.

'Now, sit up straight, because I'm going to read you all a story.'

And that was that until the next time and this name-calling would go on for years.

Later that evening, I was out rioting and throwing petrol bombs and bricks at the Peelers and running amok. I thought about the wee boy that I'd grabbed by the scruff and shook like a rag doll, and it didn't bother me in the slightest, because if he said it again, I would probably have done same thing.

What a wee cheeky fucker, I thought to myself.

October came in like an icy breeze, as did Halloween and I'd just bought my first box of black cat bangers. They were powerful and sounded like gunfire, so, obviously the army and the Peelers got tortured, as relentless waves of kids threw them at the security forces, laughing.

Two arms out wide and spluttering like a Spitfire, we sought out and fired at the enemy bombardment after bombardment, as Tommy G would say, until it was dinner time, and we all flew back to base.

'Alpha, Charlie, Foxtrot,' we cackled to each other, 'next mission at nineteen-hundred hours, over.'

'That's a Roger, squadron leader, over and out.'

It was a Sunday morning and Kieran and I were to go to mass. Da always went to 10 o'clock mass with all his friends, or sidekicks. So, we decided not to go to the 11 o'clock service. But we would always walk past and pick up any service pamphlets, in case Da would ask us any questions. It was absolutely freezing cold, and we went down to Thompson's Shop for two 10p mix-ups and a penny book of matches. We walked up to the back of the pensioners maisonettes that ran parallel to the streets where we lived.

There was a big lead bin filled with newspapers and rubbish, which I set alight. Soon after that, another bin caught fire, then another, and another. Kieran and I stood with our hands held out, all nice and toasty and rubbing our faces with our hands from the heat of the fire. Suddenly, the entire bin-chute went up in flames. I could see the panic on Kieran's face.

'Jesus, fuck,' he said, 'We're gonna get killed again.'

Flames and black smoke came billowing out of the back of the building. And we could hear someone shouting, 'Fire! Fire!'

Kieran squealed, 'We're gonna be swingin from a rope fer this.'

'Aye, but they have ta catch us first,' I snapped back and started running.

Kieran followed quickly behind me, squealing.

We could hear the ambulances but we saw a couple of big red fire engines, flying down North Queen Street towards the fire. I burst out laughing, probably with nerves; I don't know, actually.

Da and my brother John caught up with us at Collin's fruit shop on North Queen Street and we were dragged home by the scruff, kicking and squealing like two wounded pigs. Da told us to go up to our bedroom and said he would be up in five minutes.

We watched from the bathroom window, as all the old dolls and old boys were being stretchered into the back of the ambulances. Tubes appeared to be sticking out from them, everywhere. We quickly put on an extra pair of jeans, extra t-shirts and pullovers, trying to cushion our bodies from whatever was going to be used to beat us with. Da came bursting in the door.

'What the fuck am I supposed ta do with yis two dickheads? I just pray ta God nobody fuckin dies.'

I could see tears of pain on Da's face, as he looked almost bewildered or shocked at what we had just done. Da put his hand into his cardigan pocket, and pulled out a leather dog lead, with a chain on the end of it. He whipped us to within an inch of our lives, and I'm sure the squeals were deafening for miles. I managed to grab Kieran by his coat collar with one hand and slip my other hand into the loop of his jeans, and I backed up into the corner of the bed. Da whipped us for twenty minutes or so, but I used my brother Kieran as a human shield, as I swung him about like a rag doll. By the time Da was finished, Kieran was like a zebra and had lash marks from head to toe and I had barely a scratch. Da left the room and I laughed, as I checked my body for lash marks. I glanced over at Kieran, who was now down to his trunks.

'Holy Fuck,' I said.

You couldn't count the number of thick chain-shaped raised foot-long lashes that were over his body. Tears were streaming down his face, and I went into the bathroom to get a flannel and soaked it in cold water. I gave it to him to try and ease the pain but he smacked me up the face with it.

'Bastard, bastard, fuckin bastard,' he shouted, sobbing uncontrollably. The tears were dripping off his chin.

Da shouted up the stairs, 'Youse two fuckin numbskulls better nat leave this house, till I decide what I'm gonna do with yis.'

Eggshells, I mean we walked on fucking eggshells, for a fortnight, because otherwise Kieran and I knew we were dead meat. My brother and I still argue to this day, forty years later, about what happened but we laugh about it now.

Run, Darby, Run

I got into school earlier than usual the following day and no one was in class yet. There were kids in the playground, hanging onto the backs of each other's jumpers, and having chariot races, acting out the famous *Ben Hur* scene, where he destroys everything.

I went into the classroom and lifted a bottle of milk out of the crate that was in the corner. You know the wee bottles I'm talking about? I drank the milk and set the empty milk bottle on the teacher's desk. I lit a banger and stuck it inside the bottle.

BANG!

Smoke and glass everywhere and I ran out and into the playground, laughing, as I nearly shat myself, because of how loud it had been, in our wee small classroom. As the noise had reverberated off the massive windows, they actually shook.

I'd stolen a few boxes of drawing pins and some play putty (*Plasticine*) from the classroom and went to work in the graveyard later that night. The graveyard was one of the few places that I actually felt safe. I poked a big blob of putty into a bottle and poured in some of the drawing pins. I then opened a banger, by tearing the paper at the top. Being careful not to damage the fuse, I emptied the contents of the banger into the bottle, poked in some more putty and the rest of the drawing pins, some more putty, and then stuck a banger into that, after I'd attached the other fuse to it. I set it on a flattish branch of a tree that had grown up out of a grave over the years.

'Anyone here?' Tommy G shouted, as he dropped down the graveyard wall.

'Aye, over here,' I shouted excitedly. 'Yu're just in time.'

'In time fer what?' He asked.

I pointed to my contraption, which sat ominously on the tree branch. I went over and lit the fuse and hid behind a headstone.

'Fer fuck's sake, Tommy, duck, ya stupid cunt.'

Tommy dove behind me. 'Whawhawhat is it?'

He had no sooner spoken than BANG! it went off. The deafening noise was immense, as it echoed and bounced off the graveyard walls.

'Wawawawat Da fuck was that there?' he shouted.

We stood up and waited for the smoke to clear, as we fanned the smoke with our hands. The tree branch was all scorched and there were wee pieces of metal stuck everywhere.

'Holy fuck,' Tommy said, 'that sounded like a real bomb.' He rubbed his eyes, nearly blinded by the blue flash. 'Hohoholy fuck, wewewe wanna make loadsa these,' he said eventually and laughed.

We had a closer look around and there were drawing pins stuck everywhere. Most had melted into wee metal blobs, like pellets, and had cooled, as they hit the headstones and were now embedded into them.

We heard police Land Rovers pulling up outside the wall that was on the Antrim Road side of the graveyard, so we scarpered.

The October mornings were cold and wet, and you were chilled to the bone when walking to school. I had just eaten breakfast and Ma was in the living room, doing the girls hairs, as usual. My brothers were upstairs, getting ready for school. I was looking through the kitchen drawers, trying to find a box of matches and I came across a small holy water bottle, which was plastic, with a wee small plastic statue of Our Lady of Lourdes on it. I grabbed it and went over to the built-in larder, where all the bottles of booze were kept. I filled the holy water bottle with whiskey, I quickly screwed the lid on and put the bottle of *Black Bush* back onto the top shelf of the larder. It was up there, where no one could reach it, without standing on a chair, but not me, I could reach it no bother at all.

I got ready for school and hung back, so that my brother, Kieran, would have left already. I walked around to the school, taking the scenic route, and got in around 10am. I'd take a swig of whiskey throughout the day and suck away on my polo mints, which I had taken off another boy at playtime. I should have been studying for my eleven plus but instead I was in primary one, drawing and making paper aeroplanes. When I got home for lunch, Ma brought up the subject of the eleven plus.

'Ma,' I said, 'I don't care, I'm nat doin it.'

'I'm nat sayin y'are,' Ma said, 'I'm just talkin about it.'

'I don't care, I'm nat doin it.'

In fact, when I didn't feel like it, or when I was tired, I would just say to Ma, 'Don't wake me in the mornin, I'm nat goin ta school.'

'Y'are, so y'are.'

'I'm definitely fuckin nat,' I'd shout back.

Ma wouldn't wake me.

I didn't like school. I hated anyone telling me what to do, especially the teachers.

They would say, 'Boys, open up your catechism and colour in page seven, and I'll pass the crayons around in a jiffy. And remember to try and stay inside the lines. Liam, open your book.'

'Fuck aff, I'm nat doin anythin.'

'Liam, open your book.'

'Go fuck yerself.'

'Right, get out. You can't be disrupting the class like this.'

Most of my primary school days were spent sitting out in the school corridor, talking to myself.

I had just started going to Artillery Youth Club at the weekends. It was good craic. We would down a bottle of cider and head on in for a few games of pool, darts or table tennis but most of the time we just wrecked the place. We'd be throwing pool balls or darts at each other, play-acting out the riots. Nevertheless, we were inside and out of harm's way.

On Sunday nights, 7.30pm sharp they would show a movie, which was projected on to the back wall, so that it was like being in the picture house. And I don't think any of us had ever been to one yet. If it was a kung-fu movie, all I can say is, New Lodge, beware. I was 5 foot, 9 inches, and 14 stone: an almost 11-year-old ninja. So, when I jumped off a wall or railing, with my deadly ninja head-kick, you were going down. Unsuspecting passers-by would probably be traumatised for life, as a gang of us ninjas swept their feet, head kicked, and body slammed our way to victory, showcasing our latest tiger palm, throat-crushing moves, nearly killing ourselves as we jumped, flipped and flew about, demonstrating our braveness.

One time in the graveyard, where eight of us were all sniffing glue or drinking, we started knocking the fuck out of each other, when Curley dared me to stab one of the other boys. I jumped up and climbed over the graveyard wall and went home and took a big butchers' knife out of the kitchen drawer, and called around for Tucker, the chosen candidate. His sister said he wasn't in, so I rammed the knife into the door and shouted through the letter box.

'Tell yer brother he's a fuckin dead man.'

The knife was left, still stuck in the door as a reminder. My anger had no limits when the rage built up to the point where it would explode in my head, so that I couldn't control my actions. I would have probably murdered him, had he been home.

When I was out rioting, I didn't care if I lived or died. There was many a time I would be standing 30 to 40 feet away from the Police line, daring them to shoot me.

'Go on, shoot me, yis murderin bastards!'

Then *boomph, boomph, boomph,* as they fired the baton rounds.

I'd sidestep out of the way, with two halfers in my hands. These were half-bricks that I'd lifted from the street.

Across the road from my house was a place called Harding Street, where my Da had grown up. It lay derelict, run down, with no doors or windows: just empty wee parlour houses. Memories left to the bitter elements, most of them didn't even have a roof. Ghosts from the past were said to still live there, as such. Most people avoided the wee ghostly street. I didn't. As my Da always said, 'It's nat the dead ya should fear, it's the livin.'

So, we turned Harding Street into an assault course, for The Pinkies, which was the name of our gang. We ripped up floors and laid sheets of cardboard over them, and on the floor beneath, we'd have planks with nails pointing upward and broken bottles everywhere. So, when you fell through, you were well and truly fucked. We set loads of booby traps for the unsuspecting army, if ever we were getting chased. This was our playground, where we practised countless manoeuvres to outsmart the unwanted army. This was our turf war, so kill or be killed. We had balls to burn and feared no cunts, especially the English Hun. Schoolboy vigilantes, who wore warpaint like the suppressed Native Americans and wore our battle scars with pride, like badges of honour.

The very bottom half of Harding Street ran on to North Queen Street and was getting rebuilt, so it was all fenced off, for security, using huge metal fences. We had no trouble, getting into the site, as we dug, beat and chopped our way in. Even the barbed wire fences were a piece of piss, as we'd pulled many apart before. We stole half a pallet of bricks and took them to our training camp, where we smashed them into four or so pieces for ammunition, which we hid away for emergencies. A load of us would go down into the Belfast docks area and break into warehouses, or builders' yards. We got a "blunder bus" tyre, a nickname for tyres as big as a tractor tyre and loads of smaller tyres, then we wheeled them up to Harding Street. Our hands and faces were always black. I spied this big cylindrical tube, about a foot high and a foot wide, with a metal lid on it. I pried it open, and it was three-quarters full of ball bearings. So, I took it with me.

When we got back to Harding Street headquarters, we broke into the site at the bottom of the road and stole a cement mixer. Later that evening, I went to HQ and emptied the big heavy cylinder of ball bearings into the cement mixer. I then chucked in four or five bricks, and hand-turned it for about an hour or so. I threw in a few big heavy wrenches and spanners for good measure. The ball bearings came out all spiky and anyone who pressed too hard on them with their fingers would be cut. We all took off our socks and loaded them with 20 spiky ball bearings, and then knotted the top of each sock. We got hold of three Black Widow catapults that had been swiped out of Braddel's on Lower North Street. We stashed them all away and returned the cement mixer. For the next four weeks, we had the security forces tortured, as we attacked with deadly force, armed to the teeth.

'Nigh yis know how it feels,' I'd shout and then fire the spiky ball bearings at them. 'Get aff our streets. Yis don't belong here, yis rotten bastards.'

'SS RUC, SS RUC,' we'd all be chanting and giving the Nazi salute.

The initiation into the Pinkerton Mob was tough. First, you went through the tunnel of death: that's where you stood a foot or so out from the wall, leaned over and then someone would have to run up the tunnel you created. You'd get knees to the face, elbows slammed onto your back, and kicked stupid. Most times, you would come out with a broken nose, black eyes, cracked ribs; all of which took a long time to heal.

The next one was even more severe. First, we would grab an old mattress from HQ in Harding Street and place it up against the wall, facing the streetlamp at the end of Pinkerton Walk. The lamp had been knocked out of action, so that we could operate in the dark.

There was an inch-thick black wire poking out of the side of the metal lamppost, with black insulating tape around the end of it. We would peel off the tape to expose the bare wire and you would have to lick your thumb and then touch the wire with it. BANG! You would be hurled against the mattress in a fit. Most people shat or pissed themselves. It may have been hard or extreme but so was life and nothing came easy. You only had to look at all the dipsos or alcos that roamed or lay in the Belfast streets.

One alcoholic in particular was old Tucker, who would go around singing and people would throw pennies at him, which he collected in his hat, to go towards his next bottle of *Mundie's* wine. We thought we were fortunate to have a huge *Co-Op* near us in York Street, as their security guards were buck eejits. We stole countless tins of *Evo-Stik* and *Time Bond* glue to sniff then we would stop at Joe Rocktown's to buy bottles of *Mundie's* wine for a pound each.

'Red or white?' He always asked.

We would reply with a laugh and then say, 'Red.'

We stole the glue, sold half of it and that paid for our *Mundie's*, and that was party time on the graveyard shift. Yeeha!

I was in Glenravel Street lifting a half crate of petrol bombs when I ran into a foot patrol who then kicked the shit out of me. I managed to dig under the metal gates that led into the graveyard. I was badly winded, because of the kicks to the ribs and was struggling to breathe. Blood ran out of my nose and down over my shirt and I had a cracker of a black eye. I crawled down the crypt stairs to lick my wounds and catch my breath. I went to our stash, which was behind a loose brick: a half-bottle of *Mundie's* and a few tins of *Evo-Stik*.

'Oh, happy fuckin days,' I yelled.

One hour led into another, and five hours had passed. I could hear like a banshee calling in the wind. It went on for ages, so I finally went out to see what it was.

The sun was just coming up over the graveyard wall and it was blinding. I put my hand up to shield my eyes, like a vampire in one of the old movies. My eyes had only started to focus and there he was, just hanging on the cross.

'Jesus Christ,' I yelled and fell to my knees in repentance. 'Oh Jesus, oh Jesus. I promise ta go ta school an' stap drinkin. Oh please, God. I won't sniff glue anymore.'

And I looked up, by now my eyes were fully opened. There was a young man tied to a cross, it was a big Celtic Cross tombstone, and he was stripped to his monks, and he was covered in blood. The Back Street Mafia, as we called them, had caught him sniffing glue and tied him to the cross. They had entwined thorn bushes together and made a whip and had been whipping him for hours, to teach him a lesson.

'Fuck's sake, I thought I heard a banshee earlier, but when I came outta the crypt, I thought ya were Jesus on the cross, I thought I had a vision, fer fuck's sake.'

I cut him down.

'A Banshee,' he said, 'fuck's sake, mate, ya musta been well lit.'

'Lit?' I said. 'Like a fuckin Christmas tree.'

I helped him over the wall and out of the graveyard, to hobble home like an injured streaker.

Later on, I went to the youth club and told my mates and the youth leaders what had happened to me. They were in stitches laughing.

'Ya must be the immaculate contraption,' they shouted.

Pat Henry, the head youth leader said, 'Don't tell the priests, over in St Patrick's chapel, or they'll be out ta yer Ma's, doin an exorcism.'

We all had a good laugh about my so-called vision.

And I then said, 'There was even one time I was talkin ta the devil himself an' he was tryin ta pull me down ta hell, which I thought would happen soon enough, because I always thought that I'd be dead before my 30th birthday. I would talk ta him fer hours, as he lay trick after trick ta try an' capture me.'

'Fuck me,' they said, 'were ya nat scared!'

'Nah. My Da always said yu've nathin ta fear from the dead, only the livin.'

That expression always stuck in my head. Plus the fact that I would be standing on the roof of a two-storey house, ripping the slates off to throw at the Peelers, and swinging a block hammer at the pavements, breaking them up for ammo, while getting fired at with numerous baton rounds, so why in the name of God would I think anything else?

There was death and destruction all around you, and the pain showed on the people's faces, especially when the BBC news would come on and talk about more atrocities, like Bloody Sunday, justifying it from the perspective of the British propaganda war machine. People looked worn out and tired, life was brutal and harsh, and you'd no choice but to make the best of it.

I headed back over to the graveyard and the usual gang of hoodlums were there, so I joined them in a neighbourly bag of glue, as you do. We were all tripping off our skulls, when all we could hear was this pixie music like out of *Darby O'Gill and the Little People*. We all looked at each other in disbelief, as we were all having the same trip, so, one-by-one, we danced out of the crypt. De-deedle de-deedle de-deedle de-de, and we followed the music, while swinging our arms and skipping which took us to the far back wall of the graveyard. There was a row of shops that ran along the Antrim Road at Carlisle Circus, so we climbed up the wall and ran across the roof of the first shop, which was a corrugated fibreglass roof that belonged to the fruit shop underneath.

We climbed up another wall, and along the second roof, and finally the third. We stood and looked about, to see where this magical pixie music was coming from, and then we saw the Orangemen marching down the Crumlin Road and through Carlisle Circus. We all looked at each other and burst out laughing and calling each other, 'Wanker.'

We stood and slagged the fuck out of each other, until we heard sirens. We looked over the edge of the roof and about a dozen Land Rovers pulled up. Loads of Peelers piled out of them, looked up and pointed at us. We hadn't realised that we were on the roof of the Bank of Ireland and must have set off the silent burglar alarms.

'Fuuucck,' we all shouted and made a run for it.

We jumped off the first roof, landed on the second roof, and scrambled to our feet, ready to hit the next roof. But I made this huge leap, missed the next roof and landed on the corrugated fibreglass roof of the fruit shop. I hit the roof like a sack of spuds, and it sprung me up about six feet into the air, catapulting me over the graveyard wall and safely onto the grass, then the fibreglass roof landed on top of me. I was ecstatic. I'd got away and I was laughing.

Meanwhile, all my mates had just jumped off the second roof, which was Specky Reynold's record shop roof, and they landed smack-bang in the middle of the now roofless fruit shop. They were dragged out one-by-one by the Peelers, kicking and screaming, and slung into the back of a Peeler jeep.

I wished I'd brought my ninja invisibility cloak, but I couldn't find it; someone was looking out for me, nonetheless. I was like a greyhound, as I ran through the graveyard, jumping over our pre-laid traps, dodging the lower branches of the trees and finally leaping up the wall, monkey style, over the gap and away like Flynn, whoever he was. I laughed the whole time; it must have been the adrenalin and the nerves from the chase. I got home and sat down in the kitchen to a cup of tea and toast. I was only in the house for 10-15 minutes or so, when my brother Kieran came in, saying that all my mates had been scooped by the Peelers.

'Really? I said.

'Aye, I was talkin ta one ah their das, as he marched along North Queen Street, an' he was swingin a big thick leather belt. He's nat happy about havin ta go ta the Peeler station.'

'Nah, no one ever is,' I said,

'It's a fuckin wonder ya weren't with em.'

'Who, me? Fuck's sake, I haven't seen my mates all day.'

He looked at me and shook his head.

I quickly fired my toast into me and headed along to the Cop Shop. I could hear one of my mates get the living fuck beat out of him by his Da, to appease, and even humour, the cops, in the hope that they wouldn't press charges. I split like a banana. My mate was black-and-blue from head to toe, when we eventually met up again, about a week later.

'Silent roof alarms,' was the first thing he said to me, 'we won't make that mistake again, an' that's fer sure.'

We were always made to go to mass on a Sunday and it was the same crap every week.

The priest would say, 'We raised one-thousand, seven-hundred-and-fifty-pounds last week, to go towards a new roof, so we're going to do two collections today.'

Just to be sure they get your last few shekels anyone had rattling about in their pockets. I was always led to believe that the Catholic Church was the richest church in the world, and that the Vatican was paved with gold. If that were the case, I often wondered why they needed to bleed their own poor people dry.

Pay for your own fucking roof and feed your hungry people, instead of robbing them, I thought.

I dared not mention this at home, or Ma would say, 'I don't wanna hear that kinda talk, ya fuckin heathen,' and then she'd give me a clout round the ear.

The collection baskets would be passed around by people in the chapel: along the rows and down the aisles, and they would be stuffed with money and paper envelopes. Each envelope had a serial number on it, so that the Church could keep track of how much each household was giving. A scam of the highest order, as those who gave least would then be prayed for, and practically shamed into giving more. The people of the New Lodge had little to nothing and struggled to make ends meet. Feeding and clothing their children should have been their top priority, not putting a new roof on the church. The rumours about the Catholic Church were mounting over child abuse but these were quickly swept under the carpet, and then the particular priest in question was simply moved to a different parish. No warning or anything was given to the community that a suspected paedophile was moved into the parish, and a priest, no less, who could access all areas. The abuse must go right to the top, as wave after wave of accusations eventually came out. It was a fucking joke, the priests all drove new cars and had housekeepers to cook their every meal and clean their parochial houses. What the fuck do they know about the poverty-stricken neighbourhoods, where families were going hungry? Fucking shame on you, you hypocrites. Well, that's my stand up on a soapbox finished, for now.

Later that evening, I was in a full-scale riot. Some kid lost an eye, while shouting abuse at the soldiers. They shot him with a baton round, at almost point-blank range, standing about fifteen feet away from the youngster. The whole place erupted, the kid who was shot came running past me, screaming for his mammy. His eye was hanging out, because he had been hit on the side of the head.

We were rioting at the top of the New Lodge Road, and I would later learn that a Saracen, an armoured six-wheel monster of a machine, fired the point-blank baton round out of one of the wee slots in the side panel. The kid was hitting the Saracen with a stick, it looked like a brush pole, only half the size, he was only six or seven years old. What damage could he have done to this reinforced armoured monstrosity of a thing? His eye dangling down his check, being held in by a gooey thread.

North and west Belfast went ballistic, Ardoyne, the Bone, Twinbrook, Andytown, Broadway, it was madness. And through chaos came opportunity and the IRA took full advantage, blowing up shops in the town, and taking crack shots at opposing armies. The entire city ground to a standstill, as buses, lorries and cars were hijacked and set on fire. It was total meltdown, as the carnage spread to the Short Strand and the Markets areas.

I got pulled into the incident centre by the IRA, and a hood was put over my head. I heard men's voices saying that I was being charged with anti-social behaviour.

'Anti-social behaviour?' I screamed.

I got a knock on the side of the head and told to be quiet.

'Aye, it's bin reported that ya were sniffin glue durin a riot.'

'Really? Really? Well, yu'd better shoot me nigh an' get it over an' done with, cos yu're borin me ta tears. D'ya fuckin actually see what ta fuck is goin on out there?' I screamed at the top of my voice.

'Yer Da's on his way,' one of the men said.

I tried to stand up and someone pressed my shoulders down, then I got another bang to the head and told, 'sit,' like I was a dog or something.

'Okay, okay, no more shoutin,' I said. 'D'ya nat think em English bastards aren't shootin enough of us or what? An' I've ta sit here an' listen ta this shite.'

BANG! Another knock to the head.

I screamed, 'Shoot, me yis yella cunts.'

'Jesus fuck, it's the devil himself,' one of the voices quipped. 'Will we shoot him nigh?'

'Nah, fer fuck's sake,' another said, ''is Da would only end up shootin us.'

So, I got off with a warning and let go.

I immediately grabbed an old scarf that was lying on the street, half-soaked it in petrol and wrapped it round my face, covering my mouth and nose. I got a great buzz from the fumes of the petrol.

Madness ensued as hordes of us rampaged through the streets. We hijacked cars, vans, lorries and buses. Nothing was spared, as we set them on fire and the flames licked the skies. Black ash and orange embers floated everywhere, as if snowflakes were on fire. The heavy fumes from the burnt tyres and tarmac filled my lungs, as I coughed up some of black soot that I had just breathed in. And those bastards were worried about antisocial behaviour, while we had to live in this shit, day-in and day-out. Plumes of black smoke billowed from a double decker bus we'd set on fire. Kids a lot smaller than me but older were trying to break the windows, as the bus creaked and crackled in flames. One kid was in nappies, and he was throwing stones at the bus and mimicking Indian noises from old western films. His nappy had come off and there was a big dark brown lumpy shit streak halfway up his back. They danced around the bus like Native Americans circling a wagon train. The smoke and fumes were hard on my chest as the windows popped, letting the roaring flames through. I realised that the boy, who was now nappy-less, was Tommy Kelly, so I went over and grabbed the wee imp by the ear, and brought him home. He lived on the next street to me, in Bruslee Way.

Later on in life, he would regret that night, playing cowboys and Indians, as his new nickname was wee Tommy Treacle Trunks, which I still call him, forty years later.

My Ma's a Geg

Ma was always full of songs and jokes. She was bonkers. For example, my brother Kieran had a speech impediment, and he couldn't pronounce his r's correctly: rabbit was wabbit, etc. So, my Ma used to send him up to Ma Steele's, a wee house shop, around the corner. Kieran would walk in and say, 'Could I have a Maws Baw, a Staw Baw, and a waspbewwy wuffle baw?'

Cathleen Steele would look at him and say, 'Did yer Ma send ya up ta the shop.'

She knew my Ma well. They used to go to school in their bare feet together, as Ma would say.

When my brother came back, we would all be in wrinkles laughing at him. Kieran would charge upstairs, in a huff, because we were all laughing at him.

Ma would then send me up to the shop for a 50p mix up.

'Son,' Ma said to me, 'go an' get ya an' yer brother, Kieran, a 50p mix-up between yis, ta cheer him up a bit.'

Ma gives me 50p and before she could say anything else, the front door slammed behind me, because I was away like a rocket.

Ma shouted after me, 'Don't ferget ta tell Cathleen ta put some seagull's water boots in. The green ones, cos they're my favourite.'

'Over and out Ma, message received, loud and clear.' As I bolted around to the shop, banging off walls, as if I'd lost control of my rocket ship.

Cathleen Steele looked up at me and asked, 'What would ya like, son?'

'A 50p mix-up,' I blurted out.

'Jesus. Yu're a big spender.'

'It's for me an' my brother. Oh, an' be sure ta put some seagull's water boots in. The green ones, cos they're Ma's favourite.'

'Seagulls water boots? What're they?' Cathleen said.

'They're wee jelly things, about this size,' and I held my finger and thumb up, about a centimetre apart.

Cathleen looked around, 'Nah, son. Don't seem ta have any ah em, but here's some jelly wellies. Okay?'

'Over and out,' I shouted and sped down home with a massive bag of sweets. I flew in through the front door and slammed my reverse rockets on.

'Ma, they don't have any seagull's water boots.'

'Are ya sure? Did ya even ask?'

'Ma, honest, I did.'

'What did ya say, exactly, son?'

'Well, I told her that I wanted a 50p mix-up fer me and Kieran. An' then, I asked her ta put plenty ah seagull's water boots in. She looked about an' said, tell yer Ma I don't have any. So, I said, are ya sure? They're wee jelly things about this size an' I held my finger and thumb up, just the way ya showed me, Ma.'

Everybody burst out laughing. Only then did I realise that Ma was making an eejit out of me. 'Fuck's sake, Ma, the fuckin shap was packed, I'm nat goin back there. Fuck's sake, Ma, people already think I'm simple, an' then ya go an' do this.'

'Son, I didn't think ya were gonna ask. Like, seagull's water boots, like. Fuck's sake, it was a joke. I really didn't think yu'd ask.'

'Well, I'm nat goin fuckin back there.'

The tears of laughter were running down her face, while she was trying to hold back.

'There, there, son,' she said. 'Go y'on upstairs ta Kieran an' share em wee sweeties out between yis.'

Ma was a geg but we were the ones who had to live with her. Even when the ticky, ticky man would come round, looking for his pound of flesh and Ma would let on she wasn't home. I would open the door. He would be on one side of it, looking for his coin, and I'd be making excuses.

Aye?' I'd say, then he would ask where my Ma was and I'd respond with something like, 'Oh, sarry, Mister, but she's at the doctor's.'

'Oh, is she now?'

'Aye. Dunno when she'll be back, Mister, but I'll tell her ya called, lookin her, okay?'

Meanwhile, Ma would be standing on the other side of the door, swinging her arms like a gorilla and scratching her head and trying to ape the debt collector. He had the shakes all the time, and he fumbled to get his wee book out. Ma, hiding behind the door, would have her arms outstretched, shaking them vigorously, and she'd be making funny faces, to try and get me to laugh.

She was brilliant at doing impersonations and especially of one my mates Tommy, 'Tommy Gun' who had a really bad speech impediment, as she would spit and splatter her words out, slapping herself on the back of the head for emphasis.

She was bonkers, like the time she told my four kid sisters that she could have been a big movie star, like Doris Day in Hollywood but gave it all up to be a mum, and raise her family!

One day, Ma said, 'Fuck it, we're goin ta America, an' we're gonna be movie stars on the big screen. Girls!' She shouted, 'Pack yer bags, Hollywood, here we come.'

The four girls were nearly in convulsions, 'We're goin ta America! We're goin ta America!' They were screaming.

Ma was in the kitchen, putting the dinner on: cabbage and spuds and bacon ribs, all done in the one enormous pot that took up the four rings on the cooker. The four girls were running around laughing and giggling between themselves, then they all flew upstairs. Ma just carried on with dinner, as she strained, flopped and chopped the ribs to dish the dinner out.

'Jesus, Ma, that went down like a whore at an hockey match.' I said.

My oldest brother, John, said, 'What did I tell ya about talkin like that in the fuckin house? Keep that fuckin bad language fer the street, where ya belong, ya dirty fuckin animal dog ya.'

The following morning, we went downstairs for breakfast and my four sisters were all sitting in the hall on top of black bin bags, filled with their clothes, and all their prized possessions. They each wore a light blue anorak and had hats and scarves on.

'Where yis all goin?' I asked.

'America!' they all said.

The rest of us just burst out laughing but we did feel so sorry for them, when their wee faces dropped: they looked so sad and were fighting back the tears. Ma came down and scooped them all up in her arms.

'There, there, my darlins,' Ma said as the girls broke their wee hearts.

It was priceless humour, and forty years later they would never live it down, as the story is told at every wedding, anniversary and family get-together.

Green Carpet and Burnt Orange Walls

At night, we hid in the shadows with our ammo of bricks piled high as we guarded our turf. We were always on high alert, as we crept about the piles of rubble, waiting on foot patrols or the so called 'dawn raid' squads, so that we could stone them, and alert everyone to what and who was coming; not knowing that, forty years on, we would be called the child soldiers of urban guerrilla warfare.

Other nights, we would sit at the bottom of Dill House, a twelve-storey high-rise at the end of my street, and we would tell jokes, have a laugh and muck about. We would watch the lightning, far away in the distance, flashing on and off, just over Gallagher's roof, the cigarette factory in North Queen Street at the bottom of the New Lodge Road. We would sit for hours upon hours, watching the rain getting blown about in all directions, as the wind howled, as it ran through the tall block of flats, whistling and screaming, banging doors and scaring the crap clean out of you, when you weren't expecting it. Someone would pull out a packet of biscuits, and it would end up a free for all. Or a 'pile-on', as we called it, digging your elbows in, until you got to the bottom where the prize was. A packet of *Jammie Dodgers* was gold at this time in the early morning. You were locked in a scrum for them. The poor *créatúr* who was on the bottom of the pile-on, who would be holding on for grim death for the spoils, was lucky to get any at all. And who would be regretting every moment.

It always seemed so peaceful, at this time of the morning, as it was still dark, and not a sinner about. Well, except for the milkman. As he pulled up, he would bring half-a-dozen crates of milk into the foyer of the flats and load them into the lifts, and he just travelled up and down, delivering the milk. Most of the time, as soon as the lift door closed, we all bounced over to the milk lorry, and started chugging down pints of milk and bottles of orange juice. And if, by any chance, he came down and caught us, we would smash everything up or set his lorry on fire. You have to pay protection; we would tell him. At that time, you would see a white river of milk stream down from the back of his lorry and down the street.

'This is fer the cause,' I shouted.

'What cause?' he yelled back.

'Cos we'll kick yer bollocks in, if ya say another word!'

Dowah would normally do all the talking. He was nicknamed Dowah because he was always fighting, and shouting 'Yu'll do wah? Yu'll do wah?' And then he got stuck into you. He was a likeable big character. Well, unless you crossed him, that is. He was tall and built like a brick shithouse but was always smiling and laughing, even when he was in the middle of a digging match, you could hear him laughing and chuckling away, as he swung the digs and boots in.

'Are ya talkin ta me or chewin a brick?' He'd yell. 'It doesn't matter, either way, yu're gonna lose yer teeth.'

Tommy Gun or Tommy G for short had a really bad stammer and he sounded like a machine gun when he spoke. 'Dadada, dadada, dadadada,' but before he could spit out the words someone would shout, 'Shots fired! Shots fired!' And we would all dive on the ground and take cover behind each other. Truth be told, we tortured him, slagging him always but he was good for it.

My Ma wasn't the full shilling either, you know. She would send me down to the shops for a large loaf, so I would run down to the bakery, all five-foot ten and fourteen stone of me, even though I was only eleven years old, swinging my arm above my head like a helicopter blade, because I believed that made me go faster. I'd burst in the door of the bakery.

'Could I have a large loaf, please?' I would shout.

'A large loaf?' Dolly said.

'Aye, a large loaf.'

'Son, son, calm down. Did yer Ma send ya down here?'

'Aye, Ma sent me down fer a large loaf.'

The counter staff and customers pissed themselves laughing.

'Are there no mirrors in yer house, son?' Dolly said.

'Just gimme a large loaf,' I screamed, and gave them all the evil eye.

They would put their hands up to their mouths, and try not to look at me for laughing. So, I went home and told Ma and Da what happened. Ma burst out laughing.

'C'mere, son, c'mere,' and she gave me a big hug, as she wrapped her arms around my chest. 'Yu're my special son.'

'Aye, special fuckin needs,' my brother John shouted.

'Yu're a bucket ah laughs.' I replied.

Da chirped in, 'Ya shouldn't mock the afflicted.'

'Ma, Ma, am I afflicted?' I didn't know what it meant.

You soon learned to be thick-skinned, because that was the only way to be back then; well, in my house it was.

That evening, as darkness fell there was a huge orange glow in the sky emanating over the roof of the recky. The recky was a huge recreation hall around the barracks that had a boxing club upstairs and a large hall that was used for discos. We ran past the recky, down onto North Queen Street and someone told us that the paint shop got firebombed, at the top of North Street. When we arrived, we looked at the three-storey building and it was ablaze. The flames licked fifty feet into the sky and thick clouds of black smoke billowed out. The heat was fierce, and you could barely look at it, as it was so bright and scalding hot. The firemen were at the front of the building, hosing the place down but it was futile, as it was burning well out of control.

We ran around to the back of the building and kicked in the back door. We pulled our jumpers up over our noses and ran in. There was thick black smoke everywhere and everybody just grabbed what they could. I took six big tins of paint, rollers, brushes, putty knives, you name it…I had it. And in no time at all, I was loaded up like Sister Mary's mule and walked the half-a-mile home.

'Ma, Ma, Ma,' I screamed.

My wee Ma was sitting at the kitchen table, drinking her tea out of her wee fine bone China cup, with a gold rim.

'Ma, Noblett's paint shop went up in smoke! It musta bin a firebomb!' I screamed out, trying to get a breath.

'Ach, son, how'd ya know…I'd like ta decorate the house.'

Six one-gallon tins were banged down onto the kitchen table and I started pulling the brushes and rollers out of everywhere. The brushes were all around my waistband, twenty or so, the rollers were down my sleeves. I pulled plumb lines, *Stanley* knives, measuring tapes, putty knives from every pocket and socks.

'Oh, here Ma, there's a couple of measuring tapes. Right Ma, that's me away.'

'Where are ya goin son?'

'I'm gonna go back down an' see if anythin else fell out the back door.' And I was gone like a shot.

I was back over in North Street in no time at all. There were loads of kids, at least twenty or so, lifting everything that wasn't bolted down. Part of the roof came crashing through the ceiling and the lights exploded, sending sparks everywhere. A giant plume of smoke blew outwards, and the ceiling collapsed onto the ground floor, half-roasting us, as we ran to the back exit. One of the kids' arms was on fire, so I quickly took my jacket off, to wrap around his arm and put out the fire. His fingers and thumb just melted like candle wax, to leave a bloody gooey puddle on the ground. I put the fire out quickly, and he screamed and screamed for his Ma. The Peelers and an ambulance arrived, and everyone just seemed to sink back into the shadows, as the boy got attended to. His high-pitched squeals and screams of agony still haunt me, as I was right next to him.

'Jesus, fuck,' I screamed. 'What's that on yer hands?'

'It was like acid,' someone said.

I just thanked fuck that it wasn't me.

A week or so had passed and the entire house had been painted. Every wall in every room had been painted with luminous orange vinyl silk. I felt so proud and loved the attention. Ma sat me down at the kitchen table.

'Here, son, here's a wee cuppa tea.'

'Thanks, Ma.'

'Don't be tellin anyone,' she said as she leaned over and took a packet of dark chocolate digestive biscuits out of the washing machine. 'Here, take a handful ah these, an' stick em in yer pockets, in case someone comes in.'

'No sweat, Ma,' I said, smiling and took a huge handful. It was like dying and going to heaven, as I dunked each one into my tea and scoffed them.

I went outside and stood at the front door, while Ma puttered about the kitchen. There was a huge furniture lorry that was just about to be hijacked on the New Lodge Road. The driver shouted over to me.

'Excuse me, mate, excuse me…do you know where Carlisle Terrace is?'

I just noticed three or four men approaching the driver, about to pull him out of his lorry.

'Yo,' I shouted. 'What the fuck d'ya hallions think yer gonna do? That's my fuckin uncle an' no-one's gonna touch him. An' I mean fuckin' no-one.'

The driver had a puzzled look on his face but seemed relieved, as I clambered up into the cab.

'Mate, ya were just about ta get hijacked,' I said, 'go down the road, an' turn right at the bottom, take the next right, an' fally the road on up. I'll go with ya. No one will touch ya, or yer lorry, with me here.'

We drove up the road to a house, where the man delivered a bed and a big wooden dresser.

'No one will dare give ya any jip or lip, with me here, cos everybody knows me, or knows of me.'

'Sure,' he replied. 'I thought I was going to get burnt out there. I can't thank you enough, mate.'

'Ya don't have a spare bitta lino fer my Ma's kitchen, d'ya?'

'I'll check when we get round there,' and he dropped me home.

I ran into Ma and shouted, 'Here, Ma.'

'What is it, son?'

'I might be gettin a bitta lino fer ya.'

Ma went out to the front door, as the man slid open the big roller doors at the back of his lorry and hopped in.

'No, mate, no lino.'

And Ma's face dropped.

'Hold on, hold on,' he checked his clipboard. 'There's a roll of carpet. It was to be sent back, because there's a flaw or tear, I think, every six feet or so.'

Ma said, 'That's great.'

He rolled the huge roll of green carpet off the side of the lorry and it landed on the road with a giant wallop. Ma and her mates were there, each holding a piece of paper, with measurements on them. I went into the house, grabbed a tape and a *Stanley* knife, and started slicing the carpet up. Ma got the four bedrooms done and she was over the moon.

Ma's mates were shouting, 'Twelve by ten!' and 'Twelve by twelve!', because all the houses were identical, so the dimensions of the rooms were the same. I got everyone sorted and there was still a bit left to do to our front hallway, which measured about eight-by-six. The women rolled up their carpets, lugged them onto their shoulders and marched away home. Ma was elated with the free carpet and was as happy as a 'dog with two dicks' as Da would say.

The next morning, I was awake early, and went down to a huge Ulster fry with tea, bread and butter. I lay down on the sofa afterwards, absolutely busted and one of Da's mates came rushing in.

'Scalper, Scalper,' he shouted, 'that wee boy died.'

'What wee boy?'

'The one in Turf Lodge. Brian. Brian's 'is name.'

'Dirty bastards,' Da shouted, 'that's em plastic bullets. Safer, my hole! They don't even bounce em off the ground, like they're supposed ta. They just fire em inta the crowd, shoulder high, but ah course, the Prods are allowed ta go apeshit, especially around July time. They don't get opened up on. None ah their kids're dyin, after gettin hit on the head with plastic bullets. One-sided, per fuckin usual. So, ya may tell everyone ta batten down the hatches, cos this town ah Belfast's gonna be up in flames, before the night's out.'

The entire nationalist community came out in protest and blocked all the major arteries in and out of the city, bringing it to its knees. To add fuel to the fire, the Shankill Butchers had just claimed their first victim.

Belfast erupted. Thousands of people were rioting about the injustices, or plight of the nationalist community. The wee boy, Brian, was an innocent victim; now just another statistic. And the Shankill Butchers were just lifting innocent Catholics, who were then brutally beaten and tortured for information. If they weren't killed, they were beaten to within an inch of their lives. We all knew that the RUC was a one-sided bigoted police force, who knew who was killing the Catholics but the gang was allowed to move freely between the peace walls, as such. Everyone knew of the collusion and corruption between the loyalist gangs and the security forces but it was always vigorously denied by the high ups in Downing Street. Don't make me laugh, years and years later, all would be corroborated, even the shoot-to-kill policy. And what do you do? Make that murdering bastard, Maggie Thatcher, a Dame, instead of being done for war crimes against humanity and towards the nationalist community. She alone caused more division between communities than anyone else, illegal organisations or not. In my eyes, there was no hope, no future, and no kind of life worth talking about, and when you have nothing left to lose fear goes out the window and pure hatred and rage take over, as you've gone past the caring stage and into the 'don't give two fucks' anymore mode.

The rioting went on for days and was not looking like slowing down at all. There were a few hundred of us, making a stand, up at the bottom of the seven hills, and we needed more petrol bombs, as they were just about to break our ranks. When I say 'they' I mean the British army. We ended up at the bottom of Dill-house, which was halfway up the seven hills, just before the grotto, in no man's land. The security forces were all around, firing at us. It was a proper warzone: bricks, bottles and petrol bombs were flying in from all sides. There was thick black heavy smoke everywhere from the burning cars, limiting your vision and hearing. BOOMPH CRACK CRACK CRACK as shots rang out, and we were caught in the middle. I heard a girl's voice, and I turned around instantly, she was leaning over the front railings at her house. I couldn't make out what she was saying.

'What?' I shouted.

Everything stopped, and then went into slow motion, as she mouthed something to me. I still couldn't make her out, then, as if a volume switch went on to maximum output:

'Run, run, run,' she shouted, 'it's the snatchies.'

Snatchies was short for the snatch squad who were ruthless paratroopers, who let nothing nor no one stand in their way, and who took out all the ringleaders and the most violent rioters. They were right on our tails, so we had no choice but to run. Me and two other lads had bolted in the same direction, BOOMPH, BOOMPH, CRACK, CRACK, CRACK.

Fuck, em there fuckers are shootin live rounds, flashed through my brain in a millisecond.

Now the adrenalin really kicked in. I was like *Action Man*, as I leapt over car bonnets that were still on fire, almost laughing with excitement. The fella on one side of me fell, hit with a plastic bullet that knocked his knee out and made him collapse onto the ground. The other fella stumbled and fell and, as he lay on the ground, he got shot in the heel with a bullet. The bullet travelled up his leg and out his kneecap.

On the news, it said that he had been caught in crossfire. 'Crossfire' my arse, it looked and sounded as if the cunts were just shooting at us and from behind. I was like a racehorse, and away I went.

Denise, the girl from Bruslee Way, who was leaning on her garden railing helped me to hide in her coal shed. Three nights, I spent there. And she brought me out grub daily. Tea and sandwiches, whatever they had in the house. She smelt like flowers, only sweeter and was a definite ray of sunshine for me. A big mug of tea, with four rounds of ham sandwiches, wrapped all nice and neat in tinfoil, with a coconut *Banjo*.

'Here, this is fer you,' she whispered. 'An' be quiet. The soldiers are goin mad lookin for ya, an' they've already raided yer house.'

I slept in the shed at night but during the day Denise would let me into the house to wash up, and stuff. We would just sit and watch TV and talk.

'Here Liam, there's a disco on in the Vic on Saturday night if ya fancy it?'

'The Vic? Sure, that's a Stickie club.' I said referring to the term used for the official IRA. 'Nah, I don't dance' I said. 'An' besides, I might be headin ta the graveyard fer a bag ah glue an' a bottle ah wine.'

'Well, whatever ya decide, the offer's there. There was talk ah crossfire on the TV there, about that wee boy who was beside ya. Same oul shite. Crossfire? Sure, it came from the direction ah the paras.'

She then gave me a big bowl of vegetable soup, made with a shin. It was lovely, different from my Ma's, as my Ma always used boiling fowl.

I ended up in the graveyard that night and didn't give the disco a second thought. Denise and I met up a few times at Artillery Youth Club. She was absolutely beautiful, and she was thirteen. I was almost eleven and I was still in primary one at school. Even now I find this fact incredible. What must my brain have been thinking, one minute I was out rioting and the next moment I was in school learning how to read and write. Is it any wonder that I thought I was a giant! But then nothing made sense, neither the riots nor the way people had to survive.

Zootopia

Denise was very wise and mature for her age and used to organise wee day trips up to Bellevue Zoo, which was only ten/fifteen minutes up the Antrim Road on a bus.

'Be at my house by eleven themarra mornin, an' bring a packed lunch, an' have two bus tokens, an' any odds ya can scrape together fer the fairground rides.'

I didn't even know that there was a zoo in Belfast, let alone only ten minutes away. We didn't have to pay in, as Denise knew where there was a wee gap that you could squeeze through, that her Da, Dindo, had shown her before. She had the cutest smile and I always felt calm and relaxed around her. We would lie down on the grass, look up at the sky and watch the clouds go by. And Denise would talk about The Eagles or Barbara Streisand, none of which I had a clue, as to who they were. The sun was splitting though the trees and there was a lovely cool breeze that came down from Cave Hill. It was so relaxing. You didn't have to be on your guard. You didn't have to watch your back, and you definitely weren't going to get chased by Peelers or paratroopers. No shouting, no fighting, just fresh air. We would spend hours going around the zoo, looking at the animals and making up nicknames for them.

'Denise, ya do know that I'd never let anyone hurt or harm ya in any way.'

'I know that,' she said. 'But, Liam, d'ya ever think that the troubles will end?'

'Nah, nat in my lifetime anyhow.'

'Yeah, me neither, there's too much bitterness an' hatred in-bred.' She said. 'I don't care about the political side ah things. I just wanna be left alone.'

'Aye, me too. Left alone, ta do whatever ya want.'

'Y'know I can see a softness, a kindness, almost, in ya?'

'Really?' I said.

'Yeah, yeah, definitely, deep down.'

'Deep down,' I said, laughing, 'it must be deep. Yu'd need a shovel ta get at it.'

Denise gently reached out and touched my cheek, 'Don't ya worry, I'll look after ya.'

'What,' I said, laughing, 'yu'll look after me?'

The two of us were in stitches, laughing. We ended up in the playground and went on the bumper cars, where I drove around, protecting her car from all-comers, as if I were her bodyguard. We then went onto the big wheel and you could look out over Belfast at all the lights coming on, as it was starting to get dark.

'Let's go,' Denise said, 'we need ta be gettin home.'

'Denise, d'ya think this is what freedom feels like?'

'Freedom? Like nat havin a care in the world and doin what normal kids do elsewhere? Well, aye, I suppose.'

'Jesus,' I said, 'I could live up here.'

'What, in the zoo?' Denise said.

'Aye, in the fuckin zoo,'

Denise laughed. 'No way, yu'd be too scared, up here, with all the wild animals.'

'Are ya fuckin havin a laugh? Sure, the New Lodge is worse than any zoo. Sure, there's more wild animals there, an' it's definitely more dangerous.' I gave a big guffaw.

Our bus arrived and we were home in the blink of an eye, or so it seemed. We got off the bus at McLaughlin's Pub and dandered down the New Lodge Road. There were burnt out cars strewn everywhere, and bricks and rubble were being stockpiled by the natives. The stench of burnt ash and rubber was nauseating, like the diesel smell in a lorry. Especially after being on a trip to paradise, where the air was crisp, clear and fresh. We pulled our jumpers up over our mouths, to filter out the floating pieces of ash. Half the New Lodge was in an abandoned state: bricked up old houses, half tumbled down houses lying derelict, while kids played hide and seek in them. SS RUC painted all over the walls. IRA and PIRA painted in big black letters. Although the people in the New Lodge Road had little or nothing, you were never stuck for a cup of sugar or a loaf of bread in an emergency. People generally didn't lock their front doors at night, because when you were being chased by the Peelers in the wee hours of the morning, you could fly into anybody's house, and they would hide and feed you and expected nothing in return. I got home at around 7pm and Da asked me where I was.

'The zoo,' I said, smiling. 'I was up at the zoo.'

'I hope ya weren't up robbin the place, cos there's enough fuckin monkeys down here an' we don't need anymore.' He gave a huge belly laugh.

'Aye, yu're a laugh an' a half,' I said, 'an' is that my stew, in the pot over there?'

'Aye, son. It's all yours.'

I grabbed the spoon and started shovelling the food into my gob, as it was lukewarm, and I didn't even heat it up. The spoon crashed and clattered off my teeth, as I was starving. Da laughed as he watched me devour my dinner.

'Did y'even chew any, before ya swallyed it?' he asked.

The HP sauce dripped down my chin, leaving big blobs on the table. I set the empty pot up on the cooker.

'Just leave it.' Da said. 'I'll wash it later.'

'Cheers, Da, I'm away on upstairs,' I rubbed my now-swollen stomach and went to lie down, full as a lord.

I was wakened by the sound of a bomb blast that shook our house. I quickly jumped up to the window, to see what direction the blast came from. I was excited. We were like Native Americans, looking to see what direction the pigeons were flying, so that we could determine where the bomb blast came from. People were running about the streets frantically, shouting to one another. Apparently, a car bomb had gone off prematurely. Peeler jeeps arrived, along with ambulances, in case of injuries. No casualties, just a lot of windows smashed with the blast. A few shots rang out, *CRACK, CRACK, CRACK,* you could hear the bullets ricochet off the Peeler jeep. A hail of bricks came out of nowhere, along with a few petrol bombs, thrown in for good measure.

I had opened the window and could hear the commotion. My adrenaline was pumping, and my heart was beating fast in my chest and my face was glued to the window with excitement. The Peelers were in a state of panic, having been caught out in the open, as they tried to make it to their jeeps, one of which was now in flames. The other jeep had two tires that were on fire and, as they spun, the flames and sparks flew out about six feet, before they disappeared into the darkness, leaving black lines of burning rubber trails, still on fire from the petrol. The crowd that had gathered just sank away into the shadows.

I couldn't get back to sleep, as Denise was on my mind, and the lovely time we had at the zoo, with no one judging you or looking down on you. Everyone else in the house was fast asleep, because I suppose you get used to the noise of gunfire and explosions. You were almost afraid to hope, because when you did, some other atrocity in the armed conflict would be on the news, and it took something out of you. Piece by piece, you seemed to be getting more lost, more desolate and went past the stage of caring, just straight into survival mode. Bombings were normal to us, as most people didn't bat an eyelid. People just carried on with their normal lives. Shots would ring out, CRACK, CRACK, CRACK. Okay, people may have ducked but then they just stood up, and carried on doing whatever they had been doing.

I went downstairs, made a cup of tea and lay down on the sofa. I thought of Denise and the zoo, trying to grasp onto that wee bit of normality we had in this hellhole of a place. Nobody had anything, really, but you never seemed to go without. People begged, stole and borrowed, just to survive. You got a pair of boots, second-hand of course, handed to you, and you couldn't help thinking that somebody had died in them. Okay, they were two sizes too big…

'Okay,' Ma said, 'but ya'll grow into em.'

You clunked about in the boots and had to wear two pairs of socks. Ma would spit on the toecaps then rub them on her apron.

'Look here, son, they're as good as new.'

Nothing went to waste, and you were thankful for small mercies. As soon as you got your new boots on, you had to test them out: climbing walls, playing football, jumping on roofs of burned-out cars, while trying to inflict as much damage as possible. But the ultimate test was going to artillery youth disco and kicking the living shit out of each other. Because after all, we were all friends and that's what friends do. There were loads of gangs, every couple of streets had one, and if you weren't fighting the Peelers or army, you were fighting each other, in a battle of nerves and tactics. We all made makeshift huts out of planks and bits of scrap lying around, with flattened out cardboard boxes to sit on. We would pull all-nighters to watch for unwanted visitors, or early dawn raids from the Peelers. Bin-lids to the ready and piles of bricks for ammunition. We would light campfires to keep warm, an old metal mop bucket with loads of holes in the side for ventilation, made with a hammer and rusty nails. We would set in some bricks and fill it with paper and sticks, some wood and a wee drop of petrol, and the mop bucket would be glowing red and giving out loads of heat, as we warmed our extremities. We would wrap potatoes in tinfoil and bake them on the really cold nights and they'd be so hot, you had to shuffle them from hand to hand, blowing on them and trying to eat them as quick as possible. Oh, oh, oh, ah, ah, ah, we looked like a troop of monkeys dancing to any onlooker, not that we cared.

Tensions were still very high because of that wee boy, Brian, who was shot in the head by a plastic bullet in Turf Lodge, who died just five days later. Everyone stayed in their own area and only ventured out for essentials. People dated and married girls from the next street, so community relations were very tight, because everyone knew one another, and most were related through marriage or whatnot.

The rioting went on for weeks and all the streetlamps were knocked out of action. Roads in and out of the New Lodge were blocked and manned with armed men. We were left to our own devices, and we ran amok and did whatever we wanted to do; bearing in mind that we were between the ages of ten and twelve. The Back Street Mafia, or the IRA, protected us, as such, and took no shit from anyone. This was urban warfare at its finest, and we would have done anything to survive. No one really planned ahead, as I actually thought that I would be dead before I was thirty years of age. No one's future looked bright, and you just lived for the day. Yes, the day you are in now, as tomorrow was promised to no one. You just had to suck it up and accept the fact that you were on a road to nowhere. A life in the shadows, where brutality reigned supreme, where the weak were discarded and set upon.

Sliced and Diced

We headed up to The Waterworks that night. The Waterworks was a park that had two ponds and was otherwise known as Queen Victoria Gardens, although, nobody called it by that name anymore, but it was adorned as part of the iron work on the gates. The Waterworks was built in the 1840s to supply water to the factories and houses and when it rained heavily the water from Cave Hill ran into the reservoirs causing them to fill to capacity.

The ponds were full of swans and ducks: huge white swans that shone bright during the summer days. The Waterworks was always busy: parents with their children having picnics and feeding the birds. It had two playgrounds for the kids, and even a wee stream, where you could catch tadpoles, as long as you had a net on a bamboo pole and a wee jam jar. The kids would have played ball and tippy-tig and everything looked grand in the scale of things. But at night-time it was full of winos and glue-sniffers, basically undesirables. They would light fires and sit around with their carryouts. After dark, the place was notorious for riots, as the top pond backed onto a Protestant estate and the sides and the bottom of the park backed onto Catholic estates, so fierce battles often erupted. Most people thought you would be mad to go in there at night-time, but it didn't stop us, and we were tooled up to the teeth: crowbars, hurls and dog-chains. Most of the time, the police dared not to come in at night, because it was so dangerous. There were loads of trees and bushes; any sniper would have been in his element, hiding amongst all the foliage.

When we arrived, there was a massive riot already in process. They were fighting hand-to-hand and beating the bollocks out of each other. So, we got stuck in, as you do. A few hours passed, and the crowd dwindled then the Peelers moved in to pick up the stragglers. Everybody just split like a banana.

There was a guy on a bike, with a pole that had six-inch nails hammered into it. He was swinging it around and around his head. He managed to crack me on the forehead and then gave chase, as I bolted. I managed to get to the big steep hill that separated the two ponds. The guy had the pole now fixed to the front of his bike, like a spiky battering ram. He came flying down the hill towards me, and I looked about the ground frantically for something to lift, in order to defend myself. I spied an old rusty chain that must have come off a Moped scooter. I picked up the heavy rusty chain and hurled it at the fella. It caught him on the forehead, wrapping around and tightening as it went. I heard a massive crunch and looked on in disbelief: his forehead lifted about half-an-inch, as the chain ate into the bone. He screamed and fell off his bike and lay in a heap. Blood spurted everywhere and he rolled around in agony, with the bike twisted around him. I sprinted home in no time at all, as the adrenaline spike was maximised in me. I ran into the kitchen, nearly taking the front door off its hinges. I ran to the sink to get a drink of water. As I looked up, I saw blood running down the wall. I turned slightly and watched blood trickle down the window.

'Jesus, son, what happened ta ya?' Ma screamed.

'Nathin, Ma.'

'Jesus, fuck, son, look at yer head.'

I raised my eyes, and saw a fine spray of blood shooting out of my head for about five feet or so. Ma folded a tea towel and pressed it to my noggin.

'Fer fuck's sake, son, what am I gonna do with ya? I'm gonna have ta get ya a taxi up ta the hospital.'

'To the Mater Hospital, Ma? Sure, it's only five minutes away, I could run up. Ma, I'm alright. I don't need a taxi.'

Off I went, up to the hospital, spraying as many people as I could, while laughing away to myself. I stopped to write my name in blood on a white-painted wall, thinking it would look cool. When I eventually got to the hospital and the nurse asked what was wrong, I lifted the tea-towel and blood hit the ceiling tiles. I don't remember anything after that, except for the floor hitting me on the face, as I did an Indi-nose-bone dive onto it. An Indi-nose-bone dive was a made-up term for when you were on roller skaters and fell over hitting the tarmac face first.

I didn't wake up until the next morning, in a hospital bed and with a terrible headache. The nurse came to me.

'Well, aren't you the lucky one?'

'Lucky?' I said, 'I feel as if I've been through a mangle.'

'Here, pop this into your mouth,' she said.

The nurse put a thermometer into my mouth and then took my blood pressure. She removed the thermometer, looked at it, gave it a shake and put it into her pocket.

'You're fine,' she said and smiled.

I could barely open my eyes, as the light streaming in the windows was blinding.

'What the hell happened?' I asked.

'Well, you lost a tremendous amount of blood, and your pulse was so weak, we could barely find it. Your heart al Cave Hill most went into arrhythmic shock, as it was working so hard. We had to give you almost four pints of blood. You're a very lucky boy. What happened to you?'

'All I can remember's that I was up in the park, feedin the ducks, an' then I woke up here,' I mumbled.

'How old are you?' She asked. 'And are you still at school?'

'Still at school? It must be the oil ah ugly I use.'

And she gave me a big smile and pinched my cheek.

'How old are you?' She asked again.

'Well, I'll be eleven in a few months.'

She looked at me is disbelief. I butted in, to save her from the embarrassed look that she had.

'Aye, nearly eleven, but, as I said, it's the oil ah ugly.'

The two of us laughed.

I couldn't tell the nurse what really happened, as she would have had to phone the Peelers.

'Well, you won't be going anywhere for a few days, and your mother is on her way. She was on the phone all night. Well, that's me away, I'm on the night shift. I'll see you later on.'

I thanked her very much and gave her the thumbs up. I had just closed my eyes, when I heard my Ma's voice.

'Where ta fuck is that big lug?' She shouted and came flying in the doors, as if she was going to rob the place. 'What'd I tell ya? What the fuck did I tell ya?' She scolded me. 'Yer head, yer head, ya have ta take care ah yer head. Back when ya had yer accident, the doctors said that yu're always gonna have a hairline fracture and yu're gonna have ta be careful.'

'Ma, I was just standin there, an' this fucker cracked me over the head.'

The tears were rolling down Ma's wee rosy cheeks and she whispered, 'I honestly thought I'd lost ya again, son.' And she started squeezing me.

'Ma, Ma, get aff me, fer fuck's sake, get aff me. Everybody's lookin over.'

But she had me in one of her strangleholds, trying to kiss me on the dome.

'I'm gonna be here a few more days, fer observation, fer fuck's sake,' I said.

'Well, I can't get back up the night, as I'm workin in the Felons, but yer Granny and yer Aunt Jean can.' Ma said. 'God only knows who else may stick their s in.'

'Ma, just go home, I'm fine! Breakfast will be here soon an' my fuckin head is splittin.'

'I'll go on then, son. Try an' have a wee doze.'

'Okay, Ma,' I said.

The next few days couldn't pass quick enough, as my arse was making buttons. I was bored shitless and thought about just getting up and walking home but decided to bite the bullet and wait. Ma and Da came up to collect me and brought me up fresh clothes. As I got dressed behind the curtain around my bed, I could just about hear the Doctor say, 'Keep an eye on the wound, in case of infection, as there are several small holes and the artery was nicked. Oh, and we gave him a tetanus injection.'

We thanked the Doctor and off we went.

Ma started, 'Son, I'm sick tellin ya ta be more careful.'

'Fuck's sake, Ma, give over, I'm alright.'

'Son, are ya even listenin? Son? Son…'

Da interrupted, 'Listen ta yer mother,' he said in a very stern voice and threw me a sly wink.

We walked home. By the time we got there, my legs felt like jelly: the short walk had exhausted me. I crashed out on the sofa right away, as I felt light-headed.

Again, the following days were uneventful for me, as I didn't leave the house. Tiredness came on very fast; sometimes, it was like trying to breathe through a wet flannel. The house resembled a train station: doors banging, whistles and the constant chatter and hustle and bustle. The front door never stopped rapping, you could hear kids screaming and shouting at each other. Ma would get our coffin-like radiogram lifted and sat outside the front door, where it would be turned up full whack. Records played constantly: *For My Name, it is Sam Hall, Chimney Sweep*, from the album, "Four Green Fields", was Ma's favourite. Ma and the singer, Kathleen Largey, had met quite a few times. The music thumped away all day and I soon knew every word of *Sam Hall*. Songs such as *Armoured Cars and Tanks and Guns* and my favourite, *The Broad Black Brimmer*. I only ventured out when I felt up to it, especially when Ma gave me a 'Bob Dylan': a shilling, or 5 new pence. I'd scoot down to Thompson's shop for *Chelsea Whoppers*.

I'd only arrived at the shops and heard lots of shouting coming from behind the row of buildings, where a burnt-out car was still smouldering away. A few men in balaclavas had dragged a man from Artillery Flats and pulled him behind the shops. They shot him in the knees and ankles. Four loud *CRACKS* rang out and they left him, lying there in a heap, with blood pishing out of him. It was early morning, in broad daylight. They must have got him going to or coming from work. It was bad enough that all these other corrupt fuckers, the RUC, the British Army, were trying to silence us and we were actually shooting our own.

A woman who was in the butcher's shop appeared and wrapped her shawl around the man, who by now had an audience of people around him.

The woman said, 'Did anyone see what happened?'

Everyone denied it and skulked away into the background, as the ambulance arrived. The blood was a blackish deep red rose colour, as it oozed out of his wounds and lay in what looked like lumps on the ground. He was fully *compos mentis* and was talking away, as if it didn't faze him one bit. He just lay there on the ground.

'Fuckin bastards,' he said, 'that's the fuckin second time. The first time, they only done my knees. Here, anyone gat a feg?'

'Nah mate, I only smoke when I'm on fire,' I said.

'Aghhhhhhhhh. Don't make me fuckin laugh,' he said, as the blood came out in spurts and bubbled even harder.

The ambulance arrived and they carted the man away. I went into the butcher's shop and asked for a bucket of water.

The butcher said, 'Just leave it. The cops will be here soon, an' ya don't wanna be about when they're askin questions.'

I bolted out the front door and up the seven hills and back home.

Ma said, 'Are ya okay, son? Ya look a bit pale.'

'Nah, Ma, I'm fine,' but I was thinking about the large blood clots that looked like lumps of meat that had been hanging off the man.

I called up to Denise's house later that day and we went upstairs and sat for hours. She was recording songs off the radio onto cassette tapes. *Silly Love Songs* by Wings was playing.

'I love this one, it's one ah my favourites.' Denise said.

Don't Go Breaking My Heart by Elton John and Kiki Dee came on. She told me to shush, as she was recording and she was listening for the end, before the DJ spoke, so that she could press pause and wait for the next song. Billy Ocean, Queen and the chart show was soon over.

Denise had a wee two-foot pool table, which had tiny cues and we played pool. To be honest, I didn't care what we did, as long as I was near her, because she never judged me for the way I looked, or made any funny remarks about me.

'Oh my God,' she said, 'that's some whack ya got, there on yer dome.'

'Agh, it's nathin. Just another war wound.'

'Well, it looks painful.'

'It is, but only if ya press on it or hit it against somethin.'

'Well, ya need ta be careful.'

'Fuck's sake, ya sound like Ma, only yu've got a full set ah teeth!'

'Liam Kelly! That's yer mammy yu're talkin about.'

'Stap! My Ma is madder than I am.'

'Well, I would never say anythin like that about my mammy.'

'Fuck's sake, my Ma takes the piss outta everyone an' takes no prisoners. She's full on, yu'll find that out, if ya ever meet her. She imitates the house doctor. Y'know the one with the shaky hands? Or anyone with a speech impediment, or tic, or twitch. She works in the Felons Club, an' if yu've a lisp, or hair lip, she tortures ya. When the band takes a break, halfway through, she gets up onstage an' grabs the microphone an' starts givin people dog's abuse. She's a geg.'

Denise's Ma, Marie, shouted up the stairs, 'Is Liam stayin for dinner?'

'Nah, Mrs. Brown,' I said. 'Ma's makin us champ.'

'Okay, son,' she replied.

My Ma and Denise's Ma grew up together on Upton Street in Carrickhill, and had worked in the mill together, so they knew each other very well. Marie was quiet and mainly kept to herself, Ma had told me.

I was walking out Denise's front door, when her Ma called after me, 'Oh, an' tell Donna I was askin after her. Nigh, ya won't forget, will ya?'

'No probs, Mrs. Brown, will do!'

I only lived two small streets away and was home in two minutes.

Ma was standing at the door, 'Did ya nat hear me callin ya? Get in, it's gonna kick aff here an' I don't want ya stuck in the middle of it.'

I went in and sat at the kitchen table and Ma plopped a big plate of champ in front of me, with a lump of butter oozing down the mountainous load of potatoes. Six big fat pork sausages were then stuck in the sides of the mound. They looked like charred trees on a mountainside. A tall glass of ice-cold milk was then placed on the table and slid over towards me. *It doesn't get any better than this*, I thought. Then Ma put her hand into her apron and pulled out a *KitKat*.

'Ma!' I yelled, 'Yu're a superstar.'

I cleared my plate and devoured the *KitKat*, washed down with the last of the milk. I wiped my mouth with the back of my hand.

Ma said, 'Nigh, yu're nat goin back out, we're watchin a film.'

'A film? As long as it's nat that singin musical shite,' I chirped. 'You an' the four monsters watch that shite all the time.'

'Be quiet, don't call yer sisters monsters.'

'Ma, I'm only slagging, but they are monsters.'

'Fuck up, you,' Ma said. 'An' yu're an oil paintin, are ya?'

'Why is it gonna kick aff?' I asked.

'None ah yer beeswax, ya nosy wee fucker.'

I went into the living room and all the seats were taken, except Ma's. I walked over to the rocking chair, where three of my sisters were sitting and I rolled the chair over, tossing them onto the floor.

'Move,' I shouted, and they burst into tears.

'Mammy, Mammy,' they cried, 'he took our sate, he took our sate!'

'Fer fuck's sake,' Ma screamed, 'no fightin. Can yis nat act like normal decent people?'

She then placed two large pillows on the floor, directly in front of the TV, for my sisters. We watched *It's a Wonderful Life*. Ma was in tears and so were the girls, sat on their cushions.

'I love this film,' Ma said and shuffled off to the kitchen for party bags.

We sat, not a peep nor whimper, till the very end. Ma grabbed a tissue from her sleeve, to blow her nose. We scanned around, to see if we could detect anybody else crying.

'Look, look he's gurnin,' we all yelled and pointed at Martin, the quiet brother.

'Ya wimp,' I shouted. 'Cryin, ya wanna be ashamed ah yerself. Cryin, like some wee girl.'

'Enough!' Ma shouted. 'Nigh, get up ta bed an' stay away from the windies.'

We all got up and made to leave the living room.

'Houl on,' said Ma. 'Everybody, sit down again. *Abbot and Costello Meet the Werewolf* is comin on.'

'Yeahhh,' we all shouted and dived back onto the chairs.

We watched it the whole way through, and it was really funny; we were in stitches laughing at it. Ma made tea and toast for everyone, then we all went to bed. You could hear a barrage of gunfire and it went on for an hour or so, then the rioting began and lasted throughout the night. I tried to sneak out but Ma heard the squeaky floorboards, which had not been nailed back down properly, after the army had pulled them all up.

'I hope yu're nat outta bed an' tryin ta sneak out,' hollered Ma. 'Ya'd better stay up em fuckin stairs.'

'I'm fuckin eleven years oul an' yu're talkin ta me, as if I'm a kid. D'ya think ya own me, or somethin, fer fuck's sake?'

Da's deep voice sounded, 'Listen ta yer Ma, fer once. It's really dangerous out there. Eleven years oul an' only in primary one.'

'Ma, I'm nat goin back. Fuck's sake, Ma, I look like a freak, compared ta the other kids.'

'Son, yu're nat a freak, nor a giant, fer that matter. Son, yer just different, that's all.'

'I can hear people sayin my head's so big, cos I've gat water in the brain, an' if there's ever a drought, it would come in handy. Ma, I get so angry at times, I just wanna bash all their skulls in.'

'Look, Son, I've been in touch with the Christan Brothers, who are in charge of the big school an' all, an' there might just be a chance ah ya gettin in there.'

We were still shouting across the landing to each other.

'Jesus, Ma, the big school. Secondary school?'

'An' don't ever get worried, as yer two older brothers will be there, to keep an eye on you.'

Smart Street

I remember being on the school bus and then setting fire to the back seat. Don't ask me why. Also, if a bus stopped and was overshadowed by a tree, I would pull a branch in the window and then hold the window shut, so that when the bus pulled off, the window and the black rubber seal would be sucked out, accompanied by the sound of a huge pop, and the window would be left hanging off the tree branch, before crashing to the ground.

I sat in class and listened to the teacher rattle on about my two older brothers and how they were exemplary students and that no less was expected from me. Blah, blah, blah, the conformity in terms of behaviour at secondary school was hard to get used to. So, half the time I escaped up the Hightown hills and came out at Bellevue Zoo and then on to Belfast Castle. I would sniff a bag of glue as I went, so you can imagine how bright the flowers and trees looked. I would stand atop the Cave Hill, look at the clear blue sky and feel that if I just reached up high enough, I could touch it. It truly was beautiful up there, as the view overlooked Belfast and the harbour. The two big yellow cranes, Samson and Goliath, stood proudly in the docklands. If anyone ever approached me, or asked why I wasn't at school, I just told them that I was doing nature study for class, although most times I just told them *"Fuck aff an' mind yer own business."*

Belfast Castle was surrounded by trees and looked like something out of a Disney cartoon. The air was fresh and clean and full of floral aromas; nothing like what I was used to. Then 3.30pm would come around, and it was back to reality, as I sauntered home, starving with hunger. If other pupils from another school got on the same bus as my school used, well, it became a free-for-all boxing-match from the get-go.

As I walked down the New Lodge, I could see the Sheridan Street gang, just standing guarding their turf. There were loads of different gangs, typically named after the street their members came from, except for the Piggy, who were from North Queen Street. We all battled each other to reign supreme and show our dominance but when a riot broke out, we all banded together, no questions asked, against the security forces and their heavy-handed tactics.

At times, two-to-three-hundred of us would go apeshit and hijack cars and lorries, siphon their tanks, then set them on fire. We ran about with sledgehammers, breaking up the pavements to throw at the Peelers, or stockpiling chunks of concrete as ammunition. We'd block roads by hammering metal poles in at 45-degree angles to stop the jeeps from coming in, or sling a bus across a road and set it ablaze; it was like a timed tidal wave of violence. Once we had created unimaginable havoc and destruction, we would return to playing 'hide and seek' or 'rallio' and the best game was 'kick the tin'. These, believe it or not, are happy memories for me. Late at night, if we weren't on watch patrol, we would play 'rap the doors' or 'Belfast', where you ring a door's bell and run like fuck. Only snobs had doorbells back then. The dark murky streets of Belfast overshadowed everything, and no matter what you were doing or playing, bombs and shots could happen in the blink of an eye, and you'd be nothing more than a statistic read out on the news, then the event was swept under the carpet by the English government, with their bureaucratic ideals for a place that belonged to them and not to us, as part of a united Ireland.

I listened to my Da very carefully, as he shouted at the BBC news about the British propaganda war machine, and what he deemed a one-sided bigoted perspective. ITV was an alternative but even they had sanctions imposed on them. Things reported on the news could trigger riots that often lasted for weeks. Somehow, you couldn't stop listening to the news and imagining that one day someone might tell the truth.

Da always said not to fear the dead, only the living, especially when someone in the family was having a nightmare. Maybe that's why the graveyard never frightened me, and it was one of the few places where I felt safe. It was an old run-down graveyard that had been closed to the general public for years. Most times, you could hear a pin drop, it was that quiet. There were tombs, crypts and huge headstones. It was all overgrown and dark in places. So much so, you couldn't see the entrances to some of the crypts.

For two solid months, Curley, Kev, Sean, Skin, Tucker, Joe Baker and I collected for the August 9th bonfire. Later, we were down at the docks, raiding a used tyre depot but couldn't get in the gates. We were just about to move on to another depot when a voice called out through the gates. Unbeknownst to us, Joe Baker had slipped away and had been hiding in the depot all day, until the workers went home. He was delighted to see us.

'Happy days,' we all shouted and slid in the narrow opening through the gate that Joe opened. We all picked the biggest tyres we could find and rolled them out two at a time, up to our bonfire site. We gathered our army together, The Barrack Boys, and did run after run, almost clearing the tyre factory. It was well after midnight, before we were all done. Day after day, we gathered material to burn: mattresses, pallets, sofas, until our bonfire was finally built. And it was huge. The barrack 'bony' was always the biggest between all the different street gangs and the Barrack Boys were known for being tough as fuck and took no crap from anyone. It was also the biggest gang. It didn't help that arrest after arrest, and sheer brutality in the area had the barracks like a tinderbox: everyone was on edge.

Curley, Kev, Sean, Skin, Tucker, Joe Baker and I met in the graveyard for a carry-out the following night.

It was raining lightly, and we were all sitting in a crypt drinking bottles of *Strongbow* cider, with a few cans of *Carlsberg Special Brew*, when Sean pulled out a bottle of poitín that his brother had given him. We started chanting: 'We are the Barrack Boys, we are the Barrack Boys, we are the Barrack Boys, booyah!' Then we took swigs from the poitín. Considering that we were all between the ages of eleven and thirteen, we polished off the alcohol. Kev was outside the crypt, dancing in the rain. Beep, beep, he shouted down to us. 'Everyone on the bus,' and he turned his imaginary steering wheel.

We piled out of the crypt in single file and followed Kev singing *The Broad Black Brimmer*. First stop, *Henry Joy's*, then on to *The Green Fields of Freedom*. For hours, we followed each other, in single file, singing all the republican songs we could remember, before retiring back down into the crypt. On reflection, I am convinced that Kev McGran invented the party bus! We drifted off into a drunken stupor and woke up at 7am, and when we looked at each other, we burst out laughing. We lifted the bottles, to check if there was any alcohol left but none had survived. One-by-one, we dragged our sorry asses over the graveyard wall and headed home. We said our goodbyes and we jumped down off the derelict garages behind the graveyard and landed on the old burned-out cars.

Later that same night, August 8th, we stood, looking up at our massive bonfire: the flames licked 50-to-60 feet into the sky. But the topic of conversation was the riot the night before. Apparently, it was one of the fiercest nights of rioting Belfast had ever seen. And we were sitting in a graveyard, safe as houses, singing and dancing, with only the dead to keep us company. Our laughter and singing had drowned out the gunfire, the 80 or so baton rounds that had been fired in Victoria Barracks, which was a small housing estate that ran from the bottom of Churchill Street/Lepper Street, all the way down to North Queen Street, which included Churchill Flats, next to our bonfire site. The Barrack Boys gang was huge, and they were fierce. Curley and I were the closest in our clique but we all got on. Well, Skin was just bonkers. Kev and Tucker were so laid back, until provoked. But Sean was always cracking jokes and was good for a laugh. The craic we had through the darkest days of the troubles forged bonds between us that would last a lifetime.

If a huge bomb went off that actually shook the ground you were standing on, you didn't bat an eyelid, except if it came from the direction of the town, then we all looked at each other and shouted, 'Bomb-damage sale tomorrow!' And we would laugh.

Everyone fed everyone. The feeds I had in Curley's house, I couldn't count, and my Ma was exactly the same. When anyone called the first thing they were asked was 'Are ya hungry?' It was a close-knit community, and everyone looked out for everyone else. The worst crime of all, which brought shame on your entire family, was getting your name called out at Sunday mass. Then you just hid.

In 1977, four men were shot dead and another eighteen injured in an internal feud between the Provisional Irish Republican Army (PIRA) and the Official Irish Republican Army (OIRA) and everyone felt the tensions. An off-duty Royal Ulster Constabulary (RUC) man was shot dead by the Provisional Irish Republican Army (PIRA) and security forces and prison officers were on high alert. During the seventies Belfast city centre was crippled by security checkpoints and everyone entering and exiting the city was lined up and searched. The security forces had steel railings, barbed wire and gates installed everywhere, it was called the Ring of Steel, and the city centre was like a fortress; people were regularly stopped and searched, day-and-night. The town at night was like a ghost town and very few people ventured there. The British army and the Peelers had a free hand to do what they liked.

The RUC sealed off part of West Belfast, while they were searching for weapons. A few men died, many more were injured, and 337 men and women were arrested. The Women's Movement blocked off a police station/barracks, to prevent anyone from going in or out, and the blockade would have lasted much longer than it did, if it wasn't for the Women's Movement. Women came from all over with food parcels to feed hungry families and bring supplies like medicine, nappies, soup, tea, bread, butter, sugar: basic day-to-day provisions. No one could go to work and the shops were empty. Ma told me many a time about this action by the women, who were the backbone of the community, as far back as 1971, when 350 men were sent to Long Kesh, with more to follow every year, until '78 or '79. Women, for the first time, had to run the households, find jobs and fight for their family, their communities and their husbands' civil rights. They were always out picketing, and were beaten with batons and the boots of English soldiers. Women smuggled guns and grenades in prams, and any other ways they could.

Ma had three jobs to feed and clothe our family, because she had eight children. She told me of the times when these wee Belfast women would surround huge Saracens, block off entire streets in protest at the illegal arrest and internment of their loved ones. They were dragged by the hair many times during house raids. I used to sit, listening to her talking, hypnotised, as I had seen with my own eyes how evil and vindictive the security forces were towards men and women of the nationalist community.

Fifty bombs exploded across the North within a week of each other, with little to no warning given. The La Mon House hotel was devastated by a firebomb, killing and injuring many people, as the PIRA and Irish National Liberation Army (INLA) stepped up their campaigns. A paratrooper shot and killed a young joyrider in west Belfast, which was said to be a tit-for-tat killing, for the IRA shooting dead three soldiers in Armagh the day before.

People cheered every time a member of the security forces got murdered but every time, I could see the pain in Ma's eyes, as she knew that the backlash from the Ulster Defence Army (UDA), Ulster Volunteer Force (UVF) and the Peelers would often overshadow what had happened the day before.

The 'armed struggle' or 'armed conflict' seemed endless. At the time, human rights organisations went to the Haig to demand better treatment for prisoners and people living in nationalist communities. These people were on TV but nothing was done or changed. Da said to me that the English draconian laws hadn't reformed in years, so the British government just selected the bits that suited them at any given moment in time and dumped the rest. Well, that's the way it seemed, at least.

One time, I was at Artillery youth club, minding my own business and a few lads stood about 10 feet away, talking.

I heard one lad say, 'Aye, ya should call him Sandy.'
Another lad said, 'Why Sandy?'
'Cos he's gat water in the brain an' every time he tilts his head, he can hear the waves. D'ya get it? Sandy, sandy shore.'
'Ah, ferget it,' another one of them said.

I went into a blind rage. I mean, I grabbed the pool cue and cracked the guy over the head breaking the pool cue in half, and nearly splitting it down the middle. I tried to stab the other guy with the broken cue. I had a big deep voice, and I was screaming. The two young guys squealed like little pigs, as I got stuck in, kicking one of them until he was nearly unconscious. It took half-a-dozen people to get me off them. I got barred for six months from the youth club, and I fell deeper and deeper into depression. Almost every night was spent sniffing glue in the graveyard. I'd talk to myself all the time but only in my head, *I don't want people ta think I'm nuts*. I would question myself *Why this? Why that? Keep calm, don't let em annoy ya* but nothing seemed to work. The only saving grace I had was Denise, because every time we were together, I didn't feel conscious of how I looked, as it didn't matter to her. Every time she touched my cheek with her soft scented hands, the only way I can explain it: it was like being touched by an angel.

Ma was playing her *Four Green Fields* record and singing away, and she shouted upstairs, 'Liam, there's someone at the door for ya. It's a girl.'

'Fuck aff, Ma, an' stop messin about,' I shouted down.

'She says her name's Denise.'

I was down in two seconds, as I bounced off the stairs on my ass the whole way down and nearly broke my neck. I landed in the hall on my ass, picked myself up, and tried to look as cool as possible.

'Hi, Denise, c'mon in.'

Ma shouted, 'Did that fucker steal yer handbag?'

She burst out laughing.

'Fuck's sake, Ma,' I mumbled.

'He's always at that, ya couldn't watch him, if yu'd a bucket ah eyeballs.'

'Ma, is there any fuckin chance?' I yelled. 'Denise yu'll have ta excuse my Ma, she only gat outta Purdysburn. She's all wired-up an' nat plugged in. C'mon in.'

'Nah, nah, I can't. I only called in ta let ya know I'm babysittin fer my mammy's mate an' just wanted ta know if ya fancied callin up?'

'Aye, aye, definitely. Where is it?'

She handed me a piece of paper with an address on it and a time.

'I've gotta scoot,' she said, 'I'm cleanin the house.'

I watched her walk back up the street, until she turned the corner.

Seven-thirty couldn't come quick enough, as Ma shouted, 'Have ya a bee up yer hole?' Yu're traipsing about there, as if yer arse is makin buttons.'

'Ma, leave me alone. Yu're startin ta do my fuckin nut in.'

'I'll fuckin do you in, ya cheeky monkey,' she said, laughing.

At seven-thirty, I was at the door where Denise was babysitting, and we sat for hours, talking about anything and everything, while listening to the radio. A song came on, *Denis Denis* by Blondie. That song changed my life, as I loved the lyrics and even though Denise's eyes were hazel, it didn't matter. *Denis, Denis, oh with your eyes so blue, Denise, Denise I got a crush on you. Oh Denise be do I'm so in love with youuuu.* I couldn't get it out of my head the whole night.

We talked about the pledge Denise had made to her Granny, to never drink or smoke, because her Da was a heavy drinker and could be abusive to her Ma at times. We talked about the Troubles and how they affected day-to-day life, as most families were on the breadline, and the New Lodge Road was poverty stricken. She was so mature and wise for her age.

'Ya need ta get aff that oul glue an' all,' she said. 'Ya know yu've already had a bad injury an' all, an' that glue isn't helpin ya in the long run ah things.'

'Don't care,' I said, 'sure we'll all be dead soon enough, if all this crap doesn't stap.'

'I'm just tryin ta help ya,' she said sincerely. 'Look, instead ah goin ta the graveyard an' diggin up those bodies…'

'We don't dig up the bodies.'

'I know, I know, I'm only slagging. Well, instead ah sniffin glue, I mean. Just call up fer me an' we can get a video out an' watch it. Sure, it'll do ya no harm ta try.'

'Y'know, Denise, I don't care if I live or die, an' this place's so fuckin cruel.'

'That's no way ta be.' she said, and I could see the sadness in her eyes.

'We'll that's how I feel, an' ya know that I would die protectin ya, ya do know that, don't ya?'

'I know, I know, my hero,' she said and looked up at me.

'Stap fuckin about, I'm fuckin serious.'

'Here, calm down, I know y'are.'

'Well, I'm only sayin.'

'Well, Liam Kelly, if yu've someone ta die fer, well, then yu've gat someone ta live fer and' all. I can see a sadness in ya, a kinda softness, and yu've got wee sad puppy dog eyes.'

My face went as red as a beetroot.

'Stap fuckin about, ya balloon begh.' I snapped, trying to disguise my embarrassment. 'Well, it could be worse. I could be cross-eyed, like y'are: one eye goin ta the shap, an' the other one comin back with the change.'

'Really?' she said.

'Nah. I'm only slaggin. Yer eyes are amazin. Oh, *Denise, do be do, I'm in love with you*, can't get…can't get that bastard song outta my head.'

The two of us started laughing.

'Y'know, it feels like yu're the only friend I have in the world,' I said.

'Have ya anythin else ta say? I can feel as though yu've somethin else ta say but ya won't say it. What's on yer mind? I can smell somethin burnin ya know,' she said and smiled.

'Burnin,' I said, 'it was probably that toast ya made earlier.'

'Haha,' she said, 'very funny. Liam, ya know I always feel safe, when yu're around.'

At that particular second it was as if someone threw a bucket of courage or male hormones or something like that over me and I said, 'Ya do know that I fancy ya an' I feel I wanna spend the rest ah my life with ya. Jesus fuck, did I say that out loud? I think that there's somethin wrong with me.'

'Liam, I'm turnin fifteen an' yu're turnin twelve. Yu're runnin about, mad as fuck, sniffin glue an' God knows what. We're friends, really close friends an' let's just leave it at that, fer nigh. I do have feelins for ya, but I just don't know what ta do with em.'

'Aye, me too,' I agreed.

Denise gave me a big hug.

'Look, Denise I'm just gonna go. I'm kinda scundered, y'know.'

'Liam, please don't be embarrassed,' she said and clasped me by my big red-rosy chops. 'I really do feel safe with ya, an' I need ya as a friend right nigh. I love yer company an' I love yer pwetty wips an' yer big puppy dog eyes.'

'Oh, ya must be thinkin of someone else,' I said and the two of us went into a wrinkle.

I waited until her Ma's mate came home and I walked her home.

On the way, we called into a Chinese takeaway called Provie Charlie's, for curry chips, peas and onions. We were standing in the queue, and I piped up to the girl at the counter, 'Here, why d'ya call the place Provie Charlie's?'

'Ya don't, it's called the Weo Ping, but there was this one time, ages ago, when these men came in and robbed us, and the wee Chinese fella that owns the place, Charlie, ran out into the street with a meat cleaver shouting, "Me-Provie! Me-Provie!". Hence the name, Provie Charlie's.'

I told Denise that Charlie had been caught with a van load of pigeons about six months ago.

'Oh my God, are ya serious?' she said, really concerned.

'Nah, I'm only slaggin.'

She hit me a tap on the shoulder with her fist. I fell to the floor and lay there, as though I had been knocked out.

'Get up! Get up! Everybody's watchin.'

I stood up and shouted, 'Abuse! Abuse! Did anybody see that?'

Denise's face went rosy-pink.

'Nigh y'know how it feels,' I said, 'an' have ya noticed, whenever we're together, all we do is laugh?'

'Yeah, it's funny that, isn't it?'

We started laughing again.

I understood why Denise's Ma called her Smiler, as she was always beaming.

We went around to my house and sat in the kitchen, eating our curry chips, along with tea, bread and butter, and then I walked her home. I walked back down to the house and Ma was now in the kitchen.

'Where were ya?'

'I was babysittin,'

Ma burst out laughing.

'You? Babysittin? I wouldn't trust ya ta mind a dog.'

'Very funny, Ma. Me and Denise were babysittin. Well, Denise was babysittin; I was just there ta keep her company. An' she gat curry chips fer us outta the money she gat.'

'Listen, Son, her Ma and Da are Stickies an' there's a big feud on at the minute, so ya need ta steer clear, son. Son, are ya listenin ta me?'

'Ma,' I shouted, 'if anyone goes near her, or her house, an' she gets hurt, Ma, I'll fuckin kill em,' I screamed. 'I'll bate the cunt ta death, whoever the fuck it is. I fuckin mean it.'

Even though I was only 12 years old, I was 5ft 10, 14 stone and had shoulders like a grave digger; I feared nothing and no one.

I was always referred to as the black sheep of the family and was never out of trouble. Inner city poverty was widespread in our community, and we were constantly under attack from the security forces and the paramilitary wings of the loyalist politicians. Collusion between the security forces and the loyalist paramilitaries was rife, although denied many times over by the government, and everyone knew it. The dogs in the fucking street knew it. The paratroopers would come into our street on foot patrol, looking through their telescopic sights, and kneel down, hiding behind children playing. They used us for cover, as they pointed their rifles at us. Especially in built-up areas, they would call kids over to talk and give them sweets, all the while using kids as human sandbags, in case someone took a crack shot at them. We fought in the darkness, shadows of the war in a concrete jungle, like urban guerrillas, we knew our turf, and no one was taking it from us. Okay, we did not have the weapons or technology the British government had but we had heart and soul and we put it into every battle. We watched our Mas taking on Saracens and armour-plated Land Rovers with nothing but their hearts, screaming about the injustices, the torture and mistreatment of the nationalists, and how many of their loved ones were in jail.

Ma had one coat, 2 pairs of trousers and one pair of shoes, a couple of aprons and a few headscarves, and that was her full wardrobe. Everything else went on us, or food and other essentials. She bought nothing for herself and put everyone before her and expected nothing in return. At the dinner table, everybody else was fed first, until they had their fill, and then Ma would eat, usually a small dinner or whatever was left.

I always felt a bit estranged from my family. I knew the adults were my Ma and Da because of photographs and stories, the same for my brothers and sisters but I didn't know them, really, and after the accident, everything was new to me. I felt alone, most times and that I was beyond help, with regard to my temper. I wanted to be normal. I'd ask myself over and over in my head, *Y'know it's wrong but why'd ya do it? What the fuck is wrong with me?* I was never out of trouble and the only person who calmed me down was Denise. I always felt at ease in her company, and I never had anything to prove to her.

Ma went nuts at times, and shouted at me for always being in bother but she never once lifted her hand to me, or any of her kids, for that matter. Ma and Da often exchanged words: mostly over what to do with me but he never lifted his hand to her. Okay, they would argue about what to do with me but that was that.

Da, on the other hand, beat the crap out of Kieran and me, as I dragged him into a load of shit. We got a hiding with a dog lead the time we set fire to an old person's maisonette. And there was another time, when we were down at Gyles Quay, a caravan park between Dundalk and Omeath. We were out for a walk and my brothers began throwing stones down a big grassy bank that led down to the beach. I thought they were trying to hit this wee dinghy out on the water.

'Move outta the way,' I said and shoved them aside.

I lifted a massive rock and hurled it with all my strength. It went right through the middle of the dinghy and nearly drowned half-a-dozen kids that were sitting in it.

'Why ta fuck did ya do that?' My brothers shouted, 'ya coulda killed someone.'

'I thought that's what yis were tryin ta do.'

'Nah, ya stupid fucker. If that rock hadda hit one of em kids on the head, ya woulda fuckin killed him.'

Word soon reached my Da, compliments of Mr. Hegarty, father of the entire family that I nearly drowned. We were in the caravan, ready to bed down for the night, and Da came in, furious. He went into the bedroom, took off his bedroom slippers, and put on his Oxford shoes. He must have kicked me for half-an-hour. My four sisters thought I was dead, as I lay unconscious on the floor in a pool of blood. I can't really remember much, except for the first few blows to the head. The next morning, I got up to go for a shower and could barely move. My body felt twisted, I couldn't stand up straight, and could barely breathe. My eyes hurt and my nose was busted: all caked with dried blood. My ribs and spine were heavily bruised, and I walked like a hunchback, dragging one of my legs. I was beaten to within an inch of my life, for being stupid and not realising the potential consequences of my actions. I did deserve it. I nearly wiped out an entire family of kids, although they were mostly the same age as me, eleven years old or so.

My sisters, 40 years on from the event, still talk about it, as they screamed the whole way through it and thought I was dead. I'd stopped moving long before he stopped kicking me. My own children disagree with what was done to me but I try to explain that it was a different life back then and anger and violence seemed the only way to get your point across. Death and destruction were everywhere. Whatever hand you were dealt in life, you just had to run with it. Very little mercy was ever shown towards each other, never mind towards the security forces.

The late 1970s had arrived, along with Punk, Ska and Crombie coats, Oxblood Doc Martens, short jeans adorned with braces. Punk music, especially, sent the youth of the time into a more rebellious spirit. They rebelled against the system of right-wing government. A new type of rioter emerged, as more and more youths became involved. They seemed to thrive on the pain of repression, as Margaret Thatcher did her worst. Airey Neave, the shadow secretary of State for Northern Ireland, was blown up in a car bomb planted by the INLA, just a few weeks before Maggie got elected. Airey and Thatcher were good friends, so when she took office, she already had a bitter view of the Nationalist Community and Northern Irish politics. Airey Neave was a very public figure for the Tories. He was a writer, a barrister and a politician, as well. He had also escaped from Colditz prisoner-of-war camp in Germany, during the second world war. He worked with and advised the British intelligence services and operated closely with MI5 and MI6. He played a crucial role for Thatcher and her Northern Irish policies. His main job was to defeat Republican terrorism, but he was unable to implement his reforms into the system, as his car exploded with him in it, in an underground car park of the House of Commons. He was still breathing but his face was burnt beyond recognition, when they found him: both his legs had been blown off below the knee, and he died later that day in hospital. When Thatcher received the news, she was quoted as saying, 'These devils must never triumph'.

The INLA, formed in 1975, pledged to establish a Republican and Socialist state and had approximately 70 members. But after Airey Neave's death their ranks expanded rapidly, with people queuing up to enlist. Neave's sole purpose was to suppress the Nationalist community, even more than it already was. That is why he was handpicked as a target: first, to deliver a fatal blow to mainland politics, and second, to expand their ranks. Thatcher was furious, which reverberated down through to us, by means of supplying the Unionist death squads with weapons, as well as intelligence, names and so on of suspected members of Republican paramilitary groups. These were handed over and a green light was given to execute people by the English Government. Thatcher caused more division between the people of Northern Ireland than anyone or anything else ever did. The paratroopers and the Peelers carried out assassinations, under the auspices of the shoot-to-kill policy. The ramifications were further felt in HMP

Maze, or Long Kesh, among others, as the inhuman treatment of prisoners common place and worsening. And these orders came from the top. The Prime Minister herself, Thatcher, was by now the most hated person in Ireland. She went on TV to talk about the political prisoners and the state of Long Kesh. She used phraseology such as *These are not political prisoners, they are criminals with barbaric attitudes and will be treated as such.*

Anarchy seemed to be sweeping through the United Kingdom. The Punk and Ska movements took over control and people went onto the streets in protest of Thatcherism. People who had never before taken note of politics and policies stood tall and protested. She took apart unions and broke the will of the common man. The entire place was up in arms, people came out of the woodwork in droves, as she shoved her Tory right-wing capitalist views forcefully into our faces, stripping any hope that common folk had of a fair and just system. *The rich get richer, an' the poor get poorer.* I heard my Da use that phrase many a time.

Ma always seemed to get her children's names mixed up and normally went through all of our names, before she finally got it right.

'C'mere, ya dirty wee trollop,' she shouted. 'Are ya lightin fires again?'

'No, Ma.'

'Are ya sure?'

'Aye, Ma.'

'C'mere, you. Look in that mirror.'

I'd look in the mirror and my face would be black with soot, except for my teeth. I'd have a big dark black ring around my neck, where soot had stuck to the sweat.

Ma would often grab me by the ear and say, 'Jesus, ya could grow spuds in there. Get up em stairs, ya dirty fuckin cow walloper, an' get a bath!'

'But, Ma, I'm starvin.'

'Starvin, starvin, I'll give ya fuckin starving, ya dirt bird. Get up em stairs, before I call yer Da. I'll make somethin fer ya fer when ya come down. What'd ya like?'

'Anythin, Ma. I'm so hungry, I could ate the scabs aff a child's head.'

'Ya dirty animal dog ya! The scabs aff a child's head.'

'Ma, stap talkin ta me as if I'm a child.'

'But y'are, son. Yu're only eleven an' that's a child. I dunno what I'm gonna do with ya. Yu'll be startin secondary school soon an' they're nat gonna know what's hit em. My fuckin head's gonna be turned, cos ya couldn't watch ya. Nat even if yu'd a bucket ah eyeballs. Yu're a slippery wee fucker.'

'Fuck's sake Ma, alright. I'll behave but I'm nat wearin a uniform.'

'Get in the fuckin bath. I'm nat listenin ta any more ah yer crap.'

I gave in and went for a bath, scrubbing myself clean. When I got out, there was a centimetre of black scum floating on top of the water, like an oil slick. I dried myself quickly and pulled out the plug and went downstairs for a munch.

Ma looked in my ears and checked the back of my neck. She took a plate from under the grill that had sausages, eggs and beans on it, and she carefully set it down.

'The plate's hot,' she said.

Ma buttered me six slices of bread and I got stuck in. I had only started, when Dolly, my Ma's friend, called into the house and the two of them went into the living room for a wee natter. I wolfed down my grub-steaks and went into the living room.

'Get out, nosy Oliver, we're talkin.'

Dolly excused herself and asked to use the toilet, 'Liam, talk ta yer Ma, I'll be back in a sec.'

Dolly was only away about thirty seconds, when she shouted, 'Donna? Donna?'

Ma shouted back, 'What is it, Dolly?'

'Are ya keepin coal in yer bath?'

Ma looked at me, 'Did ya nat clean the bath, ya dirty fuckin hallion…'

Just as she got the word 'hallion' out of her mouth, I was already out the front door.

'Bye,' I shouted.

I looked over at the maisonettes we had set fire to, most of the doors were kicked in and there were scorch marks everywhere. I remembered the old folk getting carried out on stretchers and the firemen with their masks on putting out the blaze. Some of the old folk had tubes and stuff coming out of their noses and they had looked half-frightened to death. I had set a bin on fire to keep warm. Kieran was with me at the time and the bin set another bin alight until the whole place was in flames. Kieran and I got pulled upstairs by Da, and he was furious. We had put on extra jeans and tops to soak up the blows. We were on the bed when Da came in with a dog chain and whipped the fuck out of us.

Kieran, being half my size, was used as a human shield. I lopped two fingers into the belt loop on the back of his jeans and grabbed him by the coat collar. I think Da only caught me with the chain 3 or 4 times but Kieran was nearly whipped to death, because as I said, I used him as a human shield. I know that I laugh about everything and think that I'm brave but inside I felt as if I was dying and there was no one who could help me.

Da was like a Tasmanian devil muttering as he got stuck into us. As he whipped me, he screamed, 'Yer nat my son, y'evil bastard! What the fuck's wrong with ya? Ya coulda killed all em oul people! Have ya no fuckin conscience? Yer a fuckin monster!'

After he left, I lay on the bed sobbing and praying for death to take me. *I can't go on like this, I can't take it anymore*, and that night I went down to the kitchen and took a knife out of the drawer. *I'll fucking show him*, I thought, and I scarpered over the back wall and away. I went to an old derelict house, where the front wall had collapsed, and I lay down behind it, just out of sight. I took the big butcher's knife out of my coat and cut my wrists. I was 11 years old and felt as though I'd had enough pain in my life and couldn't take it anymore. I lay there for ages in the icy ruins. I lay on the freezing cold ground and a light drizzle was blowing from all directions. I could feel myself getting weaker and weaker. I prayed to God to forgive me and take me up to the heavens. I confessed all of my sins and started drifting in and out of consciousness. I was mumbling for God to come and take me.

I heard God's voice, 'Who is that talking?'

'It's me, Lord,' I mumbled.

'Who is that? The voice again.

'It's me Lord, Liam Kelly,' I was expecting God to lift me into the heavens.

'What ta fuck are ya doin, lyin there?'

I opened my eyes and saw that Nifty Burns stood there, looking down at me.

'Fuck's sake, big lad, things couldn't be that bad.'

Nifty helped me to my feet and brought me into his home and put a big Indian blanket around my shoulders. He made me a cup of tea.

'Big lad, yu're gonna have ta go ta the hospital. Yu've lost a lotta blood.'

'I'm nat goin ta the hospital, em cunts will ring the Peelers.'

'Fuck's sake, man, I can't stap the bleedin.'

'Just tie a few tight bandages around them, I'll be okay.'

He rubbed my back to get some heat into me, as I couldn't stop shivering. He made me eat some biscuits, dipping them into my tea, and popping them into my gob.

'Drink some more tea,' he said.

'It's fuckin roastin.'

'I know, ya need ta warm up quickly. I know yer face, cos I've seen ya with Denise a loada times.'

Nifty and Denise lived six or doors apart in Bruslee Way.

'Why would ya go an' do somethin like this?'

'Nifty, none ah yer business an' I don't wanna talk about it. As soon as I'm done with the tea, I'll head on home.'

'Yu'll need a few stitches.'

'Look, I'm nat goin ta the hospital an' that's that, awright.'

'Awright, awright, I'm only tryin ta help. We have ta be quiet,' he said. 'We don't wanna wake the whole house up.'

'Okay,' I said, 'look I'm gonna slide on nigh, I'm okay.'

I walked the two streets to my house and barely made it upstairs through sheer exhaustion. I had to stop several times, as I felt as if I were about to pass out. I got into bed at 3am.

The following day, I didn't make it downstairs until 12pm or thereabouts. I staggered into the kitchen to make a cup of tea.

'Hangover,' Da said. 'Go an' sit in the livin room an' I'll bring it inta ya.'

'Okay, Da,' I mumbled.

I dragged my feet into the living room and sat down.

'Son, d'ya know where the butcher's knife went outta that drawer?'

'Nah, Da, I don't.'

Ma came in with a wee custard bun, 'Here ya go son, enjoy.'

I had a cup of tea in one hand and a custard bun in the other and then she gently tugged up my sleeves ever so slightly to reveal the bandages. Her eyes quickly darted to mine. I saw tears on her face.

'That's the end ah it,' she said, as she tried to hug me.

'Fuck's sake, Ma, I near roasted myself with the tea.'

'Son, don't break my heart, I love ya so much.'

'I know Ma, but I'm just sick ah always bein in trouble, I just feel like a stupid cunt. I get somethin in my head an' there's no shiftin it. Ma, I feel as if I don't even know who I am. Y'know what I mean?'

The shame and embarrassment landed on me like a ton of bricks, and I burst into tears.

'Who am I?' I said sobbing, 'or what am I? Da said I was a monster an' I feel like a fuckin monster.'

'I'll sort yer Da out about the knife.'

I don't think he ever lifted his hand to me after that and I was given free rein to do what I wanted. I used to come in steaming drunk and was told to go to bed. I didn't have to go to school if I didn't feel like it. They left me to my own devices. No one could control me and beating me didn't help.

When a riot broke out, I would disappear for days on end, as we took shifts during the mayhem. Every now and then, if I needed a kip or food, and people said you looked wrecked, I'd go off somewhere quiet. Then I'd come back, the next person would go for a kip. Riots moved like clockwork, as we endlessly tried to outsmart the Peelers and soldiers.

Da would bring me to 10 o'clock mass on a Sunday morning and afterwards he would bring me over to Marshals, a well-known newsagents and tobacconist on Clifton Street. Da always got his Sunday papers there and they knew him well. The shop's interior was almost completely covered, floor to ceiling and wall to wall, in comics; Marvel and DC. My eyes were fixated on the comics, *The Hulk*, *Spiderman* and *X-men*. I was frozen to the floor, as I scanned the superheroes. *Wow, freaks like me*, I thought, and was so mesmerized I didn't hear my name being called.

'Liam, are ya corned beef?'

I jumped, startled by my Da's loud voice.

'D'ya want one?' He smiled and pointed to the wall of amazing, colourful and bright characters.

I went straight for *The Hulk*. I picked it up carefully and handed it to my Da. He paid for it and rolled it up in his newspapers.

'Ya can have this when ya get home,' he said, 'because I don't want ya tryin ta read it nigh an' walkin out in front ah a bus or somethin.'

As soon as I got home, Da gave me the comic. I flew upstairs, lay on the bed, and started flicking through it, studying every picture intensely. My brother John came in and he read it to me, putting on four or five different voices. I was amazed. He made all the sound effects, as he flicked from page to page. Afterwards, anytime I had enough money, I would dander over to Marshals and buy a comic and my brother John would read it to me. We were hooked, he would give me the money and I would pick up our comics. Two or three comics and that's how our Sundays were spent for what seemed like ages.

I arrived over to Clifton Street one particular Sunday, and it was sealed off by the army. There were half-a-dozen Saracens in a line, blocking the pavement and the main road. They had twenty-foot-high screens to stop anybody throwing anything, as the Orangemen were marching. I knew a wee lane that went out the back of St Kevin's Hall, at the back of the chapel, so I snuck down there and got onto Clifton Street but to my bitter disappointment Marshals was closed, due to the parade. I could see shadows moving about inside, so I banged on the big heavy steel shutter for ages but they wouldn't open up.

Curiosity then got the better of me, so I went to see what all the palaver was about. I got up near North

Queen Street and the bands were marching past. I tried to squeeze between the barriers, to get onto North Queen Street. A spectator, who was following the bands, ran over to me, smashed a bottle over my head and then stuck it in my ear. Blood pished out, like there was no tomorrow, and I was drenched with it in no time at all. The Peelers watched and did nothing. I was 11 years old, in shock, and no one wanted to help. I don't know how I got to the hospital. I remember walking along North Queen Street towards the New Lodge and woke up in the hospital. I had sixteen stiches in my ear and thought how things would have been different if I were *The Hulk*, tossing the Saracens out of the way. I ran different scenarios through my mind about what I would have done, were I a superhero.

'John, from nigh on, yis go ta get yer comics together, I fuckin mean it,' Ma shouted. 'If brains were dynamite, he wouldn't have enough ta blow 'is nose,'

'Fuck up, Ma,' I said, then shouted, 'leave me alone.

'D'ya nat think he's been through enough the day already?' John said, 'Ach Ma, stap cryin…'

'Okay, son,' she sobbed and shuffled on into the kitchen. 'Dinner's nearly ready, so no one's goin out that fuckin door.'

'Okay, Ma,' we all shouted, looking at each other and rubbing our bellies.

Ma came back into the room with a big tall glass of ice-cold milk and gave it to me. She then got out the wee fold-up table, took a fork and knife from her apron pocket and set them down. She shuffled back into the kitchen and returned with a chicken dinner.

'Someone go an' get the brown sauce,' she said. 'Right, the rest ah yis animals get inta the kitchen, I'm dishin out in a minute.'

The kitchen table was small, and only four people could sit around it, so the boys ate first and the girls either stood and waited for a seat or went into the living room and sat in front of the TV.

'How come Liam gat a whole leg ah chicken?' I heard one of my brothers shout. We all sound the same and sound like my Da.

'Fuck up, you,' said Ma. 'A leg? A leg? Yu'll get a toe up the hole, if ya don't button it. An' you, ate yer dinner nigh. I don't want any more slabberin at the table, or yis won't be getting any ah this jelly an' ice cream afterwards.'

Everyone cheered and banged the table with their forks and knives. Then silence fell and was broken only by the rattling and scratching of knives and forks against plates. On a Sunday Ma filled the plates to capacity and this was definitely the favourite meal of the week. You could feel your top trouser button tighten, and you had to open it, as you crammed your food down your gullet. After dinner everyone piled into the living room for the Sunday matinee and waited for dessert.

If a movie starring Humphrey Bogart or James Cagney came on, the boys cheered and the girls booed but if it were a wee soppy movie, the girls cheered, and the boys booed. Everyone fought over the best seats and Ma would soon hand everyone their desert.

'Nigh everyone shush, the movie's startin.'

We'd watch the movie then everyone would go for a kip.

'Boys, there's a scary movie on at ten the night, if yis are interested?'

The scary movies were the best, because after they were over, there would be a mad dash to get up the stairs. We would jump out of cupboards at each other and turn lights out and make ghostly noises, scaring the living crap out of each other. You opened your bedroom door and heavy books would fall and clunk you on the head that someone had put there during a piss break.

Before the scary movie, Ma would get the girls bathed all at the same time and they would be sitting in front of the fire in the living room with their housecoats on. One at a time, they knelt in front of Ma, and she ran a fine-tooth comb through their hair, in order to check for nits. I could hear the girls crying from my bedroom, at the top of the house, and then she'd dry their hair and put ringlets in for school the next day. That was Ma's Sunday ritual, she never stopped, and spent little to no time on herself.

For a long time after the day of the march, any time I thought about how that grown man smashed a bottle over my head, I could feel my blood boil and pictured myself smashing him into bits.

The following day, I stood at the front door, trying to take it all in. I thought about Aunt Sally's lovely home in Glengormley, as I stared out at the concrete and tarmac wilderness. Broken bottles and bricks lay everywhere. Half a spool of barbed wire had been stretched from one side of the road to the other. Cars had almost been burnt out from the carnage the night before. Small skinny pale sickly kids played cowboys and Indians and pretended to shoot one another with sticks. Some were rubbing their hands together to warm them up. A car pulled up to the barbed wire and the driver attempted to move it. The kids stoned him, and he got back into his car and sped away. I wasn't sure whether the barbed wire was to keep people out or to keep us in. A burnt-out bus lay in a heap and resting flat to the ground as the tyres had been burnt off, leaving circles of wire, mangled with the heat. The steering wheel was still intact, and a young boy stood holding onto it, pretending to drive. His hands were pure black, as was his face. He wore a ripped t-shirt that looked three sizes too big for him and a pair of torn baggy trousers with huge holes in them. His two bony knees poked through the holes, he seemed to be happily playing away.

'Ding, ding,' he shouted, ringing his pretend bell.

The boy would shout at anyone who passed, 'Here, mister, have ya gat two nupe ya could spare?'

Every so often, someone chucked him a couple of pence and he shouted, 'Cheers, big ears.' He then ran down to the shop for some sweets. Ten minutes later he'd be back at it again, 'Here, mister, have ya gat two nupe ya could spare?'

The name 'Two Nupe' stuck to him like glue, as he's still called that to this day.

Two Nupe lived in the house facing us, next door was Sarah and Frankie Webb, and you could hear Two Nupe laughing two streets away. He was a bit of a character in the rubble-fuelled jungle, where anything that wasn't bolted down was chucked at the Peelers. Every now and then, a shot would ring out and everyone hit the deck. The rumble of a bomb would go off and you'd see a cloud of smoke rising in the distance.

What ta fuck is this place? I asked myself.

Everyone went about their business, regardless. One minute, everything was calm, the next, there might be a full-on army invasion: armour-plated six-wheelers with guns on top and loads of paratroopers, complete with a radio operator, whose aerial went six feet into the air. They knelt at every corner, scoping out the place.

Who ta fuck are these people? I wondered. *What do they want from us?*

It wasn't long before I found out, because four days after I got the stitches out, I got hit on the elbow with a baton round and got a plaster of Paris put on my broken arm.

At the hospital, the nurse said, 'You again,' and laughed, 'I think you fancy me.'

Da brought me down home from the hospital. I ran amok in our street, bopping all the kids on the head with the solid heavy cast on my arm, which I saw as my new superhero ability, knocking everyone out, and trying to bash their skulls in. Other Mas and Das soon queued at the front door, to complain about my behaviour.

'Right, that's it,' Da shouted. 'Yu're nat gettin back out till that's aff yer arm. Who in the name ah God's this Hulk? Three more Das said the Hulk tried ta bate their kids unconscious an' it was you. I know these kids might be the same age as ya, but they're half yer size, an' it staps nigh.'

Eight weeks, I was stuck in the house; it was driving me nuts. I was nearly licking the paint off the ceiling, as I sat and stared, almost in a catatonic state. I was like a wild dog, caught in a snare, and eating my leg off to get out. I was arguing and fighting with everybody, as it did my nut in, I was bored shitless, lying in front of the TV, watching *Champion the Wonder Horse*.

'If ya sit any closer ta the TV yu'll get square eyes,' Da said.

'But, Da...'

'Never mind, yer, 'But Da'. Go an' get yer coat, yu're gettin yer cast aff the day.'

'Yehaaa!' I screamed and off we went.

I could only get one arm into my coat and Da had to zip it up for me.

The relief I felt was immense, and when the cast came off I wiggled my fingers and bent my arm, to get the blood circulating once more.

'I have ta go see a dog about a man,' Da said, once we were home again.

'Da, Da, it's a man about a dog,' I said.

He laughed.

'Nah, unfortunately, it's a dog about a man. Be good,' he said, as I ran out the door, swinging my arm furiously around and around, like rotor blades.

'Jesus Christ, son,' Da yelled. 'Go easy, fer fuck's sake.'

He shook his head and then let out a huge laugh, as if to say: *there's no hope for him.*

I was well away, zip, zip, zip, as I dodged out of the way of passers-by and thought I was The Silver Surfer. I weaved and bobbed, firing spider webs from my fingers, and swinging round lampposts. I ducked and dived, shooting lasers from my eyes at the Peeler jeeps. I slipped and slid, covering the foot patrols in blocks of ice, like Sentry aka Robert Drake, then back homeward, saving the best until last, as I burst through the door.

'Aghhhhhhh,' I was mimicking my favourite superhero, The Incredible Hulk.

Everyone burst out laughing at this huge numbskull: me.

'Ma, are ya sure ya didn't drop him on his head when he was a child?' John shouted.

'Twice,' Ma said.

'Twice?' I said.

'Aye,' Ma said, 'twice, cos nathin happened the first time.'

Everyone was in hysterics.

'Donna,' said Ma's mate, Dolly, 'I think 'is 's fulla wee doors an' they're all slammin shut at the same time,' and she giggled to herself. 'Nah, nah, Donna, 'is 's fulla wee sweetie mice. Nah, nah, there's air gettin in an' nat gettin out quick enough.'

My family were loving it. They were all in fits laughing.

'Very funny, Dolly,' I said.

'Nah, but, all jokes aside, come over here,' Dolly gestured.

Being as daft as a brush, I went over beside her.

'Son, lift yer head up an' twirl it round and round. Y'know, like, rotate it.'

So, I did.

'Do it again, son,' Dolly said.

So, I did it again.

'Can ya hear that?' she said.

'Hear what?' I said, curiously.

'Hear that fuckin marble rollin about inside yer head.'

By now, my family was on the floor, pissing themselves with laughter.

'Fuck up, all ah yis!' Ma barked. 'Dolly, that's enough. No more, I fuckin mean it,'

Dolly backed down, knowing full-well that Ma was serious.

'He's my son, my special son,' Ma said.

'Aye, special needs,' John said.

'Enough,' Ma shouted, 'Liam, go inta the livin room.'

I noticed Ma fired dagger eyes at Dolly. Dolly put her two hands up.

'I surrender,' Dolly said and wiped the tears of laughter from her eyes and cheeks.

'Nat one more fuckin word,' Ma said and pointed her finger at Dolly.

I went into the living room and my three brothers grabbed me and tried to get me down onto the ground. One jumped on my back, one dived at my legs, one pulled on my arm. I swatted them like flies, throwing them one-by-one onto the sofa. I was as strong as my three brothers put together, I was taller and a lot broader. We were all screaming and laughing, as The Hulk, aka me, smashed them to bits.

The next day, there was a lot of commotion in the New Lodge: a massive riot was about to start. People were going door-to-door, warning people about what was happening. A Protestant workman had been murdered and the residents of Tigers Bay were up in arms. They had come over to the Catholic side of North Queen

Street and were smashing windows and beating people. They were letting off steam. There was a large security presence, who were quite happy to sit back and watch, as the fury was unleashed. They had blocked off the Protestant side of North Queen Street into Tigers Bay and although they could freely cross over to our side, we were prevented from crossing over to theirs by Saracens. Loads of windows in Catholic homes were smashed, as a big angry mob invaded. Three grown men were beating on a young fella, who was protecting his girlfriend. They were hammering him with batons of some kind. He lay over his girlfriend, taking blow after blow to his head and back. We could hear the girl screaming, just as around 70 of us or so arrived at the scene. Many people were rioting, using bin lids and blowing whistles to alert people about what was going on. They were like jungle drums in a Tarzan movie, calling on the wild animals to come out. It was a full-on free-for-all, as people got beaten and nearly bludgeoned to death. Blood ran everywhere, it was a battlefield made up of barbarians fighting for survival.

'Look at the bastard Peelers, just sittin there,' someone shouted.

I was beating a man with a hurl over his head and after a few blows he fell to the ground. The Protestant mob was on retreat. I grabbed an 8-foot piece of barbed wire and wrapped it around a fella, then we tied to him to a lamppost in No Man's Land, which was the road that separated the two opposing sides. We tried to goad the Prods over but they wouldn't come. So, we started stoning the man that we'd tied up. About a hundred of us hurled bricks at him. At first, he squealed but then he must have been knocked out, because he was hit continuously, brick after brick, and didn't utter a word. The Peelers then moved in and, as soon as they did, they got showered with dozens of petrol bombs.

SS RUC, SS RUC, everyone was chanting. *UDR, UDA, UDR, UDA*. They were struggling to save the guy wrapped in barbed wire, because every time they got close, they got bombarded from all sides. As we charged forwards, *boomph, boomph, boomph* they fired. The crowd opened and let the baton rounds through, then crossed over again. Men were now giving orders, telling us what to do and how to do it. We were merciless: a five-gallon drum of petrol was lobbed on top of a Saracen. It had holes in it and the petrol went everywhere. Someone hit it with a petrol bomb, and it went up in furious flames. Six soldiers jumped out, firing and were disorientated by everyone cheering, as the six-wheeler burned.

Bumphhh, bumphh. The baton rounds came thick and fast, and it was fucking madness. People were trying to catch the baton rounds with their jackets, as they bounced uncontrollably. *Crack, crack, crack*, someone fired again at the peace line of Peelers. They dived for cover and waited for reinforcements. An army of Peelers and soldiers arrived and were trying to clear the street, which was littered with burnt-out cars still in flames. A big heavy armour-plated truck, with what looked like two metal H beams welded into a point, pushed through the barricade, like a hot knife through butter. They pushed it aside and drove towards the crowd. *Crack, crack*, a few more shots rang out and everyone dived for cover, running frantically to get clear of the armed lorry, with a foot patrol of soldiers up its ass, firing baton rounds.

It was a cunning strategic move by the security forces, as they next tried to arrest a number of people. First, they stood by and let the situation get out of control, then they got in and arrested as many Catholics as possible. The brutality was swift and effective, and the crowd dispersed, only to move to the top of the New Lodge Road, and it was open season. Buses, cars, vans, lorries, all were fair game, as we swept in, like a tidal wave and created chaos. We blocked off the Antrim Road and everything was on fire, as hundreds of us now took control. The police and army moved in eventually to calm the situation down and we went back down to North Queen Street to pick up where we left off. Three full days I rioted, before going home. It is strange to recall that people in their homes brought out sandwiches and cups of tea for you. A tray of sarnies between four of us, gone in seconds, as we stuffed our faces. Shopkeepers handed out boxes of *Mars* bars and tins of juice and we ate on the hoof.

Three full days and nights I was out, and arrived home at 11am, exhausted and weary. Da was sitting in the kitchen, waiting upon news of my death, or for me to come home.

'Pack a bag, son, yu're comin with me.' he said sternly.

'Where are we goin?'

'Never mind, just get in the car.'

He drove for an hour or so and we came to Newry.

'Da where ta fuck are we goin?'

'Y'know that caravan we have on the wee bitta land I own up in the Cooley Mountains? Well, that's where yu're goin.'

'No fuckin way,' I shouted.

'Look, yer Ma an' I've already discussed it. It's too near the twelfth, so we need ta get ya outta the way, before ya kill someone or get killed yerself.'

'I'm only twelve years oul, Da, what ta fuck am I supposed ta do up in the Cooley fuckin Mountains?'

'Nathin, son, absolutely nathin. Just stay outta trouble.'

We reached the cottage and Da gave me £20 and a box of groceries.

'Oul Jimmy, who lives in the wee cottage next door, will give ya breakfast an' dinner, an' someone will come an' check on ya every week.'

He chucked the box of groceries inside and checked the lights and gas.

'I mean it, son, stay outta trouble. Don't annoy Oul Jimmy an' try ta help him, as much as ya can. Yer mother's head's turned with ya, son.'

I sat in the caravan for an hour.

'Fuck this,' I said.

I walked three miles down to the nearest bar and off-license and bought a case of *McArdles Ale*. I walked back up the mountain to the caravan. In no time at all, me and Oul Jimmy were steaming drunk. We were sitting in front of a crackling fire. There was a black heavy chain hanging down with a big flat metal plate on it, suspended just above the flames. Jimmy was making soda bread and flattened the dough onto the hot plate with his bare hands. He then flipped the loaf beautifully. I loved smelling soda and watching him bake, with what looked like a putty knife. Ten minutes later, he had lovely hot sodas, with butter dripping off them, filled with ham and cheese. There was also a big black teapot that swung in and out by a chain. Jimmy's hands were like shovels, with big fat fingers and hair all over his knuckles. They were like the scary hands you would get in a joke shop. The dimly lit room was filled with the smell of turf. Half-a-dozen big spuds were wrapped in tinfoil and placed around the fire. A whole roast chicken was set in front of me on a table. A crusty loaf and a big block of butter. Jimmy lifted a spud out of the fire with his bare hands, opened the tinfoil and poked a large hole in the spud. Using his thumb, Jimmy then put a large knob of butter into the hole and handed it to me. It was roasting hot, so I set it on the table. Jimmy sliced three big thick rounds of crusty bread for me. He buttered them and set them on the same tinfoil that the hot spuds sat in. He went to the kitchen and brought out a whole roasted chicken. It was on a plate and hot lovely steam from the dark crispy roasted chicken filled the room. He split it in two up the middle, using only his bare hands. The chicken bones cracked as he did. He plopped half a roast chicken on top of my bread.

'Eat,' Jimmy pointed to the food.

Jimmy was a man of few words but his food was exceptional. I got stuck in, as if there were no tomorrow. The blackened crispy chicken skin stuck to my fingers as I pulled it apart; it was sticky and sweet, as he had put honey on it. The spuds were lovely and salty, he had rubbed beef dripping all over them, then salted them before baking. This was a feast for champions. The bread was light and fluffy with a light brown crispy crust. No forks, no knives and no plates, we ate like cavemen, and it was glorious. I sat, stuffed to the neck, and Jimmy handed me a beer out from the box and grunted. We had a sup or two and I went into the caravan to crash. Jimmy banged the door and called me back in. We sat on comfy fireside chairs, enjoying the glorious heat.

I was wakened the next morning by Jimmy at 6.30am, and he took me out to show me how to milk the cows.

'Squeeze an' pull,' he said, in a real culchie accent. 'Loike dat dere.'

It took me a while to get the hang of it, but I was a quick learner.

Jimmy slid a tiny wooden stool over, as I was on my knees, which helped me and made things so much easier: we soon had enough milk for breakfast. It was warm and sweet and wee particles of cream kind floated on top of the mugs of tea. He handed me a couple of slices of thick-cut bread, which I put in a basket that opened like two tennis rackets and held them over the fire, while they went a lovely dark golden brown. A wee metal jug sat beside the fire and Jimmy poured hot melted butter from it over my toast and I watched as it soaked into all the wee holes. I've never tasted toast like it and the two big mugs of tea to boot.

Jimmy went off to work on his tractor and told me to shut the door behind me, if I were going out. Inside, the cottage looked like an old curiosity shop. Old dusty ornaments lined the shelves. The dust lay thick on everything, from a wee delicate delft mother and baby, to the big brass ornate clock that looked as if it had come off the Titanic. A stuffed fox with a pheasant in its mouth took pride of place on a big heavy carved sideboard. Brass framed photos lined the walls: images of some old fishing boats and their crew. Four bottles of whiskey, three covered in dust and one-half empty, a big clay flagon, with a cork the size of my fist and a broken lug, and smudged fingerprints on each side where he held it. A few plates stood on each side of the sideboard on wee makeshift stands. One had the picture of a woman in an old-style dress with a buckle and she was wearing a bonnet. The other was a man in a top hat and he carried a cane. It must have been knocked over many times, as it was cracked and chipped.

I grabbed a 6-pack of *McArdles* and headed up the Cooley Mountains. It was a beautiful day. The sun was splitting the trees and there was a lovely cool sea breeze. I stopped a few times to really fill my lungs with the floral aromas. I saw a huge haystack, sat in the middle of a lush green field. I climbed it and lay on top. I couldn't open my eyes fully, as I could feel the sun burning through my eyelids. I lay for ages, squinting up at the sky, while the sea breeze cooled me down. *This is how the other half live*, I thought, as I cracked open a 'dumpy' bottle of beer and took a long sip. *Can y'imagine if Denise was here, lyin beside ya*? I was in an instant state of calmness at the thought of Denise. I reminisced about our time at the zoo and how much of a good time we had. Denise's Ma then flashed into my head. There was no way in a million years that her Ma would let her be with me. The idea of total happiness fizzled out like a damp squib. I lay on regardless, in the glorious sun, and supped a few more bottles of beer. I yawned and stretched out and decided to nap.

I woke up sometime later and strolled down to Oul Jimmy's. When I arrived, he was throwing out food for the chickens. He put the bucket of feed in my hand, for me to throw out. I chucked handfuls out at them, and they followed me squabbling. Oul Jimmy grabbed a chicken by the head, swung it around and around, clockwise, and broke its neck.

'D'ya fancy chicken fer supper?' he asked.

'Aye, I suppose so, seein as it's a bit late fer the chicken.'

Oul Jimmy strung the bird up and drove off in his tractor. I sat on for thirty minutes or so then went into the cottage and took the quarter bottle of whiskey, as old Jimmy must have mauled it earlier. I walked down to the beach at Gyles Quay, which took half-an-hour. I sat on the pier, on a metal cleat, watching the wee fishing boats spluttering and gurgling in, and the crews displaying their catches. Four or five dogfish chucked up first, they looked like small sharks. I went over to touch one and the skin was rough like sandpaper. Not what I was expecting. Its eyes were white and glassy looking, and sad. I took a swig and put the bottle down. I watched boats bob up and down like corks, as they waited to offload. A steady stream of small vans arrived and went when loaded with each haul. A fella came over to me and started talking.

'Where ya from, big lawd?'

'Belfast. Why?' I looked at him sternly.

'No, nathin, at all,' he said with a smile. 'There's a loada Belfast ones here. They're my buddies.' He pointed to a small group of people.

'That's Liz, Cathy, Michael, Liam an' I'm Pádraig.'

They all gave a wee wave in my direction.

'I'm Liam Kelly, nice ta meet y'all.'

We all walked together up a long flight of stone steps that led over the pier wall, and up to a wee small lighthouse kind of place. We climbed up a rusted metal ladder that was bolted to a circular stone tower. A metal safety bar surrounded the top, where we sat and looked out to sea.

'We're all from Dundalk, an' we drive down here all the time, cos it's so quiet an' peaceful.'

Two gulls were squabbling over scraps, as the fishermen gutted the fish on a big table that had been set up for just that job. All the guts and scraps were scrapped into a black plastic bucket and emptied into the sea. Seagulls constantly dived into the water like kamikaze pilots. I took the bottle out of my coat and shared it around. Swig after swig and we sat motionless, holding onto the rusted bar at the top of the wee stone look-out post. We were forty feet or so above the waves and gulls flew against the wind. They looked as if they were hovering, waiting on their turn to dive-bomb.

We talked about the troubles in Belfast, and they were amazed at the stories. The girls especially looked shocked. I told them about my wee Ma getting booted by the solider. We exchanged stories and sat for ages, chin-wagging about every kind of topic. The pier was in full swing now and packed with people. We climbed down and walked along the beach, throwing skimmers in the sea and pushing one another onto the waves. I watched most of the others hold hands and I thought of Denise.

'Fuck this,' I said, 'I'm goin home now, I'll find my own way, no bother.'

They tried to talk me out of it, as we were oiled up. The whiskey bottle got chucked into the waves and I said my goodbyes. I walked up onto the main road and thumbed a lift. I travelled as far as Omeath on the back of a lemonade truck. I knocked around Omeath for hours. I laughed at the cop shop: their police station was off the main street, and it looked like a double-fronted house, complete with curtains, no bars or bulletproof windows. I burst out laughing, *Jesus, that place wouldn't last a crack back home*, I thought to myself. I sat on a grass bank that ran up the side of a park. Kids were playing football, while their parents watched.

I next moved closer to the carpark and started asking as many people as possible, 'Are ya goin ta Belfast?'

It only took fifteen minutes, and I got a lift to Carlingford. When I got there, it was like walking down the New Lodge Road, I knew almost everyone.

'Young Scalper,' someone shouted.

It was Blue Kelly.

'What're ya doin here? An' is yer Da with ya?'

I paused, 'Nathin an' nah, he's nat here.'

Blue was on the Felon's committee along with my Da and he knew me well.

'Was yer Da nat takin ya somewhere?'

'Aye, he did, but it didn't work out.'

'Ya hungry, big lad?'

'Sorta,' I said but I was starving.

I told Blue how my Da left me up the Cooley Mountains with Oul Jimmy, because he was worried about me acting up over the Twelfth of July. I declared my innocence and Blue went to the chippy and got me a fish supper. We went back to Blue's gaff.

'Ya can stay here with us tonight, but I'm ringin yer Da themarra. Belfast's about fifty miles away, it's too dangerous ta thumb it. Are ya mad?' he said.

'As a fuckin hatter,' and we both laughed.

'Well, as I said, I'll ring him themarra, an' he can decide what he wants me ta do with ya,' said Blue.

'I'm just goin out,' I said, 'ta stretch my legs before bed.'

'No problem,' Blue said, as he rubbed his full stomach.

I left and headed straight to the main road, and it was pitch black, no streetlamps. I sat on a low wall at the side of the road and jumped up and stuck my thumb out whenever a car came. Thirty minutes or so passed and an old minibus stopped, I didn't like the look of it but it kept on beeping its horn. I walked over cautiously; I ran my hand up the side of it and I could feel all the rust bubbles that were now hard and flaky and cracked. I walked up to the driver's window; it rolled down and a massive cloud of cigarette smoke billowed out. I fanned it away from my face and coughed. The smoke cleared. To my surprise, a wee old nun was sat there, with a feg hanging out of her mouth.

'Are you getting in or not?' she barked, her voice gruff and deep.

Nun on the Run

I tried not to show my bemusement for fear of jeopardizing my lift. I slid open the door and climbed inside. Musical instruments were strewn everywhere, a battered and well-worn base drum was tied to a chair with a rope and the seat next to it had a bass trombone securely fasted to it. The floor was carpeted and ripped in places. The ends and corners had all curled up and had seen better days. My eyes scanned everywhere, and my brain now told me that it was safe to sit down and relax. My bum had no sooner hit the seat and zoom, we were doing nought-to-sixty in seconds, the wee nun was flying like a bat out of hell. I got thrown backwards, as she accelerated. I burst out laughing, and the wee nun turned to look at me, she was mounting kerbs and knocking over bins.

'Watch out, fer fucks sake,' I yelled.

She turned back to watch the road again. This wee woman must have been a rally driver in her former life, and she flew round corners and bends and never braked once. Instruments were sliding and flying in all directions, she was like a character from the *Wacky Races* cartoons. I looked at the base drum and trombone. They were tied securely and barely moved. They sat there, like valued customers on the taxi-ride of their lives.

The wee nun lit up another cigarette and I could see the glare of its reflection in the windscreen. She looked down towards the flame and didn't even see the red light she went through. A few puffs later and I could hardly see through her cloud of cigarette smoke. Instruments clattered inside the bus as they slid about, moving in all directions, as she drove erratically around the bends. By the time we got to the border crossing, the rain was falling quite heavily and dancing on the windscreen, as the wiper blades threw it from side to side. We stopped and got out, for the army to search us and the vehicle. The nun stepped out of the minibus, and she was tiny, less than five feet tall and she looked scrawny. Her face was wrinkled and tired and looked every bit of seventy years of a hard life. Her tiny frame made her look fragile, and I couldn't get the vision out of my head of the racing driver from hell. I nursed a big lump on the side of my head, which resulted from my skull hitting on the side of the window frame, when she had almost done a handbrake turn. Her thick-framed glasses, which housed chunky lenses, almost looked too big for her. At times, she would turn her head, which made her eyeballs look huge and made me think of an owl.

I started laughing, and a Brit said, 'Oi, Mate, ya fink it's fanny,' in a real cockney accent.

The wee nun stepped in front of me, 'Don't say another word and get back on the bus.'

I did what she asked and got in.

'You can't be too careful these days,' she said in her deep raspy voice. 'Some of those soldiers think it's the olden days, you know, the old draconian laws. But we're okay now and tomorrow's another day.' Her voice did not suit her, and it must have been the smoking, as she lit up one cigarette after another.

'My Da always comments on the oul draconian laws an' how we were treated as vermin, funny enough,' I said.

The nun stared at me.

'There's nothing funny about it,' she said.

Before long we had pulled up on the Banbridge to Belfast Road.

'You're going that way. I'm going this way. Take care now.' She pointed to the Banbridge signpost with one hand and handed me a fistful of shrapnel with the other.

I got out of the van and shoved the coins into my pocket.

'God bless you now,' she said and was gone, wheels spinning as though she were in a car chase.

No On/off Switch

It was close to midnight, and I started walking. I walked for hours and didn't even see a car on the road. Army land rovers and Saracens rumbled by, going to wherever.

Daylight broke with a chorus of birds, all fluttering and stretching their wings. The sun on my face was welcome, as I was soaked through. I took off my coat and hung it on the branch of a tree. I could now feel the sun on my back and my t-shirt was soaked, misty steam rose from my coat, as the sunshine enveloped it.

I sat by the side of the road, not even standing or trying to thumb a lift when cars passed. By nine o'clock I was as dry as an Arab's flip-flop, so I stood up and started walking again. Lisburn—2 Miles—a signpost read. A black taxi approached, I did not know what side of the community the driver was from, nor did I care, I stuck out my thumb and he stopped. I explained my situation.

He said, 'Just hop in.'

Before long, I was in Andytown, west Belfast.

The taxi driver pulled up and said, 'I've a few errands ta run, but if ya hang about fer awhile, I can run you inta Castle Street.'

'Happy days,' I shouted.

Andytown Road was bumper to bumper, lorries and buses mainly. It almost looked normal, except for the skeletal remains of a double-decker bus, and a few burnt out cars that had been pushed into a layby beside the shops. Beyond the layby was a piece of waste ground where lots of burnt out remains lay. It was like a graveyard for the DOE. Kids ran about screaming, chasing one another and re-enacting riot scenes, as they chucked bricks at each other, as if they were hand grenades, making explosion noises as they fell. They were split into two teams and the captured team was lined up against the wall.

'How d'ya wanna die?' A boy shouted.

The first captive said, 'Bow and arrow.'

So, the boy drew back his imaginary bow and fired.

The captive kid staggered forward with his hands up to his chest, he coughed aloud.

'Right in the heart,' he said, then collapsed to the ground, as if he were dead.

The next captive said, 'Tomahawk.'

And so on, until a heap of bodies lay motionless. It was like a west Belfast western unfolding. I watched the alpha dog change over and over, as others got beat with poles.

'Yu're too fuckin rough,' one boy shouted and got wired into another kid. They fell out and made up a few times.

I sat on a stump watching them practicing, I couldn't stop laughing, because these kids were tiny but still had loads of spirit, as they mucked about the DOE graveyard.

The black taxi man came back and handed me a foot-long sausage roll and sachets of tomato ketchup and brown sauce.

'Choose yer poison,' he said laughingly.

I squirted on the brown sauce.

'Yu'd better ate that outside, before ya make a mess.'

I gulped down the warm sausage roll, and I could feel it warm in my belly and fifteen minutes later I was outside Rab Maguire's barber's. I stuck my head in the door.

'Young Scalper,' Rab shouted, 'there's a search party out lookin ya. Yer Da's doin 'is fuckin nut in. Get on home, straight away.'

I jumped in a black taxi and got out at Carlisle Circus at North Queen Street as the Antrim Road was blocked and I had to go up the Crumlin Road to get to Ardoyne. Once there I was able to get another black taxi down to the New Lodge. I was home in ten minutes and Ma nearly strangled me to death hugging me.

'My son, my son,' she whimpered. 'We were worried sick, son, so we were.'

'Fuck's sake Ma, y'know I can look after myself. I'm fuckin twelve Ma, I'm nat a child.'

Da came flying in the door. 'What're ya doin up here?' And before I could say anything, he said 'Yu're goin back down there.'

'Fuckin sure I'm nat, no fuckin way. Yis would have ta tie me ta a fuckin chair or somethin.' I screamed.

'How did ya get home?' Ma asked.

'Thumbed it.'

'What! The whole fuckin way?'

'Aye.'

'Jesus Christ, Billy, he coulda been killed or somethin. Billy, just let him stay. Y'know there's no talkin ta him.'

'Alright, but ya can't have the cops here all the time lookin for ya. An' no more playin chicken, tossin hand grenades at each other. Someone coulda been killed.'

I shrugged my shoulders.

'Are ya listenin ta me son?'

'Aye, Da, I hear ye.'

I had no fear or sense of danger and a tremendous amount of anger that sat deep in the pit of my stomach, making me feel sick most of the time. Denise was the only one that I didn't feel that way with, she always made me feel calm and relaxed. She made me feel soft and vulnerable, and I knew that I would always protect her and not let anything bad happen. She was the only bit of colour in the concrete and tarmac building site we lived in.

Da was tossing things around in his head, 'Okay, son. Ya can stay but don't let me down.'

'I'm knackered. I'm away up ta my bed,' Ma said and left the room.

'Bro, Bro,' my brother, John, shouted, 'do fridge magnets stick ta the metal plate in yer head, or is it just one big lump of wood?'

And we all had a good laugh.

'Very funny, but nat as funny as findin out ya were adopted,' I replied.

'Me, adopted? Yu're the one who looks as though ya ate yer own twin. Like, look at the size ah ya, and ya think I'm the one adopted.'

'Enough,' Da shouted, 'before this gets outta hand.'

'But Da, do I have a metal plate in my head?'

'Aye son, ya do, they'd ta melt one of the bells down in Saint Patrick's chapel ta make it. Nigh, I'm nat sayin yu've a big nut, or anythin like that, but they had ta use the whole bell.'

We all burst out laughing.

'That's cracker, Da,' my brother shouted out, still laughing. 'Melt a bell... melt a fuckin bell... that's a cracker.'

The more he said it, the more we laughed. Sides splitting by now and struggling to breathe. It was as if all of the oxygen had been sucked out of the room, as we all held our throats and gasped. It took about ten minutes for us to regain any kind of function to our bodies.

John, grabbed me by the cheeks, 'Bro we'll be talkin about this moment for generations.'

'Generations?' I sniggered. 'All this crap will stop at us. Generations? Who in their right mind would bring a kid inta a shithole like this?'

'Houl on bro, relax. Yu're only sayin that cos ya couldn't get a dog ta bark at ya, never mind touch fer a bird. It'll all change, mark my words, bro, it'll all change. Come on into the kitchen, I'll make us a cup of tea.'

'Too late,' Da shouted, 'there's one on, I'm just waitin on it stewin.' A few minutes later Da spoke again, here, son, take this up ta yer Ma. Y'know, she's worried sick about ya.'

I shook my head and lifted Ma's cup. Ma, apart from all her gusto and bravado, only drank out of a fine bone China cup. It had a shiny gold edge, and if by chance you'd hand her a mug of tea, she would simply say, 'Jesus, d'ya think I'm a docker,' and pour it down the sink. We had a big kitchen cupboard full of mugs of all sizes and one wee fine bone China cup that no one was allowed to use except Ma. When Da handed me the cup of tea, the handle was so small that I couldn't get my fingers inside. Da placed it on the palm of my hand and I took the teacup up.

'Here, Ma, Da sent this up.'

'Thanks, son,' she said and smiled. 'Here, what's all the commotion down there?'

'Ma, if I toul ya, I don't think yu'd believe it. Ma… we nearly died laughing. I swear ta God, Ma. I could see fuckin angels.'

'Aye, son, Hells Angels ya mean,' and she cackled like a witch. 'Son, nigh that ya mention it, y'always did have the face of a saint.'

'Really, Ma?' I said naively.

'Aye, son, a Saint Bernard,' and she cackled away, sipping the tea.

'All yis fuckers need ta be up on the fuckin stage,' I said, 'cos yis don't wanna ever stop.'

'I'll stop when they're nailin the lid shut an' nat one minute before.'

'Nice one, Ma. Did y'know that cos there's that many people dyin, they're runnin outta graveyard space, so, from next year, everyone gets buried in the standin-up position, like what they do in China.'

'Fuccccck,' Ma said spitting her tea out everywhere, 'I'm nat gettin buried standin-up, ya can be fuckin sure of that.'

'Ma, yu've ta tell the priests nigh, ta book a lyin-down grave, they gave it out in Sunday mass that yu've ta do it, before the new legislation comes from the Vatican.'

'Billy, Billy,' Ma shouted and seconds later, Da was standing there.

'What's up, wee woman?'

'Billy, did they give it out in Sunday's mass that we've ta get buried standin-up, like what them ones do in China, cos there's no more room in the graveyards?'

'Aye, Da,' I said, with a wee laugh, 'like they do in China.'

'Donna, don't fuckin listen ta him, y'know he comes with papers.'

'Papers,' I said, 'what papers?'

'The papers certifyin ya.' Da said.

'Certifyin me for what?'

'Son, certifyin yu're mental. Oh, sorry I didn't mean mental, I meant insane. Donna, don't listen ta him, sure he's barred from St Patrick's.' Da gave me a sly look. 'Aye, son, barred, ya didn't know I knew about that. Ya thought that I wouldn't find out.'

'Da, y'know that I don't believe in shite.' I said.

Ma blessed herself, 'I don't wanna hear talk like that.'

'Ma, they're all paedophiles.'

'Get him outta here,' she screamed.

'Ma, my mate told me what they done ta him in 'is own fuckin kitchen, while 'is Ma and Da were talkin ta another Priest in his own fuckin livin room.'

'Billy, Billy, get that fuckin heathen outta here. He's no respect for the Catholic Church whatsoever.'

'Yu're right, Ma. I don't.'

'Son, c'mon. Ya know how yer Ma gets on, when ya talk like that.'

'Da, relax, it all started as a joke.'

'I know Son, but ya don't have an on-off switch, like the rest ah us. Ya just keep on goin.'

'Okay, Da, I get the picture.'

Take it on the Chin

I flew downstairs and went over to my Harding Street stash. It was an old biscuit tin that I'd buried in a derelict building. A black widow duck caty, two socks of ball bearings, a knife, a hacksaw blade though rusty, it did the job. Seven darts and loads of boxes of black cat bangers. A white cue-ball, covered in chips, which I had stolen from Artillery Youth Club. This was my secret stash that only I knew about, I opted for the black widow catapult. I took my jacket off, put my arm through the elastics and tucked the handle right up into my armpit. I put my jacket back on and zipped it up. The reason we carried the catapults this way was, if you were stopped, you'd a chance of not losing it when getting searched by the army. I then untied a sock and emptied out four or five ball bearings and put them in my pocket. I put my stash away and headed up the Antrim Road. I looked about and thought about what I could do. I went to Coulters, a Ford dealership that had been burnt out, and walked to the back wall. The building had been completely gutted, and part of the roof was gone. It lay collapsed on the ground, with the remnants of car carcasses that had once shone brightly and were now burnt black and mangled with the heat.

I quickly climbed up the wall, using a burnt-out coffee machine as a starting point. I carefully manoeuvred around the fallen roof onto the next level. The walls were scorched black, with streaks running down, where the rain had washed the soot off, and I then hopped onto the roof. At the front of the once-pristine showroom, the wall of the building was higher than the ceiling and extended up at least another two feet. There was a brick missing in the centre: I could lie down and look through the gap without being detected; it was like a big peephole. I lay down and watched everyone *dootering* about their business. I saw loud crying kids getting dragged by the arm to Pim Street School just facing me. I watched a baker's van pull up outside Julie's shop. The driver got out and opened the back doors and slid out a couple of big wooden trays and carried them inside. He was in there for ages, before coming out to lift the next load of buns and baps. Getting rations for my military operation occurred to me but the sight of an army Land Rover pulling up and a foot patrol jumping out of the back put an end to my bun-robbing scheme.

The soldiers adopted defensive positions and looked through the sights of their rifles, assessing all vantage points. I crouched down, stared through the wee brick hole and waited for my opportunity to strike. The soldiers had full combat gear on, except for their headwear: instead of helmets, they wore wee berets with some kind of flower poking out the side. A big heavy Saracen rumbled up and growled to a standstill. A foot patrol in full riot gear marched out of the double doors at the back. The first foot patrol covered them, as they disembarked and as soon as the last boot hit the tarmac, the Saracen rumbled off going into a huge ROArrrrrrr as it accelerated away. This made them easy to detect at night, as you could hear them a mile or so away. I lay down and waited for my moment, I could feel my heart pounding, my hands sweating as I had watched intently, waiting, hoping to get a good head or body shot, as they ducked in behind kids in prams, while taking aim and scoping out the place. My eyes fixated on the soldier with his back to me, I just needed a clear shot. I quickly stood up and took my shot. *Whooosssh* the ball bearing had flown, and the only feeling I anticipated would be the elation as the solider fell. I missed completely, but the ball bearing bounced up off the kerb and caught another soldier under the chin. His face looked like it exploded. I dropped back down into my hiding spot again. I could still see through a hole in the wall and looked on in disbelief.

'Fuck,' I screamed aloud and watched as the other soldiers scurried about, like frantic ants, checking everywhere with their scopes. I started crawling backwards on my belly, trying to stay as flat as possible. I could hear their English accents shouting out instructions to one another. I could hear footsteps getting closer to me. I reached the end of the roof and I dropped down onto Cranburn Street and calmly stepped out onto the pavement. I looked across the road and there was blood everywhere. They lifted the injured soldier into the back of a Saracen. The soldiers went mad and shot at two big dogs that were constantly trying to bite them. Everyone nearby was put up against a wall, hands above their heads and they roughly searched them. I was slapped on the back of the head by a soldier.

'And don't fucking move,' he slobbered and yelled.

'Mate, just shoot, yu'll be doin mosta us a favour.'

'Oi, shat yer faking gob, I'm warning you,' he spat at me.

He kicked my legs apart. There were twenty of us pushed up against the wall, spread-eagled. I'd left my duck caty on the roof of Coulters but I still had a few of the spikey ball bearings in my pocket. I waited for my chance.

'Run! Run!' I shouted.

Everybody who was lined up against the wall quickly turned and ran. I offloaded the ball bearings as I ran. Adrenaline kicked in, even more than before, when I had lain in wait.

I had escaped the line-up and was in the graveyard. I poured myself a bag of glue but then decided against sniffing it, so I went back over to my stash on Harding Street. I was considering going back for my caty, when my brother Martin came in.

"Here, Da's lookin ya.'

'What's he want?'

'How ta fuck would I know?' he grunted. 'But he doesn't look happy.'

'Fuck's sake,' I murmured.

I walked casually into the house.

'Where were ya?' Da snapped.

'Nowhere.'

'Where's nowhere?'

'I was over in Hardin Street.'

My brother butted in, 'Aye Da, that's where he was, when I found him.'

'Is that right? Dog's balls.'

'Who the fuck are ya talkin ta?' I yelled.

'Shut it, the two ah yis. An' mind the house till I get back, I've ta do a wee message. Right move it, ya two balloon bags. Inta the livin room, nigh.'

We had no sooner got into the living room when Da left, and the front door banged.

'Who is it?' I shouted.

No one answered.

Then I realised my brother had split. My four sisters were serving tea in their wee imaginary cups and saucers and taking polite wee sips, making slurping noises for added effect. There were three big cardboard boxes in the Hall, sitting on top of each other, so I found a black marker and a pair of scissors and went to work, turning the boxes into dollhouses. I drew doors and windows that swung open. A back door and a wee secret side door, we could sneak out if the Peelers came, I explained. I brought the boxes into the living room.

'Right, girls, drink up. I made yis doll's houses.'

They could hardly contain themselves as they dived onto the floor. They swung open the windows and doors, as if their wee imaginary teddy bears and dolls were calling for them to come out to play. They sat for a good hour, muttering, and giggling to each other. The front door slammed closed, and all the girls shouted, 'Mammy' and ran to her.

The sweat was lashing off Ma, and she had two big heavy shopping bags. I could see the handles dug deep into her hands.

'Here, gimme em begs, Ma,' I said.

I took them off her in the hall and set them on the kitchen table.

'Careful,' she shouted, 'there's eggs in there.'

'No sweat, Ma. Just hang up yer coat an' go an' sit down. I'll bring y'in a cuppa tea.'

'Oh, thank ya son,' she said, as if she were a wounded animal and gasped for a breath.

The girls were running around her and hanging on to her for grim death.

'Girls, girls,' Ma said but they weren't listening. 'Jesus, isn't this wild?'

She laughed as she made it to her chair in safety, without tripping.

Ma shouted 'Son, when yu're comin in, bring a packet of snowballs.'

'Okay Ma,' I replied.

I went in to set her wee floppy table up.

Ma hadn't even a hand to mop the sweat off her brow as she was bouncing two kids on knees and had the other two in her arms and looked absolutely helpless.

'Right, girls, scoot. Ma's gonna have her tea.'

The four girls sat on the sofa, while age determined their place, the oldest sat nearest to Ma and so forth. Ma then broke two snowballs in half and gave them to the girls. They squealed in excitement as they got their surprise. She took one herself and handed me one and hid the other two behind her cushion.

'Em two are for yer Da, so no one go fuckin eatin em.' Ma said.

She ate the snowball and sipped from her fine bone China teacup.

'Ahhhh,' she sighed, wriggling her toes. 'Here, son, do us another wee favour an' fly up an' get my bedroom slippers. They're up the side of the bed.'

'No sweat, Ma,' I said.

I acted as if I had been given a covert mission, as I breezed up and down the stairs. I put Ma's slippers on her feet.

'Thank ya, son,' she said and was straight up and headed for the kitchen, to start putting dinner on.

'Jesus, Ma, yu're only in the door. Sit down fer five.'

'No time, son,' and she shuffled on past me.

'Ma, d'ya want me ta peel the spuds?'

'Why what've ya done?'

'Nathin Ma,' I said.

'Are ya sure son?'

'Aye, Ma, I'm sure.'

'Well, tell me then where'd ya get all them bricks from? Were ya in that fuckin buildin site again?'

'No, Ma, what the fuck are ya takin about? What fuckin bricks?'

'The ones ya used ta build the doll's houses in there,' Ma said and then burst out laughing.

'Fuck's sake, Ma, I'm nearly in shock. I hadn't a clue what ya were talkin about. Jesus.' I sighed, 'I thought I was in trouble again.'

The two of us laughed.

'Them spuds aren't gonna peel themselves,' she said and gave me an apology smirk for winding me up.

She was like a wee five-foot octopus as she unloaded the shopping, everything getting put in its right place.

'Son, go in an' get em snowballs an' put them on that top shelf there, where no one will find em.'

'No sweat, Ma,' I hid the snowballs for her and got to work on the spuds.

'Y'know, son, I used ta train as a skin-and-eye specialist.'

'Are ya serious, Ma, or are ya just fuckin me about?'

'No, son, I'm serious,' she said.

'Where was this Ma?'

'West Belfast, son.'

What the Royal Hospital?' I said aloud.

'No, son, Aldo's chippy. I used ta do their spuds for them,' she burst out laughing again. 'Got ya.'

'Ma, yu're crackers. The fuckin men in the white coats will be comin for ya, so they will.'

'We're comin ta take you away,' she sang, 'haha hehe hoho haha,'.

'Ma, yu're nuts. D'ya ever stap?'

She was so comical.

'Oh, thank God ya were in the house the day, as a solider got shot by someone on the Antrim Road. The Peelers an' the army raided loadsa houses an' found weapons an' stuff.'

'Sure, they've nathin better ta do Ma,' I said.

'Aye, they just raid an' lift whoever they want. Half the time they probably put the guns there themselves, the dirty rotten bastards. They justify it on the news, a cache of weapons found. It's a loada bollocks,' Ma said.

Da was always going on about the English propaganda shite that was never off the news.

'Here, son em, boxes were ta be fer food parcels ta go over ta the Falls Road, as them people there have nathin, as they're hemmed in. Can't go ta work, can't go ta the shops fer food for their families. All us women are goin over there on Friday. Thousands ah us, hopefully, just ta see how they like it. It's bloody ridiculous.'

'Go on Ma! Tiocfaidh ár lá!' I shouted and the two of us killed ourselves laughing.

Da came in and said, 'Fuck me, Donna, did he fall and bang his head?'

'What d'ya mean, Da? Me peelin the fuckin spuds?'

'Oh, hilarious y'are. Yu're funny but yer bake bates it,' Ma said. 'Nigh lee-im-alone, Billy Kelly. Get out ta I put the dinner on y'animal dog, ye.'

Da laughed, 'Donna did ya tell him about bein dropped on his head twice.'

'Get fuckin out, or I'll drop you on yer fuckin head.'

Da went out and shouted, 'Donna! Jesus Christ!'

'What is it nigh?'

'Where'd them boxes go? Y'know the ones in the Hall.'

'I used em,' Ma said, defending me. 'Son, when yu've peeled the last spud, will ya fly down ta Sarah Webb's an' grab some boxes?'

I finished peeling the spuds and headed out the front door and quickly turned, locking the door behind me and staying inside the house. I ran through the kitchen, passed Ma and out the back door and climbed over the back wall. A Saracen and two jeeps had just pulled up and I wasn't taking any chances. Ma and Da were left with nothing except for two blank expressions on their faces. They may not have heard the rumble of the Saracen or the screech of the brakes, or the jeeps, for that matter, but I did.

I cautiously crept through all the wee alleyways, darting corner to corner avoiding the army watchtowers on the high-rises with military precision and on stealth mode. I made my way to the graveyard. The beads of sweat were like razor blades, running down my back as they cooled instantly, and my back pressed up against the cold crypt wall. I sat all day, not knowing what to do. I believed that the Peelers were looking for me and I tried to imagine what for: breaking into places and stealing tires for fires, ball bearings, hitting the soldier with the catapult?

Tommy Gunn and a few others gathered for a swalley.

'Hahahaha've ya bin hehehehere all day?'

'Why?' I said.

'Yer Da's bin everywhere lookin ya an' so are the Papapapapeelers. What did ya do?' he asked.

'Nathin,' I snapped.

We all kept quiet, we could hear a tin can hit another, someone set off our alarm system. We took off in different directions. Five or six men in balaclavas were hand-signalling to one another. They made a few strange whistling noises then I felt this sack go over my head and tied up with a piece of rope placed around my neck. I heard the clunk and creak of big metal gates being opened, and I was thrown into the back of a car. No one spoke the entire time and I was then marched into a building on Glenravel Street and made to lie face down. The sack was still on my head but rays of light were breaking through the fibres. The bag was roughly woven and likely was a Hessian bag used for potatoes. But I couldn't make anything out. I thought my abductors were SAS, because of the hand signals and shit. My two hands were tied behind my back and both my feet were tied together. They bent my feet back until they touched my ass and then tied them to my hands. I was truly trussed up like a pig. The pain was immense as my legs cramped, my shoulders and the back of my neck went into a spasm, and I tried to wriggle free.

'Fuck's sake whaddyas want?' I yelled.

I heard three or four footsteps then I got a kick on the side of the head.

'Ya yella bastard! Lemme fuckin up an' have me a fair go, ya yella cunt!'

I could hear footsteps and braced myself for another kick.

A voice guldered, 'ENOUGH!' and everything stopped.

'D'ya know who we are?'

'Aye, Ken Dodd an the Diddy Men!' I said. 'How ta fuck would I know? SAS, maybe?'

The man laughed, 'No, we're the Irish Republican Army.'

'The backstreet mafia. Well, yu'd better let me up, before my Da gets here,' I said in a cocky manner.

I could hear Ma's voice and knew she was outside the graveyard. She was crying, 'Nat my son, please, he's nat right y'know.'

I could barely make her pleading words out, as people started walking about and making noise. Panic struck me like a bolt of lightning as I feared the inevitable.

'Go on, do whatever ta fuck yis want. Ma doesn't deserve this.

I could hear her pleading and stressing out, so I yelled, 'Hurry up, ya yella cunt. Fuckin shoot me!'

Ma was getting hysterical, and her wee voice started to break. I tried to stretch out a tiny bit to ease the cramps, but nothing helped. I felt the cold metal bar to the side of my head. BANG, I heard. I was like a fish out of water, as I flip-flopped about the ground. I opened my eyes a few moments later, wondering what to fuck was happening.

'The next time, we'll put bullets in the gun.'

By now I was hyperventilating and couldn't breathe. Ma was beside me comforting and calming me, pleading for me to breathe.

'Ya can't keep bringin em black bastards into the area y'know. Ya cause so much fuckin trouble.' One of the provos said.

I knew he was talking about the Peelers.

Ma loosened the rope around my neck and loosened the sack but didn't take it off. I felt the cool air coming in, and my brain started to get back to normal.

'Here, yo,' I shouted, 'the fuckin Peelers are already in our area, so wat ta fuck are ya takin about?'

'Have ya learned nathin at all, big lad? Like, nathin at all?'

'Lemme fuckin up, an' I'll show ya what I learned.'

'Jesus, son,' said Ma. 'What ta fuck am I gonna do with ya? Please, please, be quiet.'

I could feel the fire burn deep inside me as my anger built. Ma's voice settled and calmed me.

'Ma, I heard the bang.'

'What bang?'

'In my head, the gun. The gun went off, Ma. I thought I'd shat myself, Ma.'

Ma looked at the puddle of pee where I must have pissed myself. I don't really remember much when the hammer clicked in my ears, I must have gone into shock or something. I'll never forget that cunt's voice that's for sure. People say that you don't hear the shot that kills you and even though there was no bang, once the hammer on the gun clicked, in my head I heard the bang which sent shivers down my spine, almost electrifying me.

Ma and I walked home, and she gave me a kiss on the forehead.

'Ma, I'm alright fer fuck's sake.'

'Aye, son, I know yu're alright fer nigh, but will ya be alright themarra, or the next day, or the next day?' Ma sobbed relentlessly, as she broke her heart worrying.

'Ma, themarra's promised ta no one. How many times have I heard ya say that yerself?'

'I know, son, c'mon in fer a wee cuppa.'

I looked down at Ma's wee tired face, her heavy brow and bloodshot eyes filled with tears of pain. *Why, why, why do I keep doing shit like this?* I asked myself. I hadn't meant to hurt my Ma but it always fell back onto her. I would have felt better if the cunts had killed me, as the shame and embarrassment of Ma coming to my rescue and having to listen to her pleading to those animals was heart-breaking. I was twelve years of age, and the scenario was beyond comprehension.

We sat down to our cuppa and Da came flying in the door.

'Jesus Christ are y'okay,?' he said, catching his breath.

'I'm fine,' I said.

'I'm nat talkin ta ya, empty head, I'm talkin ta yer Ma. Donna, are y'okay?'

'I'm fine, Billy,' she cried.

Da put Ma's head on his shoulder and rubbed her back to comfort her. Da fought to hold his tears back and I'd never seen him cry before.

'It's bad enough we're takin on the British Army an' the Peelers, now yer Ma's takin on the IRA. Nigh this has ta stop, it has ta fuckin stap. Nigh, can ya get it through that big fuckin thick skull ah yers: she doesn't deserve this? She really doesn't, like Jesus, there's eighta yis an' yu're the one, the only fuckin one. Come on, stand up, be a man an' take responsibility fer yer actions. Fer every action there's a reaction, that's what yu've ta remember, son. The security forces are fightin an unwinnable war, they just don't know it yet. We're an invisible army, whose life's blood runs through the wee cobbled streets, like veins in yer body. We're embedded inta every street, corner an' alleyway. We're the mortar that holds the very bricks tagether. We don't need ta be worryin about a loose cannon like you all the time. Are ya listenin, son?'

'Fuck's sake, Da, I thought ya were gonna start singin fer a minute there.'

'Get out! Get out! Yu're a heartless bastard of a child! Get out! An' don't come fuckin back!'

'Billy, please, please. He hasn't even turned thirteen years oul yet, Billy. An' he's never bin right from the accident. Nigh, y'know that, Billy.'

'Donna, he can't be allowed ta keep doin this ta ya. Ta us. Cos everybody suffers, so they do.'

I left, banging the front door behind me and shouting, 'Aye, fuck ya an' fuck the horse ya rode in on.'

I disappeared into a dark alleyway. I wandered round the streets and ended up walking through Tigers Bay, a Protestant estate nearby.

Their wee parlour houses looked exactly the same as ours. Drunks littered the street corners, and they were living exactly like we were. All the atrocities were committed against the Protestant people, not the Protestant paramilitaries, the real working-class people came flooding to my thoughts, bombarding my mind. I thought it would have been completely different, a yellow brick road but they lived exactly like we did, hand-to-mouth working-class. I thought about the man I'd tied up with barbed wire and stoned. These people were no different to mine. Busted streetlamps, rubble everywhere. My heart sank, because, somehow, I thought they'd be different. I was in shock, because these were normal people, going through exactly what we were, to an extent. I realised then that it was never going to end.

I must have had a death wish because I then walked to Carlisle Circus and along the Crumlin Road and stopped at the Ardoyne/Twaddel Avenue roundabout, where I turned left and dandered down the Shankill Road. I looked at the murals on the walls, all bright and well-kept; oul dolls rushing about with their shopping trollies, headscarves tied tight. Drunks outside bars, arguing with the door men, trying to get back inside. The place was a hive of activity.

I kept myself to myself and walked the entire length of the Shankill Road. They were on the breadline too, nothing special, nothing different to us from the New Lodge. Everyone trying to make ends meet and searching for bargains. I eventually got down to the top of North Street, with Unity Flats on my left. Immediately, two fellas ran over with hurls, ready to do me in.

'Houl on, fucks sake,' I shouted, 'I'm a Taig.'

'Here, that's young Scalper,' a man shouted, 'what in the name ah good fuck are ya doin, over on this side ah the Shankill?'

'If I told ya, I'd have ta kill ya,' another one of my Da's sayings. 'None ah yer business anyhow, the less y'know the better.'

The Stowaway

It was getting late, and I was looking for somewhere to bed down for the night. I was physically and mentally exhausted. My hands and feet were like blocks of ice, and my spine felt as rigid as a brush pole. There was a big lorry parked outside Bannon's Furniture shop at the bottom of North Street and as I got closer, I realised it was a big curtain slider. I slipped through the side and retired behind the heavy tarpaulin. I sat on a massive armchair and blew on my hands and rubbed them together. A large white sheepskin rug lay draped over a table that was held tight by ropes. I wrapped the sheepskin rug around me and feel asleep.

I was awakened by a loud thud. My eyes rolled around, as I tried to get my faculties together, since I didn't know where I was. I stood up, holding on to furniture and getting bounced about like a ball. I peered out through a small hole in the tarpaulin and saw green fields and trees everywhere. I managed to get back to the armchair safely. I didn't know where I was going, nor did I care; anywhere would be better than my home. I was bumping and sliding for a few hours, before the lorry stopped.

The driver got out of the cab and shouted, 'Micky, get the coffees, I'm nippin ta the loo.'

I could hear his footsteps get farther and farther away, I untied the tarp and jumped out.

Holy fuck, tricolours everywhere, well, this coulda bin a lot worse, I thought.

It was a very busy main street on a hill, with loads of people hustling and bustling past one another to get in and out of shops. There was almost a sign of panic on their faces, as they rushed about. I quickly and quietly mingled in with the crowd and faded into the background.

I went into a bakery and walked up to the girl behind the counter.

'What's this place called?' I asked.

'Brennan's bakery.'

'Nah, nat the name of the shop, the name of the town, or village, or whatever it is?'

The girl stated laughing, 'I take it yu're from Belfast. What part, north Belfast?'

'Aye, the New Lodge,' I replied and kind of lowered my head, in shame, almost.

'I'm from Twinbrook, west Belfast,' she said.

'Oh my God, a fuckin Westie, I may keep my hands in my pockets, so they don't get dipped.'

'Hahaha, yu're a geg,' she said, smiling. 'This is Keady.'

'Oh, hello Keady, I said.

'Nah, this town is Keady, ya buck eejit.'

'Sorry, I thought ya were talking about yer cat.'

'What cat?'

'Oh, y'know, yer Keady kat,' and we burst out laughing.

'I think yu've a screw loose,' she said.

'Aye, so have I,' I said, 'I'm kinda tossed out, hidin from the Peelers at the minute, or I'd ask ya round fer a cuppa tea.'

'Ock,' she said, 'I'm too busy, but thanks anyway.'

'Of all the people I could manage ta bump inta, it'd have ta be a westie.'

'Shut up, an' eat these here sausage rolls. I won't be needin em. Everywhere's closin early today, cos ah the march. An' there's gonna be murder at it.'

I snatched the sausage rolls and crammed them into my gob.

'Slow down, big fella, they're hot.'

'Oh, thank you,' I said licking my lips, 'they were lovely. So that's why everybody's rushin around? Cos the march is nearly startin?'

'Yeah, ya should be a detective,' she said.

'Aye, just call me Detective Inspector-sausage-roll.'

'Jesus, you an' Mícheál musta bin separated at birth. It's just like listenin ta him.'

'Who's Mícheál?' I asked.

'Oh, my other half, but nat ta worry, yu'll meet him soon enough. I'm Orla, I own this gaff.'

'Wow, a westie who actually owns a house that's nat a squatter.'

'Ya cheeky bugger. Here do us a big favour an' pull the shutter down fer us.'

'No bother,' I said and did just that.

'Sit down,' she said, 'I'm makin a potta tea.'

'Happy days, I do love a wee cuppa tea,' I burst out laughing. 'Fer fuck's sake, I sound like my oul Granny, *I do love a wee cuppa tea*,' I said, in my best croaky voice. 'By the way, I'm Liam, but my legs are better now.'

'Ya deserve ta be shat fer that one,' she said, smiling.

Orla brought a big pot of tea to the table and started pouring. A large plate was banged into the middle of the table, filled with buns. A large torpedo, (a torpedo-shaped yellow scone, sliced at the top and filled with mock cream and jam. If you stole one of these, you would be eating it for days), was cut into thick slices and formed the centrepiece, with chocolate éclairs and jam doughnuts up each side of the plate and a big cream-filled flaky pastry.

'I think I've died an' gone ta heaven,' I said.

'What, cos of the buns?'

'Nah, cos yu've the face ah an angel.'

Orla blushed.

'Aye,' I said, 'Hells Angel.'

She dove for me and dug me in the arm.

'I'll fuckin Hells Angel ya.'

We finished the food then Orla and I next went over to Mícheál's gaff, as he was off work that day. Mícheál was sitting at a kitchen table and looked like someone who had all the answers to every situation. I was immediately in awe of him, he was confident, and I thought this guy is cool. Orla told him I was here because I was on the run and Mícheál burst out laughing.

'Yu're on the run an' ya come ta Keady. There're more helicopters than cars here, cos Gosford Castle never stops. Twenty-four-seven. Y'know what they say?'

'No,' I replied.

'The whirly bird catches the worm.'

'I take it that yu're referrin ta the helicopters?'

'Aye, ah course,' Mícheál said. 'Someone take him outside an' put him outta 'is misery.'

Orla laughed as she said, 'D'ya wanna beer?'

'Aye, no problem.'

'We'll have ta be quick, the rally will be startin soon. Y'know, the one against police brutality?'

Mícheál boasted a t-shirt with a big red triangle on it and the dark silhouette of sniper. Underneath, in black bold letters, it read "SNIPER AT LARGE". He wore skintight blue jeans, with a heavy-looking studded leather belt, fastened by an American eagle buckle with its wings outstretched, and the stars and stripes flag in centre. His hair rested on his shoulders in a heap of black curls.

He took off his belt and wrapped it around his hand, with the big pointed studs facing outwards. He swung it around his head and the heavy buckle just missed my chin.

'Yehah!' He yelled, like he was a cowboy in a movie and burst out laughing.

Orla came in with two bottles of ice-cold beer and popped one into my hand.

'He always gets excited, when he goes ta these things.'

He lifted up his shirt to reveal a number of scars.

'That one there's a bullet hole,' he said and poked his finger into a roundish pink scar.

'A knife, a knife, another bullet hole, an' a Stanley blade,' he identified each scar while laughing.

'Yu're fuckin nuts,' I said and looked over to Orla and thanked her for the beer.

'Mícheál' Orla said, with a smile, 'Liam here hasn't even turned thirteen yet.'

'No fuckin way, yu've seen that on someone's door, are ya messin?'

'Nah, I'm turnin thirteen.'

'Jesus fuck almighty, yu're a big brute ah a lump, aren't ye?'

'Aye, my Ma said I'm a twin, but I ate em'.

'That's a cracker,' he screamed as he rolled about the sofa, laughing. 'An' there was me thinkin I had it hard.'

'I knew yis two balloons would get on, yis are like two sixes. E's nat long outta the Kesh,' Orla said. ''Em bastards tortured him fer months on end.'

'Wee fuckin buns. IRA all the way. Fuck the Queen an' the UDA.' Mícheál chanted, as he stood and gave the Hitler salute. 'SS RUC, SS RUC.'

'There's fuckin wiser people locked up,' Orla said. 'But sure, look at 'is wee gorgeous smile.'

'There's fuck all gorgeous about him; he looks like he's escaped from an asylum,' I said.

The two of them quickly turned towards me, looking pretty serious. They both stared at me for 20 or 30 seconds, then burst out laughing.

'Ahhh got ya there big fella,' they yelled.

'Fuckin right ya did, I didn't know where ta look. Fer fuck's sake, I was cut ta the bone.'

Mícheál and I headed down towards the rally, and he knew everyone we met, and they knew him.

'Ya must be a big celebrity round these parts,'

'Nah, nat really. They just know what side their bread's buttered on, if y'know what I mean?' He said in his best cowboy accent.

'I surely do.'

We arrived at the rally and there were a few thousand people there. I couldn't believe it! Burger vans, poke vans, people selling flags, others taking collections for the prisoners.

'It's like a wee fair or somethin.' I said.

'Mosta the people here are from Crossmaglen an' Jonesborough an' I know mosta 'em.'

'Here we go again, from the chip pan ta the fryer, I thought. There was a big stage set up, and a man was speaking in Irish. Two helicopters observed from a distance, as speaker after speaker got up and spoke about our civil liberties and acts against humanity. The state of the prison laws, and prisoner rights. A woman got up next, and the crowd went ballistic, cheering and whistling. She spoke of how the woman's place had changed

dramatically, by taking a more assertive role in the armed struggle and in the civil rights movement:

'Women an' children woulda starved, if nat fer us. We rallied an' we conquered. We brought the security forces to their knees in west Belfast, Falls Road. We brought another injustice to light, with nathin more than the fire in our bellies an' the hunger fer our civil liberties.'

The crowd were ecstatic!

'Our men are being rounded up like cattle an' imprisoned. No judge or jury. We need justice fer the people of Northern Ireland. Bloody Sunday was viewed by millions all over the world. This atrocity of pure bloodshed shocked the world, but we grow stronger by the day. I say nigh, the British Government must be held ta account.'

The Crowd shouted and cheered; my hair was standing on end. The buzz in the crowd was electric.

'People around the world are rising up an' shouting, 'Enough is enough!' an' no matter how many times we are beaten down, we will rise up, like the phoenix from the ashes, ta pursue a just life an' equality for all. We are one nation, livin' in the shadows. We are one nation, one Ireland. Our ranks are swelling, due ta the atrocities inflicted upon us by the brutal, bigoted, murderous British Soldiers an' their one-rule-fer-one-an'-one-rule-fer-another excuse fer a police force. People ah Northern Ireland, the world is watchin. Go raibh maith agat.'

A deafening round of applause, cheering and anger swept through the crowd. I looked up and saw four helicopters hovering in the sky above.

'Don't worry, they won't come any closer; we nearly shot one outta the sky last week,' Mícheál said. 'We're all goin fer a pint or two, ta loosen up the joints before the night's performance, an' don't be worried about cabbage, it's all covered.'

'No bother, great,' I said. 'My Ma was involved in that Falls Road sit-down.'

'Are ya serious, man? Fair play. I take it yer Ma's well-connected, somehow.'

'Aye, defo. My Da an' Frank Hickey raised the money ta build the Felon's club in the New Lodge.'

'Jesus Christ, I've actually been in there a few times.'

'Holy fuck, that's mental. Aye, my Da's the treasurer an' my Ma runs the bar.'

'I get the picture nigh, nudge-nudge, wink-wink, say no more. There's bin five murder attempts on me: shot three different times, stabbed twice.'

Orla shouted, 'Six times! What about that hit an' run?'

'Fer God's sake, Orla, he was probably as drunk as me. That's why he never stopped.'

'Yeah, I know, but he mounted the kerb an' sent ya flyin about ten feet in the air.'

I nodded my head with agreement.

Everyone was still on a knife's edge from the rally, as we went to the pub. The Pub was silent, except for the news on the TV. It was covering The Step Inn Pub Massacre: police colluded with the UVF to plant and detonate a car bomb.

'Fuck this,' someone shouted. 'We'll take it ta their front door, an' we'll see how em English cunts like it.'

'C'mon nigh, let's focus on the matter at hand.' Mícheál said. 'Seven grand was raised ta sort out bus runs to an' from the Kesh with food parcels. Two-thousand, five-hundred went directly ta West Belfast, ta relieve the British repression an' feed families on the Falls Road. This here's Liam.

'We already know. Orla rang the Felons an' he's good ta go.'

'Go where?' I said in a low voice to Mícheál, who laughed.

'Ya wanna pinta Harp, is it?' He handed me a pint and said, '*Sláinte.*'

I knew this meant, 'Health', in Irish.

'*Sláinte,*' I said back, and we had a long sup.

We had two or three pints each and someone gave Mícheál the nod and we had to go. It was dark now and a large bonfire cracked and hissed not that far from the pub, on the main road. Two or three hundred people stood around it, with hoods up and scarfs wrapped over their faces. Ten crates of petrol bombs had been piled up in two lots. There were two large bread crates, filled to the top with rocks from the quarry. We stood at the top of the hill, guarding the entrance to a housing estate. The army was at the bottom of the road, as were the

Peelers, their riot shields all in a line, tightly pressed together. They were steadily advancing.

Boomph, boomph, boomph, repeatedly interrupted the near-silence. Then we unleashed a hail of bricks and petrol bombs. There were that many, they were like stars falling from the heavens. We could hear squeals and shouting, as the petrol bombs landed. They still advanced about ten feet or so, deflecting everything with their shields, because they overlapped each other to form an impenetrable wall.

A wee hardware shop stood beside the pub. I ran over and grabbed Mícheál.

'Come with me!' I yelled over the racket of the crowd.

I nearly had to drag him across to the hardware shop. We kicked in the front door and grabbed two large steel canisters of *Calor Gas*. I searched out the back and found eight or nine boxes of nails and bolts. I ran over to a parked car, smashed the side window and opened the door. We placed the gas bottles in the boot, along with a case of petrol bombs and all the nails. We doused the interior with petrol then I took the handbrake off, and we turned the car, to wheel it down the hill backwards.

'Don't light it yet,' I yelled.

The car rolled slowly down the wee hill.

'Nigh!' I shouted, and we unleashed a hail of petrol bombs.

The Peelers pressed up against the car, so I ran down a wee side street and tossed a lit petrol bomb in through the window that I'd already broken.

BOOMFH!

Flames shot six feet out of the window, as if a rocket had gone off. It set me on fire: my coat was aflame and my hair alight. I quickly took whatever was left of my jacket off and slapped my head to extinguish the flames. I could hear the bastard Brits and Peelers laughing at me, as I flapped about like a headless chicken, trying to put the flames out.

It wasn't long before I was up with the others, who continuously patted me on the back.

'Ya dunno how lucky ya were,' one guy said. 'Cos they musta fired a dozen baton rounds at ya, but every last one ah em missed.'

'I didn't even know they were firin at me, I was too busy puttin out the flames.'

BANG!

The gas bottles in the boot of the car exploded, sending nails, nuts and bolts everywhere. The Police line was broken, as they tended to the wounded. The crowd went mad, were shouting and cheering.

Mícheál said, 'Look.'

As I turned, a huge fireball plumed into the sky like a mushroom cloud from a detonated atom bomb. The crowd fell silent; they hadn't been expecting that. They charged. The Brits and Peelers were pelted with a barrage of bricks and had to retreat rapidly.

A while later, we gathered around the bonfire, talking and one guy said, 'Fuck, did yis see that there fella who set himself on fire? Thon fucker's lucky they never shat him.'

'Well, it wasn't fer the want ah tryin.'

'I'll have ta remember this one, ta tell the kids. A fuckin legend, he is.'

Mícheál pointed to me, 'There's the big man himself.'

Half-a-dozen or so clapped and the man who had been doing all the talking came over with his hand extended.

'Put it there, big man, fer keepin em there fuckers out.'

'Cheers, mate. That's how we do it in Belfast.'

'Holy fuck, the car near done a backward somersault inta em fuckers.'

'Who owns the wee hardware shap we broke inta?'

'Fer Jesus's sake, don't ya be worryin about that, we'll sort all that out.'

We sat round talking for hours, sharing stories about the brutality that we lived with on a daily basis.

It stayed very quiet over the next few days; nothing exciting happened.

Sunday came and Mícheál took me to Jonesborough Market. I'd never seen anything like it: the whole place packed with people, all haggling for bargains. A guy was selling fireworks, the largest with heads on them like coke cans, right down in size to wee bangers. Perfumes, aftershaves and all types of cosmetics. Burger vans, fry stalls, doing a full Irish breakfast, with wee picnic tables and chairs for people to sit and eat.

'Extra black puddin an' a shovel ah beans,' someone shouted.

The atmosphere was electric, cases of wine and whiskey were being hand-balled out of a van.

'Get em while they're hot!' The vendor shouted. 'Get em before the Peelers get us!'

A huge queue was starting to form.

'Love, they're straight aff the back ah a lorry. Roll up, roll up,' he shouted to get everyone's attention, as if he were in the circus.

'If ya need,' Mícheál said, 'or want anythin, just say. I pay fer nathin here. Mosta it's my gear.'

We came up to a man, who sold jackets and other clothing. He called me over, looked me up and down, and handed me a green bomber jacket.

'Houl out yer arms. Here's a bomber jacket, ta replace yer coat what got melted,' he said and laughed.

Two *Fred Perry* t-shirts and a navy Gatsby jumper, V-neck, of course. He quickly took the hangers out, folded them in half and put them in a large carrier bag.

'Cheers, big ears.'

'That's the way it goes, big nose,' he replied.

'Nice one, an' thank ya very much.'

The three of us stood there laughing, talking about the riot in Keady.

'Everyone's family here,' Mícheál said.

Everyone greeted Mícheál, shaking his hand.

We came to a shoe stall and the guy said, 'What size are ya?'

'Oh, I'm about five-foot-ten.'

'Yer fuckin feet, I'm talkin about,' and he looked at Mícheál and laughed.

'Size nine,' I said.

'Just pick anythin over in that section.'

There were cowboy boots, stampers, Chelsea boots and Oxblood *Doc Martin* shoes. My eyes lit up.

'Are they toe-tectors?' I asked.

'Aye, steel toe-caps.'

'Brilliant, I'll have em, please.'

He put them in a bag, and handed them to me, and then stuck in a big bundle of white socks.

'I can't thank y'enough.'

I then turned to Mícheál, 'Fer fuck's sake, mate, I'm fuckin scundered. I haven't a washer on me.'

'Hey, Belfast, will ya stop worryin? Right, come over here,' he ordered.

We went over to a stall that sold jeans.

'What waist are ya?'

'Thirty-two,' I said.

He handed me a pair of flares.

'Mate, I wouldn't be seen dead in these,' and I laughed with embarrassment.

'Drainpipes, what about drainpipes? Here's thirty-two, thirty-two. Em's *Pepe* Jeans. All the young ones go fer em. D'ya wanna pair ah army begs?'

'Aye, if it's nat a problem.'

'Relax, just pick a pair an' that's the latest colour.'

There were green combats with black-and-white camouflage. He put them in a bag and handed them to me. By this stage, Mícheál and I were fairly loaded up with bags.

'There ya go, big fella. Yu're gonna look super-cool, hip-hop, fab and groovy. Jesus Christ, I loved the sixties,' he said.

'Sounds like yu're fuckin still in em,' I quipped back.

Chris de Burger Man

'Ya hungry? Cos I want ya ta meet this guy, he's a legend.' Mícheál asked and gave a sly wink.

We walked over to a burger stop. I could hear singing:

> *'It's a rainy night in Paris*
> *And the harbour lights are low*
> *He must leave his love in Paris*
> *Before the winter snow…'*

The singer pointed to a young couple, making the girl blush.

'His name's Chris de Burger,' Mícheál said, 'y'know, after the singer, Chris de Burgh?'

'Hamburger, cheeseburger, salad burger, cos everyone comes with a song,' Chris said and started singing again.

> *'These broken wings can take me no farther,*
> *I'm lost out at sea.*
> *I thought these wings would hold me forever*
> *and onto eternity.'*

He moved with ease from the lines of the song into his own pitch, 'Hamburger, cheeseburger, salad burger or the special Chris de Burger, cos everyone comes with a song.'

'Two specials, an' a foot-long hotdog cut in two, fully loaded, like ourselves,' said Mícheál.

'Yu've a fair paira lungs on ya, an' it's easy on the ears.' I said.

'Why, thank you, my good fellow,' he said and handed me the food.

It was out of this world for a burger. Runny cheese dripped off my chin, as I mauled that meat feast. Caramelized onions, mustard, ketchup, in a toasted bun. I sat at a table and looked up at his van.

CHRIS DE BURGER MAN

I mouthed the words, they were in big bold black letters, alongside an illustration of a burger singing into a microphone on a stand, with musical notes coming from it.

'Yer van's class, mate. It looks very well.'

The burger was filling, and it did the job.

'Here ya go,' said Mícheál, as he gave me half of his foot-long hotdog.

Chris sang the whole time.

> *'Some say the devil is dead,*
> *The devil is dead,*
> *The devil is dead*
> *And buried in Killarney.*
> *Some say he rose again*
> *And joined the British army.'*

The stall was packed, and his burgers were flying out like lube at a brothel.

'Now, stop everyone shouting out your orders.' Chris said. 'I'll get to you...'

'He actually does weddins an' parties.' Mícheál said.

'What, burgers?'

'Nah, fer fuck's sake, singin. 'He's in a band an' they're pretty good. Nigh, c'mon over here. I want ya ta meet Maggie Melon, but everyone calls her Maggie Melons.'

Mícheál brought me over to a stall that sold all types of hair products, wigs and the like. A tall blonde woman turned around and the only thing I could say was, 'Jesus Christ,' as she near took my eyes out. I stared, open-mouthed, at her enormous, heaving, breasts, squashed into a low-cut top.

'Fer God's sake, ya woulda thought he never seen a pair ah tits before,' she said and calmly squeezed them together. 'Somebody give him a slap, he's just froze, I think.'

'He's only turnin thirteen,' Mícheál said and laughed.

'Thirteen, sure he's nearly a beard, well, half ah one. What happened ta ya?'

Mícheál nipped in, 'Oh he set himself on fire an' kinda melted 'is hair ta 'is head. Can ya fix it?'

'Nah, there's no fixin it, if it's melted ta 'is head. I'll need ta take it all aff. Big lad, d'ya want me ta take it all aff?' Maggie said and gave me a naughty wink.

Mícheál was in stitches at my facial expression, as I nearly shat myself.

'He looks like an escaped psychopath or somethin,' said Maggie.

'Arse humpin,' Mícheál said.

'Nah, ya hallion ye, or-some-thing. An' by the way, I left my knickers under yer pillow. Well, actually, it was my G-string,' Maggie said and slapped her big curvy ass.

'Oh, is that what that was? I thought it was a fan belt fer a tractor.'

I burst out laughing.

Maggie grabbed my head.

'Sit still,' she said.

She pulled my head against her big baps. I didn't realise until later that she had winked over to Mícheál. I froze, afraid to move a muscle, as she squeezed them from side the side, with my face stuck between them. She gently rubbed moisturizer on my head, and it was so relaxing. She pulled my face out from between her boobs and kissed me on the forehead.

'I hope it was as good for you, as it was for me,' she said in a sultry tone.

My face went beetroot red, and again Mícheál chuckled away.

'Go on, get outta here ya pesky varmits,' said Maggie.

What's all this about cowboy movies down here? I thought to myself.

Maggie was like a taller Dolly Parton and as we turn to go, she said, 'Remember now, if it's nat Country, it's nat music.'

We continued to walk around the market, then Mícheál drove back to his gaff, and we put the news on. There was a news story about the troubles and it prompted me to explain what my Da had told me about a friend of his.

'In nineteen-seventy-one, somebody close ta our family was lifted by the Peelers. The cunts took him an' thirteen others. The bastards stuck hoods over their heads, and then they were systematically tortured. The Peelers are a law onto themselves and basically do whatever they wanna,' I shouted at the TV, 'the fuckin world is watchin.'

Mícheál butted in, 'Liam, no one is gonna do a goddamn thing. It's the government an' it goes all the way ta the top. People only see what they wanna see, an' by the way, we've ta get ya outta the way, big lad, till things die down. We can go ta Orla's flat, cos she's hardly ever up there. Plus, yu'll never go hungry, just ate whatever.'

'It's fuckin like I'm in a dream, it's unreal here. I've never bin treated like this before.'

'Relax, fer fuck's sake. Mosta the stuff's aff the backa a lorry. By the way, d'ya need smokes?'

'Nah, thank ya. Don't touch em.'

'Just you lie low in the flat fer a few days, ta be on the safe side. Orla will sort ya out with hot food an' stuff an' we'll come back on Wednesday night, as we're busy fer a day or so.'

I went up and took a hot shower and put all my clobber on. I felt as though I were ten feet tall. I looked down at my Doc's and bent my feet by going down on my hunkers. They were so comfortable, as I walked about the flat, feeling as if I were top dog. I sat for ages, watching the rain beat off the glass and trickling down in endless streams. The flat was toasty and soft-looking, with pillows everywhere and soft furnishings: a few bean bags, a big pouffe and heavy fancy curtains that hung from floor to ceiling, almost. It was very upmarket and well kitted-out. A small rocking chair sat in front of the window, and you could see the reflection of a red tartan shawl draped over. It almost looked out place in this bright, trendy, decorated flat. It was quiet and peaceful, and I didn't mind that one bit, I lay on the super comfy sofa with my hands behind my head.

'Aghhhh this is the life,' I said aloud and thought about how hard it was to get a seat back home and I've a whole sofa now.

Memories come flooding back to me of when I was ten years old: beaten, battered and broken; how I used to pray nearly every night that I would die in my sleep. The pains were too much, the violence was too much, and the guilt was too much. I cut my wrists and used to try and hold my breath until I died. I couldn't even kill myself right, I'd lie in a heap after getting the fuck kicked out of me. I felt of no value to myself. I had no respect for authority, as authority stank of pure rottenness and filth. Life was so cruel and unjust. The whole system was broken and one-sided. I looked around this bright colourful flat with its white-painted wooden panels that came halfway up the walls and massive pictures of glorious warm sunsets and sunrises of beaches splashed around. Well, their generosity and kindness comforted and cradled me, making me feel as though I belonged. The kind of feeling I'd had when I'd lived with my Aunt Sally, which now seemed like a lifetime ago. I kept it well-suppressed in my subconscious, as it made me soft, kind and compassionate, which made me vulnerable. My survival instinct had kicked in, and I fought hard. *It's alive, I tell you, it's alive*, as the power cable gets hit with a bolt of lightning and I emerge bigger and stronger than before. People shouted Frankenstein at me all the time and ran away laughing. I hated my life and I'd known there was something wrong with me, you know, something skew-whiff.

I wanted to be normal but my rage and temper wouldn't let me. I didn't want to be special or anything, just normal. I've nursed broken bones, bumps, bruises, scars, immense beatings that nearly crippled me at times. I've been hit with at least a dozen baton rounds, which were fired by the Peelers and the army. I've dodged live rounds, had a gun put to my head and fired, *click*, and in my head I heard the gunshot, *bang*, my body twisting and contorting, his cool calm voice saying, *You never hear the one that kills you.*

How to fuck would he know? Pain, blind fury, anger, rage and conflict were my life. I had no respect for me, yet alone others. I rebelled against the entire world, teachers, Peelers, parents and I spewed hate, pain and hurt at the people that were closest to me.

I yelled out, 'Stappp!' I'd just turned thirteen and I questioned myself. Am I beyond help or am I even worth helping? The feeling of never fitting in and being different was always there. I've no baby or toddler stories to tell or laugh about. No motherly bonding at birth, nothing. Just a white canvas that was my childhood and only dark and evil colours have splashed it. The darkness grows inside me, the hate and the rage that I cannot control. *Calm down, take a deep breath, open your eyes* and I am in Orla's flat again.

'Take ten deep breaths, that's it, in-out, in-out, in-out, just the way the priest likes it. Fer fuck's sake, concentrate. In-out, in-out.'

I waken up to a lovely homemade soda bread smell, and I think of oul Jimmy and all his stuffed animals. My door knocks.

'Liam, breakfast's ready,' Orla shouted.

'I'll be two minutes.'

I washed up, went downstairs and walked over to the table. Mícheál and Orla had already started eating. Orla jumped up.

'Sit, sit down, Liam.'

And in thirty second flat. Bang, my hot plate hit the table.

'That was under the grill, so be careful.'

A whole toasted soda with cheese and scallions baked through it, it was split down the middle and heavily buttered. Three slices of crispy bacon and four big fat pork sausage and two fried eggs.

'Would ya like sugar?' Mícheál asked as he poured my tea out off a beautifully painted tea pot the shape of a cottage.

'Fuck, have I died an' gone ta heaven? If so, I ain't going back.' I said.

'I'm here from six a.m. ta get all the bakin done an' ready fer openin at seven fer the workmen.' Orla said. 'Did ya come down at all last night fer food?'

'Nah, nat at all, I musta conked out. That sofa's unreal.'

'Aye, my dad's friend made it, he also done the chaise lounge. He's so talented.'

'What's a chaise lounge?' I asked.

'Well, y'know that wee hand-carved, funny-shaped settee? Well, that's it.'

'Aye,' I said, 'it's dark red with wee buttonholes in it. I sat on that too last night, very nice indeed. Where I live, it's a fight everyday just ta get sittin on a chair. I couldn't tell ya how many times I'd ta stand when atein my dinner, fer fuck's sake. Okay it mighta bin stew, but I'd ta stand, nevertheless. There's ten ah us, includin my Ma and Da.'

'Jesus, my Aunt Kitty's like that, sixteen ah em, fourteen weins. Eight boys an' six girls.' Orla said. 'Christmas is mad round there, but ya just can't keep away. There's so much excitement, it's like an All-Ireland cup final. Four ah em were her sisters, who were killed in a car crash, that drunken bastard ah a husband, but don't worry, he gat 'is comeuppance. Two warnin shots ta the back ah the head an' used as landfill.' Orla snapped.

'Nigh, none ah that at the table,' Mícheál said. 'Customers an' staff will be in soon, so eat up an' shut up.'

Orla whizzed around with trays of this and that and put them on display.

'Alright, calm down an' keep yer knickers on,' Mícheál grabbed her by the waist and gently kissed her. 'On second thoughts…'

'Aye, in yer dreams,' Orla quipped very quickly.

Mícheál backed up in total surrender and blew her a kiss. 'Come on nigh, big man. I'm parked out back, we can use the back door.'

'Thanks again, Orla,' I shouted as I headed to the back door and we got into the car.

'Are ya hurt anywhere? As I'm sure em plastic bullets musta hit ya?' Mícheál asked.

'When?' I asked.

'Y'know, when ya set yerself on fire. Well, they fired about a dozen or so baton rounds at ya.'

'Fuck, I didn't even know. I was too busy tryin ta put out the fire.'

'Fuck me, Liam, they were bouncin all around ya. Ha ha!' he yelled.

'Nah, nat a one, didn't see any of em.'

'Liam, yu're a jammy bastard. I've never seen anythin like it. Y'actually bent down ta put yer feet out, as they were in flames, an' when ya bent down, two bullets bounced over yer head, we thought ya were gonna get killed. I'm in fuckin shock still, it's a friggin miracle, we thought ya were dodgin the bullets, but ya were only puttin the flames out. Ya must be touched by the hand ah God.'

'Don't start that shite, fuck's sake. Yu'll have me handin out leaflets in the city centre, shoutin, 'Repent! Repent! Save yerself from the damnation ah hell!' Cos I believe we're in fuckin hell already. A livin hell, y'know?'

'I know exactly what ya mean, Liam, an' I know some have suffered more than others. No parent should ever have ta bury a child, under any circumstances.'

I agreed, 'That's heartbreakin. When I go, I wanna take as many ah the cunts with me as I can, if y'know what I mean. Yeehah!'

'Well said, my friend,' and he beeped the horn continuously in agreement. 'Yee fuckin hah, amen ta that brother.'

We drove for an hour through the countryside and pulled into a huge barn. We got out of the car and into a 4x4.

'We'll be a few days up here at my cousin's. Orla has a few messages ta take care ah, so we need ta be outta the way.' Mícheál said.

Fifteen minutes later, we pulled into a lovely big farmhouse with green fields all around. We were taken out behind the house by Mícheál's cousin, Eoin, a redheaded skinny guy with a well-trimmed beard. I thought he looked intelligent. There were two barns, and Eoin pointed to one of them.

'Nigh, that one there's outta bounds, but everywhere else's free ta go.' Eoin said.

We acknowledged his comment, and he made an apology as he had to go a message.

'Mícheál knows the craic. Oonagh's inside, go say hello.' he added.

We sat on the front porch with two air rifles with telescopic sights. We scanned everywhere looking for something to shoot at but failed miserably. Mícheál grabbed two beer cans that were in the bin and walked to the lawn to place them on it as shooting targets. Oonagh came outside.

'Put em back,' she said, 'an' come into the kitchen. I'll show ya what we shoot at out here.'

We went through the house and into the back garden which was enclosed by very tall trees and hedges and was extremely secluded. There were hay bales at different distances, and all had targets on them. Oonagh loaded and fired, *phwitt*, she loaded again, *phwitt*, and when we looked through our sights, two bullseyes.

'Fuck.' I said aloud. 'Are ya sure, yu're nat that sniper the Peelers are lookin fer?' And we all laughed.

Oonagh went inside and came out carrying a big pot of tea and sandwiches, and a load of biscuits. We stood for a few hours, shooting, chilling and laughing. Eoin came in and banged two birds down on the table and all I remember is that they weren't chickens. He locked away his shotgun and joined us.

'Anythin strange, startlin or excitin happen when I was away?'

'No,' I answered sharply. 'The last time somethin excitin happened ta me was when my finger went through the toilet paper when I was wipin my arse.'

Eoin nearly fell off the chair laughing.

Oonagh came out. 'What did I miss?'

I felt the blood rush to my face and looked around very suspiciously at everyone. Mícheál couldn't even speak through his laughter, because of the expression on my face.

I mumbled what I'd said out as if I was a naughty schoolboy, my eyes fixed on the ground in shame.

Oonagh came darting over and gently touched my cheek. 'There's nathin ta be embarrassed about,' and laughed and gave me a hug.

Mícheál shouted over, 'Speak up! We can't hear ya.'

Oonagh checked him, 'Don't listen ta that gypsy,' and fired him a dirty look, as she could see that I was hurt and embarrassed.

We ate the two birds with roast tatties and the carrots and parsnips that Oonagh picked from the garden. After dinner I went over and stripped the carcasses clean.

Mícheál quipped, 'I wouldn't like ta be on a desert island with him. I'd be afraid ta close my fuckin eyes.'

Oonagh came to my defence, 'He's a growin lad. Aren't ya?'

I told them about oul Jimmy, away up in the Cooley Mountains, asking me if I'd like chicken for dinner. But before I could answer, he'd grabbed the wee chicken by the head and swung it round in two full circles, breaking its neck. I'd looked at oul Jimmy and said, 'Well, it's a bit late fer the chicken, if I'd said no.'

We were all pissing ourselves laughing, so I went on to tell them how I'd hopped on the back of lorries and thumbed lifts for two days until I was home.

'We still can't believe that yu've just turned thirteen,' Eoin said. 'Ya look as though ya were chewed up, then spat back out.'

'Oh, here we go again,' I said. 'I fell outta the ugly tree an' hit every branch on the way down, an' when I was born, I was that ugly the midwife slapped my Ma on the face, instead ah my arse...'

'Enough,' Eoin banged his hand on the table. 'Time, please, nigh, ladies and gentlemen and yer man from the brewery. I can't take much more ah this, my ribs, my ribs. I can barely breathe,' he was laughing so much.

'We're going shootin themarra,' Oonagh said. 'We've gat plenty ah shotguns an' we don't need permission, as it's on our land, an' remember, safety first.'

Eoin nearly choked, 'Safety? How many times have ya nearly shat me?'

'Be quiet, or the next time I won't miss.'

'Ohhhhh,' Eoin said, 'I think she's serious.'

'If I was serious, ya wouldn't be sittin here nigh,' Oonagh said.

'Please, order at the bar,' Mícheál shouted as though he were the boss.

We sat in front of a roaring open fire that had a lovely, sweet turf and tobacco smell and talked for ages. I was in fine fettle and had them all in stitches. Mícheál was then showing everyone how I set myself on fire, and dodged a dozen baton rounds, accidently of course. It was such a dream. We supped on bottles of ice-cold beer, and I felt as though I didn't have a care in the world. Not one crazy thought was in my head, and I was floating on cloud nine. The company was great and the craic mighty. The food was plentiful, and the surroundings were beautiful. I thought about the time I walked down the Shankill Road and was surprised to see the deprivation and squalor they lived in. They were going through a fight to make ends meet just like me. Kids ran about mad, old dolls with trolleys and headscarves. Drunkards begged on corners, singing. Their place was in ruins, just like the New Lodge. What the fuck is going on here? Somehow, I thought the Protestant people were living in the lap of luxury. When Protestant workmen were killed, their families felt the pain, I understood none of it. I woke to a cacophony of birdsong, high-pitched tweets and low caws, it was as if they were dancing outside my window. I remember what I'd thought about last night and it filled me with sadness.

'Liam, breakfast,' Oonagh called.

A half a grapefruit with dark rum and brown sugar toasted under the grill. A small bowl of porridge topped with cream and a splash of Irish whiskey, followed by a ginormous fry and mug of hot tea. I rubbed my swollen belly while sitting at the table.

'I think I'll lie down fer an hour. I'm stuffed.'

'Nonsense,' Mícheál said, 'we're goin shootin.'

'No, guys, I just need a wee half-hour nap.'

'Okay then. Forty-five minutes, tops!'

It was nowhere near enough, but I accepted it.

Gullible's Travels

Soon I was walking around with a shotgun and my eyes were going together, because I felt exhausted. We traipsed through a thicket of heavy brush and Oonagh beat the foliage with a stick to try and shake something out. We arrived at a clearing that ran alongside a shallow river. There was an old tired-looking pony taking a drink.

'There's that oul nag we've been lookin fer. Orla said if we came across it, ta put it down,' Eoin said.

Mícheál added, 'Aye, ya don't want it fallin inta the river an' dyin.'

'He'd just rot in there,' Eoin said. 'Liam, would ya like ta do it?'

I wasted no time in even answering, I just walked up behind it and blew a hole in the back of its head. It fell onto its front knees and then keeled over. Its leg muscles were still kicking, as we all looked at each other.

'Holy fuck, big man, we were only jokin. That's Orla's oul horse. We just let it run about up here.'

I quickly tried to defend my actions and said, 'It looked in so much pain, I thought I was doin the right thing.'

In a millisecond Orla's face flashed before my eyes and how she had been so kind to me. I felt overcome with guilt. Everyone could see it in my face. Oonagh ran over and flung her arms around me and shouted, 'Don't listen ta em fuckers, they're only windin ya up. Yu've done nathin wrong an' shouldn't feel guilty in the slightest. Hey, yis two knuckleheads,' she shouted over to Eoin and Mícheál. 'Fuckin tell him, right nigh, that yis are only messin.'

'I love Orla. I wouldn't do anything, ta hurt her,' I said, all apologetic.

'Big man, we're only messin with ya.' Mícheál said, 'but we weren't expectin ya ta blow its head aff. But yu're right, it was in pain, an' it was the only decent thing ta do.'

'Fuck me!' I exclaimed in relief. 'Yis bastards gat me fuckin good there. I'm so relieved.'

Eoin turned to Mícheál and said, 'I'll get the truck ta pick it up when we get back.'

I never fired another shot the whole time I was there, not even the air rifles; I think the shock of seeing the pony's brain getting blown out disturbed me. Blood ran down the riverbank and swirled away as it mixed with the current. Blood smells like blood doesn't matter what animal it comes from, human or not. That sickly smell I've smelt so many times, as I've fell or tried to help others, and it started my stomach churning.

'Yer very quiet, big fella,' Eoin remarked.

'Nah I'm fine. After all, it was only an oul nag, like, I'm nat stupid. I know that chickens don't wring their own necks, pluck, roast an' baste themselves, like, y'know?'

Eoin looked at me puzzled, 'Yo, big man, we're nat gonna ate the horse.'

'I fuckin know that, I was just referrin ta it only as an animal.'

'Thank God,' Eoin said, 'fer a second there, I thought yis were atein horses up in Belfast.'

Everybody started laughing and the tension eased.

'Y'know Eoin, if we could catch one, we probably would ate it, but they're too fast.'

We all screamed with laughter, as normality returned and balance was restored.

'The truth ah the matter is we've been lookin that oul nag fer months, nigh yu've done us all a big favour, there.'

Three times I turned to speak to different people, and everyone ducked each time.

'Fer fuck's sake, put the gun down,' Eoin said, and everyone gave a nervous laugh.

'Oh, it's nat loaded,' I said. 'I never put more cartridges in.'

'I know, but there's still one cartridge in there.'

'Fuck me,' I was exasperated. 'I coulda killed one ah yis. Holy fuck,' and I froze and felt my chest tighten and my lungs constrict, as if I were in a chokehold.

Oonagh slapped me on the face. I took a gasp of air and quickly exhaled. It was as if my ears popped, and I could suddenly hear again. The birds seemed really loud, as cawing, warbling and chirping drowned everything out. I took another deep breath in though my nose and the pleasant aromas of the countryside flooded in and heightened my senses.

'Are y'alright, Liam, d'ya need ta sit down?'

'Nah, Nah I'm fine. I just panicked, cos the thought ah harmin any ah ya would kill me. Yis have done so much fer me an' everythin I seem ta touch turns ta shite. I dunno what's wrong with me. D'ya know what I mean, like? Sure, I blew the head aff that horse or donkey or whatever it was, cos ah the story yis toul me, I'm so fuckin gullible, it's fuckin shameful.'

Oonagh hugged me, 'Yu've been through a very traumatic accident when ya were younger, an' ya just think different ta other people. Yu're nat gullible, just too trustin, that's all.' she said. 'There's an honesty about ya, an' ya just do an' say how ya feel an' there's nathin wrong with that.'

'Oonagh, yu're a fuckin star, an' yis mean the world ta me, Orla too.'

'Right, come on you two, are we good ta go nigh?' Eoin said to lighten the mood.

'Aye, we're cool as cucumbers,' I said.

'Yeah, but just as green,' Oonagh added, and we laughed and started walking again.

The ground was marshy and one of my boots nearly got sucked off, almost throwing me off balance. I used the shotgun as a walking stick, prodding it deep into the ground. Mícheál laughed and slapped himself on the head.

'Thank fuck ya took that other cartridge out, or ya mighta lost a foot.'

Bang! Bang!

I dove for solid ground.

'Sorry, guys,' Oonagh said, as she walked over and lifted up a rabbit the size of a small dog. It was still kicking, and she karate chopped it on the back of its neck, killing it stone-dead. She looked at me, 'It's the most humane thing ta do.'

'Aye, seein as ya just shat the fuckin thing,' I added.

'I meant ta put it outta its misery, that's all,' she said. 'Yu're one ta talk, after shootin that nag!'

'Point taken, my apologies.'

I was walking about with a shotgun, even though it wasn't loaded, and half-filled with mud it gave me a kind of Godlike feeling: the ability to snuff out someone's life in an instant. I suddenly got a cold chill, when I thought of back home and the damage I could have caused. *People from both sides should not have to bury their loved ones but what do we do as we're caught in this dark and desolate vacuum* flashed through my mind. I was glad when the hunting trip was all over, and I handed the shotgun back very carefully.

'Fer fuck's sake, it's nat gonna bite ya,' Mícheál quipped.

My shoulder was sore where the shotgun kicked back at me, and I lay down on the sofa.

'I'm glad ya cleaned up first, nat like these two mucky pups,' Oonagh pointed to Eoin and Mícheál and their muddy footprints. 'At least Liam had the sense ta wash up,' she shouted again.

They both ran out and kicked their boots off at the door and wiped the floors.

'Fear's a wonderful thing, at times,' she quipped and the two of us laughed at those two buck eejits clambering to get out the front door, as if their lives depended on it.

Oonagh went into the kitchen to make some food and I just stretched out on the sofa. I asked myself if I were in an IRA training camp, or something? *Yu're gullible,* the inner voice said. *Look. There's a rifle range out the back. Loadsa shotguns. Open yer fuckin eyes. D'ya remember the last time I spoke ta ya? An' I toul ya nat ta go ta the Waterworks? An' what'd ya do? Ya went anyway an' got hit on the head an' nearly bled ta death.*

'SHUT THE FUCK UP!' I yelled to myself.

'Liam, oh Liam,' a lovely soft voice nudged me into my own conversation. I opened my eyes and Oonagh was standing over me. 'Did ya fall asleep?' she asked.

'Nah, nah, I was just thinkin.'

'Just stinkin,' she said.

'Nah, just thinkin.'

'I know, I'm only coddin with ya. There's tea, sandwiches an' a packet ah *Wagon Wheels* up there on the table with yer name on em. If yu're interested.'

I moseyed on into the kitchen and sat down.

'Won't yer family be worried about ya...' But before Mícheál could say any more, I interrupted.

'Yeah, like they were worried about me when I was stuck up the Cooley Mountains in a dingy oul caravan. I would disappear for a couple of weeks at a time, but my DA said I was like a bad smell that kept comin back.'

Ha ha ha, and we all laughed.

'I'm like that oul dog that someone feeds, an' ya can't get rid ah it. Only comes back when he's hungry. Aye, my Da's a laugh an' a half. He's about as subtle as a kick in the balls. He's disowned me many a time, cos ah the stress I cause my Ma.'

'Tough love kiddo,' Eoin said. 'Shit happens, y'know.'

'I know shit happens, but it just seems ta happen ta me all the time,' I said feeling sorry for myself. 'It's beautiful down here, a different world, actually.'.

'Well, it has its moments, like everywhere else, I suppose.' Oonagh said. 'Come on an' we'll get hammered.'

'I was talkin ta Orla on the phone there, an' we're heading back ta the bakery themarra, so what's yer poison?' Mícheál said.

'Are the air rifles an' shotguns all locked away?' I asked.

'Yip, one hundred per cent. Ya can't have em lyin around, if y'know what I mean.' Oonagh said.

Eoin burst into song.

'Jesus, he's a voice that'd curdle milk,' I said to Oonagh.

I know,' she said, 'it sounds like two cats fightin, but sure, he's happy.'

'Fuck, this is gonna be a long night, he's fully tone deaf but he's right inta it'.

Oonagh pulled out a bodhrán.

'Thank God!' I shouted, 'anythin ta drown out this caterwaulin.'

Oonagh sang and her singing voice was gentle, lovely, and had a Celtic twang to it. She tapped and sang ever so softly. I would have joined in but I'm totally tone deaf, and while it sounds good in my head it doesn't come out like it sounds.

'Let yerself go, c'mon,' she shouted.

*'And her eyes they shone like diamonds,
they called her the Queen of the land,
and her hair hung over her shoulders,
tied up in a black velvet band.'*

Mícheál came over and handed me a *Wrangler* jacket with a silhouette of Ireland on the back, outlined in metal studs and *Eire* printed at the bottom. I stared at the metal studwork.

'That's what Mícheál works at, but normally in leather,' Eoin butted in, 'he can turn his hand ta anythin.'

I turned the jacket round to the front, the collar had two triangular shiny metal tips as did the top pocket flaps. It was class looking.

'That's a one-aff, no one will have one like it, that's fer sure.'

'Yis have given me so much already.'

'Don't be daft, we love havin ya here.'

'I'm cut ta the quick, so I am.'

'If yu're still here next week there's a shitload ah *Harrington* jackets comin in. Maroon, green, black…all fully-lined.'

Eoin burst into song, '*Oh happy days, oh happy days, when Jesus washed, washed my sins away.*'

Jesus, I thought the windows were going to crack.

'It's all about the shekels, cos money makes the world go round,' Eoin stated.

'Yeah really, cos where I live people on both sides are literally livin hand-ta-mouth, livin in debt or fear ah attack. It might sound a bit biased but especially Catholics. We get fucked from all angles. Like, I watched a severely handicapped man who dragged one leg as he walked, had two hooky hands an' could hardly speak properly get the absolute fuck kicked outta him by the army fer shoutin somethin or other at them. He was drenched in blood an' half-a-dozen people of all ages ran ta his defence, an' they were bate too. Like what ta fuck is that all about? My Ma and Da were trampled ta the floor, an' Ma got pinned ta the wall, then kicked onto the floor, tryin ta protect her kids, an' don't think fer one fuckin minute I'm doin this fer a United Ireland or some cause. I do what I do ta protect me an' my family. I can't just stand back an' do nathin.

Da always said it's better ta die on yer feet than live on yer knees. That's all I can remember: fightin and strugglin ta survive. I've been near ta death so many times, I couldn't even count em. No one cares about the poor or deprived, we're treated like trash, as if we don't have the right ta a life. So, we fight fer our lives every fuckin day in life. It's the same oul, same oul.' My anger and rage were obvious.

'We'll get ya a soap box in the town square,' Mícheál tried to lighten things, 'Big Liam for *El Presidente*.'

I explained that only two years previous, I was in primary one learning how to read and write. I told them about my coma and memory loss and waking up in a fucking concrete jungle, where dog eat dog was a way of life. Violence and rage were all I'd known my entire life. I told them how Denise had a completely different effect on me and was the only one who truly showed concern and interest in how I felt all the time. She's even too gorgeous to have a nickname.

'Denise is just simply Denise and ya wouldn't have it any other way. That's love, definitely love, for one person ta have that kinda effect on ya. Phewwwww the rest is history.'

I was dumbstruck, I didn't know what to say as I didn't know what love was. I knew then that I would spend the rest of my life close to her.

They all started making kissy noises and shouted, 'Go on, big lad, get in there!'

I yelled back, 'Don't anyone talk about Denise like that, or I'll go inta the kitchen, take a knife an' stick it in yer fuckin head!'

Emotions got the better of me and tears ran down my cheeks. Oonagh came over to me, wrapped her arms around me.

'It's love,' Oonagh whispered, 'ya just don't know it yet. I can see it a mile away.' She softly kissed my forehead, 'It's rare that someone finds a soul mate when they're so young, especially findin someone that ya would die fer, it's a true rarity.' She turned to the boys and sternly said, 'Knock that shit on the head or I'll knock yis on the head.'

Mícheál stood up, his mouth agape. 'Are ya sayin ya were in primary one, two years ago?'

'Aye,' I replied.

'Jesus Christ, em kids will need counsellin, cos I'm sure they were terrified, cos I was there when ya went inta one. It's nat like yu're easy on the eyes, an' yu're a lump ah a brute.'

'Enough of the compliments,' I said, 'or yu'll be askin me fer a kiss an' chasin me round the kitchen. Course, I'll let on ta trip, so ya can catch me.'

For a full ten to fifteen minutes, we were laughing our bollocks off, because every minute or so, I would say, 'C'mon, chase me' and we went into one again.

'Fuck me, man, they definitely broke the mould when they made ya,' Mícheál said.

'Yeah, fuckin right, I am, just like the jacket ya gave me. And whatever ya do, don't say yer special needs joke, as I've heard it enough ta last me a lifetime. Pain inwards an' outwards, I'd burn myself an' everythin ta heighten my pain barrier. An' I'd show the scars on my arms, where I'd stabbed out fegs an' dripped hot melted plastic aff a stick an' onto em at bonfires. Round circular pink scars where the skin had melted.'

'Jesus, Liam, all ya do is crack people up an' make people laugh, yu're one ah the funniest people I know.'

'Aye, I know that, I take after my Ma. Even these big red rosy cheeks. I fuckin hate em cos they make me look soft, almost feminine, I think.'

'Fuck what did ya say? Soft an' feminine? My ears must be painted on. Are ya fuckin mad or what? Ya look like Boris Karloff fer God's sake.' Mícheál pointed at me, 'He's a fuckin geg, so he is. Soft an' feminine. I've heard it all now.'

We all burst out laughing.

'Liam, yu're one in a million so y'are.'

'Oh, stap it, ya, I'm fillin up here, an' yu'll be startin up a fan club, so ya will.'

We all tittered and laughed.

'But seriously, guys, I've seen blood, bone an' guts scooped up by a shovel an' slopped inta an oul metal mop bucket where different ones have bin shot an' it'll be with me till the day I die. That's why I blew the horse's brains out, or pony, or whatever the fuck it was. It was nathin ta me, I felt emotionless, uncarin an' coul.'

'Come on, big man, relax, we get it. Yu've ice-coul blood coursin through yer veins. But it's nat the gettin beat down that defines ya, it's the gettin up an' goin again an' again.'

'Aye, I suppose so, the thing that gat me the most was the smell. I fuckin dream smells, is that mad or what? I mean, I smell blood in my dreams.'

'Sure, yer senses are connected,' Oonagh said as she yawned.

We all hit the hay, and I didn't wake till noon, and I trundled into the kitchen.

'Brekkys long over but here's lunch.'

A large plate of homemade chips with garlic butter on them was set in front of me.

'How d'ya like yer steak?'

'Oh, hangin over the edge ah the plate,' I answered.

'Nigh that's funny,' Mícheál remarked. 'I'm gonna write that one down,' and he reached for a wee note pad and pen.

'Again, how d'ya like it?'

'Up the ass on my hands an' knees, while barkin like a dog.'

The guys mouths fell wide open.

Oonagh banged the skillet down, 'Is anybody listenin ta me?' she shouted and pointed over at me.

'I don't know what ya mean by, 'How d'ya like it?' Just cook the fuckin thing. No one's ever asked me before. I usually get my dinner threw down ta me, I've had a stake through the heart, oh, and a mistake tryin ta ease the situation.'

Oonagh gave me a big smile, 'I get it nigh. Just sit, I'll bring yer steak over in a few minutes.'

Eoin and Mícheál almost crapped themselves when she banged the skillet down and they were giggling like two schoolgirls.

Eoin spoke aloud first, "Up the arse on my hands and knees.' Yu're lucky she didn't bate ya ta death with that oul cast-iron skillet.'

Mícheál was wailing like a banshee, trying to hold his laughter in and not annoy Oonagh.

Oonagh came over to the table and plopped a massive steak on top of my chips.

'Nigh let it sit fer a few minutes ta let the juices flow through the chips,' she said.

I looked at the lovely lump of blackened seared meat, the fat was crispy and caramelised. It was about an inch thick, and the juices were flying out of it and adding flavour to my chips. Oonagh looked at Mícheál and Eoin to make sure that they were behaving but every time she went out of the room I loudly howled like a dog and the other two eejits went into fits of laughter and when Oonagh came back in, she kept saying, 'There's somethin fuckin wrong with you two fools.'

A bowl of mushy peas with wee pickled onions in them was set down on the table. There was a big ladle poking out of it, and I helped myself to two big scoops.

Not two words did I speak as I cut and pasted the last piece of steak. Not only did I not speak but I also didn't hear a thing as I devoured the meal. I had the plate up to my face and was licking then last wee bit of juice when I rolled my eyes over to Mícheál, Eoin, then Oonagh and we all burst out laughing.

'Is the pattern still on the plate?' Eoin asked.

'Aye, big man, ya were definitely on a mission there. We actually said, 'Slow down an' come up fer air,' two or three times an' there was no response. It's as though ya were blinkered,' and they continued laughing.

'Aye, right enough, my Da always said he was gonna get me a nosebag,' I said.

'Fer fuck's sake, don't start talkin about horses, cos he's only after atein one,' Oonagh added.

'I don't fuckin care, it was lovely.' I swirled my tongue around the plate again. 'Is that where the sayin comes from? I'm so hungry I could ate a horse, or I love horses, but I couldn't eat a whole one?'

'Aye, see what I mean, yu're always quick ta answer, Liam, so y'are.'

We all finished up in the kitchen and Mícheál and I said our goodbyes. Oonagh rushed over to me and threw her arms around me yet again.

'I can see what Denise sees in ya,' she whispered. 'It's somethin special, an innocence but yet broken.'

She kissed me gently on the cheek.

As we were gettin into the car Mícheál shouted, 'Fer fuck's sake, are ya cryin?'

And when I looked back the tears were running down Oonagh's cheeks. Eoin put his arm around her shoulders to comfort her, she looked up at Eoin and said, 'I'm gonna miss that big atein an' shittin machine.'

'Aye, me too,' Eoin said, and they waved us off.

We got back to the barn and exchanged cars and headed on back to Orla's place. She rushed over to Mícheál and kissed him on the lips.

'I love ya, love ya, love ya,' Orla muttered in between the kissing.

'Get a fuckin room,' I said aloud, all embarrassed at the open show of affection.

Orla turned to me, 'We would, but yu're livin in it,' she quickly followed with, 'I was only jestin. 'C'mere you, d'ya want some sugar too?' She asked and kissed me all over the face and head.

'Get ta fuck, ya headcase,' I tried to fend her off and failed miserably, as I didn't want to hurt her. I cowered in the corner, and we all laughed.

Orla gave Mícheál a massive hug and he instinctively grabbed her by the arse cheeks.

'Did ya miss me?' Mícheál asked.

''Course I did,' and she winked over to me.

'I saw that,' Mícheál shouted.

'Saw what?'

'Y'know what!' And the two of them locked lips again.

'Oonagh's bin keepin me updated, an' you, Big Kell, have made quite some impression.'

'I know,' Mícheál said and laughed. 'Oonagh was bawlin her lamps out when we were leavin.'

'C'mon, sit down over here, I'll organize some tea an' stuff fer yis. An' she wasn't cryin, I just spoke with her.'

'She was too, an' don't let anybody tell y'anythin different.'

'She was sayin that ya told em about Liam settin himself on fire at the riot. She really is worried about him. She knows that he's no sense ah fear or danger at times, an' she's generally worried.'

'Sounds like pity ta me an' I don't want pitied,' I added.

'Who said anythin about pity? She friggin loves the bones ah ya.'

'That's okay, I'm just lettin y'know that I'm okay with who an' what I am, an' what I've been through, an' I just wanna be treated like anybody else an' no fuckin different.'

Orla wrapped her arms ever so tightly around me and kissed me loads of time on the forehead.

'Keep calm, keep calm,' she whispered as she kissed me. 'We love ya, that's all. Oh, here comes the tea and buns…' she said, 'he must have hollow legs.'

'I don't! Ya shoulda seen the size ah the steaks we had up there, an' he'd the biggest one. It was hysterical, the big man here was growlin like a bear protectin 'is kill.'

'Button it, you, cos I don't want ya goin an' offendin anyone with yer big gob slobberin.'

'Wha', wha', wha'd I say?'

'Just sup yer tea.'

We all laughed and gorged on the sweet delights.

'The Peelers hit loadsa houses lookin ya when ya were away. They were askin who ya were with an' where ya were from, but nobody knows nathin. Anyhows only us four an' you, Liam, an' that's the way it'll be kept. They were goin crazy. Tryin ta find who Billy Big Balls is,' she pointed at me.

'Ha, Billy Big Balls, I like that one,' I said. 'Mícheál, can ya grab some ah em bangers an' the huge fireworks that we saw?' I wrote a few things down on a piece of paper. 'Get me these an' I'll show yis that wee trick I'd done in the primary one classroom.'

Mícheál laughed. 'I fuckin still can't believe ya were in Pee One two years ago! I vill get onto zizz vight avay Herr Gwuppenführer,' and he saluted me.

'He's fuckin simple, that cunt,' I said, 'right I'm goin upstairs, so yis two lovebirds can talk or whatever.'

'Oh, there's no whatever, I'm still workin.' Orla said.

I looked at her with a puzzled expression, 'Whatever.'

If it wasn't for Denise, I don't think that I would have gone back to the New Lodge. The draw she had on me was pulling me, and it was so strong, it was as though a chain was wrapped around my heart and she was tugging on the chain from Belfast. That's the only way I can describe it. I almost felt like a wild animal, now captured, and she was pulling me to safety. Little did I know then that I was going to spend nearly forty years loving this adorable creature. But that's another story.

I was waiting on Mícheál to come upstairs, so I thought I'd give him a bit of a laugh. I sat on the rocking chair by the window. I set a new mop head on my head and wrapped the shawl over my head like a headscarf and draped it over my shoulder I closed my eyes and started rocking. I was next awakened by this almighty loud scream, and I jumped up.

'Jesus fuckin Christ,' Orla, shouted, 'are ya tryin to kill me?' She grabbed a few aprons out of a box and disappeared downstairs, mumbling away to herself.

'What ta fuck did I do?' I asked myself.

Mícheál came flying up the stairs and burst through the doorway, shouting, 'Fuckin classic, she shit herself there.'

'What in the name ah fuck are ya talkin about?' I said and lifted the mop head off my head.

'Ya don't know, ya don't know,' he squealed, 'that makes it even funnier.'

'Are ya gonna friggin tell me or nat?' I spat out.

'Well, it's like this, Orla's granny opened this bakery a million years ago, an' Orla lived here with her, and when 'her granny died, she left the bakery an' the flat ta Orla. The only thing she kept, after doin the whole place up, was her wee granny's rockin chair, an' her shawl that she always had around her. Like, fuck me, can ya imagine the look she had on her face, when she walked in an' yu'd the mop ah grey hair, the shawl, an' yer rockin away on the chair? It musta scared the shite outta her. Fuck, I can't wait ta tell Eoin an' Oonagh. Fuckin brilliant! She'll never live this one down, I'll fuckin make sure ah that. Her Granny practically raised her an' taught her all her bakin skills. Whoooooooooo...' he started making ghostly noises. 'Fucking cracker. Ya musta took at least ten years aff her life bro. Yu'd better watch out, she'll maybe poison ya with laxatives, an' yu'll just shite yerself ta death. Big man, yer days are numbered, tick tock, tick tock.'

'Stop fuckin about, you!' I said. 'Is she really that upset? I didn't mean ta scare her. I was just tryin ta have a laugh, cos I thought that ya woulda bin up here first.'

Mícheál put the mop top on his head and looked in the mirror and pretended he was fixing his hair. He was adjusting the mop, which was like grey dreadlocks hanging down, and he wrapped the shawl around himself.

'Jesus fuck, I'm a double fer her granny,' he said as he parted the dreads into a middle shade. Mícheál strutted about and walked like an old granny.

'Stop fuckin about, you, in case Orla comes back up an' we end up with two boots up our holes.' I said.

'Relax, big man, I'm only messin.'

'That's a big D fer dead on,' I said in my best country accent.

'Are ya makin a cunt outta me?' Mícheál asked.
'Nat at all, at all, yu're doin fine on yer own!'
We both laughed.
'Nearly gat ya,' he said.
'Ballicks!'
'I'm just sayin, there ya go, I'm just sayin...' Mícheál tapped his chin with four fingers, Laurel and Hardy style, and laughed.
'What are ya laughin at? Cos I don't get on like that.'
'Aye, ya do, first ya say, I'm just sayin, then ya rap four fingers on yer chin an' look up ta the ceilin.'
'Jesus fuck, I've turned inta my Da,' I shouted.
'Aye, an' ya don't even realise that yu're doin it. It's funny as fuck lookin.'

Mícheál disappeared for fifteen minutes or so then reappeared with two black bin bags and set them on the table. 'First things first, put these on,' next, he handed me a pair of surgical gloves.

I snapped the gloves on and covered the table in black plastic bags, all taped together, and went to work. First, I filled a shoe box with gunpowder from the fireworks and then used window putty. Four boxes filled with rubber tubes of petrol, twenty-four empty jars, a massive box of roofing nails, and ten boxes of black cat bangers. It wasn't long before we had a wee conveyer belt going, constructing the new and improved Molotov cocktails. Mícheál lit a feg, I instantly pulled it out of his mouth and crushed it under my foot.

'Are ya fuckin mad?' I yelled. 'Just one spark an' poof, we woulda looked like a coalminer's daughter. Nat ta mention the flat'd be covered in smoke an' powder burns, an' if the Peelers ever did 'it here, you an' Orla'd be fucked.'

We worked on to well after midnight, and then spent another hour cleaning up. All we had to do now was bang a hole in each jar lid for the fuse to come out, and then put the lids back on.

'All done! Just ya wait ta see these in action.' I explained how the heat from the gunpowder being ignited melted the wee tubes of petrol and turned them into a cross between a petrol bomb and a nail bomb.

Mícheál looked at me in disbelief, 'An' ya were makin these in primary one?'

'Nah, nat this model, the first ones were just gunpowder, drawin pins, bangers an' broken glass.'

'Holy fuck, I'm all Man United nigh, I have ta get my head down or Orla will be in soon, so we'll only get three hours kip before breakfast call. I'm fuckin Lee Marvin, or is it Hank Marvin? I'm nat sure but I could ate the balls aff King Kong,' Mícheál said but was too tired to laugh.

The aromas you inhaled living above a bakery were intense, and they always made you feel hungry. It was seven-thirty before I heard Orla's beautiful voice.

'Yo, dickheads, yer breakfast's gettin coul.'

Mícheál and I both ran for the door and went clattering down the stairs, falling at the door at the bottom and laughing like two naughty schoolboys.

'Were yis two on the sauce?'

'Nope,' we both said in unison and laughed.

Orla sighed, 'It's gonna be one ah them days, I think,' and she walked off, shaking her head.

Within minutes, our plates were sitting in front of us, stuffed to the guilders with a meat feast. Orla poured the tea as I stuffed a whole giant sausage in my gob and rolled another one between my fingers, as if it were a prized cigar, ready to mangle it in my trap at a second's notice.

Mícheál sniggered, 'Here, why d'ya make faces when ya ate? Yer eyebrows bounce up an' down an' yer jaw swings side ta side, as if yu're tryin ta whistle. An' what's with the cigars? Like what ta fuck is that all about?'

'Don't know, don't care,' I said and shovelled something else into my gob.

'Yu're fuckin hilarious, ya don't even have ta say anythin, it's just yer mannerisms.'

'Is that so?'

'Aye, it is.'

'By the way, are ya gonna ate that last sausage?'

Mícheál answered, 'Yu'd know that ya were from a big family.'

'How so?'

'Well, ya devoured that as though ya were in a race fer seconds.'

'Ya betcha,' I said as I clean my plate with a slice of bread.

I'd no sooner finished when zip, zip, zip Orla breezed in, lifting the dishes, wiping the table and replacing the forks and knifes.

'Awright, awright, I get the message, I'm gonna hit the head, then hit the hay, in that order. See ya later, speedboat,' I shouted to Orla, as she was like a wee speedboat, puttering and zipping in between each table.

Orla looked back and smiled, then she sped off again.

'Smell ya later,' she mumbled under her breath.

I didn't waken up till ten o'clock that night: it was like falling down a hole and I only woke up as I hit the ground. I dragged my weary ass out of bed and traipsed into the bathroom, my eyes still half-stuck together with tiredness. I went for a hit and miss, depending on how good my aim was, and went over to the sink to wash my hands, afterwards I threw water over my face, and I looked up into the mirror and a large sheet of paper was covering the mirror with a message scribbled on it. "There are plenty of goodies in the fridge, so enjoy, and by the way, I covered the whole mirror, because I didn't want you to get a glimpse of yourself and fucking scare yourself half ta death. Haha. That's for calling me a speedboat."

I smiled and said to myself, 'Ha-ha, she's nat fuckin wise.'

I went to the fridge, and it was absolutely bunged to the dick with goodies. Two massive trays of sambos cut into triangles, and she had made wee roses or carnations out of tomato skin and rolled them up into tight wee flowers, they looked beautiful.

I didn't know if I was supposed to eat them but I ate them anyhow. One full tray of prawn salad with Marie Rose sauce that packed a punch, and a tray of mixed ones from roast beef and mustard salad, chicken and stuffing and ham and cheese and brown pickles. I made two full plates up and set them on the table, four bags of *Tayto* cheese and onion crisps and a big pot of tea. I watched a double bill of *Kojak* and shouted at the TV, 'Who loves ya baby?' I ate half of a lemon meringue pie with a spoon that wouldn't have looked out of place in a garden shed. It was massive but very effective. After *Kojak*, I turned the TV off and switched on the radio and lay down on the sofa and looked up to the stars. I could make out The Plough and it was as if I were back in the graveyard at home. Denise came flooding into my mind, like a tsunami crashing over me. My heart pounded heavily and a longing just to be near her overwhelmed me and I almost burst into tears. I stood up quickly and ran and opened the window, to let the cold breeze in, '*What the fuck is wrong with ya?*' I shouted to myself in my head, '*Cryin, fuckin cryin, yer nathin but a big wet drippin fanny. Who ta fuck cries?*' I banged my head off the window to get the voices to stop. I missed Denise and I missed Belfast and the times we had at the zoo. I fell asleep on the sofa and was still smiling when I woke and went downstairs to the bakery. I shared a pot of tea with Orla and Mícheál. Orla fetched the rest of the sambos and slid them along the table.

'Well, did y'enjoy yer sandwiches an' pie last night?'

'I thought I'd died an' went to heaven, honest I did,' I said.

Mícheál stuck his fingers in his mouth as though he was trying to make himself sick. 'Yu're a ball-lickin bastard,' he said, as Orla gave him a dig with her elbow as an act of retaliation.

Orla went to serve some customers and Mícheál spoke softly, 'What's that brown stuff on yer nose?'

'Yu're only whisperin cos yu're afraid ah Orla knockin yer fuck in.'

'I know,' he said, 'isn't that terrible?' and the two of us laughed.

'Da always said, it's nice ta be important, but more important to be nice...'

'Here we go again, Da always said, don't tell me, he writes Chinese proverbs.'

'Nah, dickhead,' I said. 'I'm just sayin. Are ya listenin or nat, ya fuckin walt?'

'Awright, awright, I'm listenin.'

'Well, Da always said, it's nice ta be important but it's more important ta be nice.'

'Aye, then he pulled up 'is knickers,' Mícheál said.

'Ya wouldn't say that if he was standin there. No fuckin way. He'd do ya fuckin in, so he would, no fuckin bother at all.'

'There'd be two 'its: me hittin him an' him hittin the deck.'

'Oh, that oul chestnut. It's as oul as the fuckin 'ills, but ten points fer tryin. An' afterwards, yu'd wake up an' ate yer cornflakes.' I said.

'Meanin that ya must be dreamin. We all wanna be as sharp-tongued an' quick-witted as ya.' Mícheál said, smiling.

'Ten points fer the A team,' I shouted. 'Ya wouldn't wanna be walkin in my shoes, cos half the time, I dunno if I'm blew up or stuffed.'

'Stuffed, definitely stuffed,' he shouted.

'I'll stuff my boot up yer arse!'

'Oh, stap,' he said in his best Belfast accent.

'I don't talk like 'at air,' and we laughed again. 'There's no hope fer us,' I said.

Mícheál shook his head, 'I surely know, we're just two sad fuckers. Oh, we're goin ta the quarry the day, ta try out our coffee jar thingies an' check the timin an' shit.'

I was buzzing and was so excited when we arrived at the quarry.

Eoin was a hundred feet or so away and was standing with half-a-dozen men. They were too far away to recognize me, if they ever saw me again. We played around for a few hours, getting the timing right and even stuck a lit cigarette in one whole jar, so that it burned down and lit the fuse. I explained how the feg didn't go out because it contained 'saltpetre', a chemical put into tobacco to make it burn down eventually.

Mícheál got a crew making these firebombs nonstop in an old, abandoned shed. They could be made anywhere, anytime and almost in the blink of an eye. Wee factories sprang up all over Armagh, improving them as time went on. I was kept well away from everything and if there were a riot going on, I was shuttled away out of sight. It was like being a prisoner in a holiday camp, as I wasn't allowed out on my own.

Well, two weeks flew by, and I told the girls first that it was time I was getting back to reality, and seeing Denise, of course. Orla burst into tears and Oonagh broke down, the two of them sobbing their wee hearts out. Soon Eoin and Mícheál were there, begging me to stay for another while.

'Guys yer lives are sorted, an' yis all have each other. I don't know who or what I am, my life feels as if it isn't mine or somethin. Fer fuck's sake, three years ago, I was running about telling people that they melted a fucking bell down outta Saint Pat's ta make a fuckin plate fer my head. An' that's why there are no more Sunday bells for the masses. I didn't know that there was work going on in the bell tower, repairs or somethin. That was two-an'-a-half years ago, I think. I'm nat the same as anyone else, I even thought that I'd superpowers, I'm almost like a fuckin outcast an' all I seem ta know is how ta hurt people. I feel closer ta you guys than anyone else. Yu've treated me like a Queen. Sarry, fuck that, a King, an' I'll always be indebted ta ya. The love that I've felt here is exceptional.'

Orla and Oonagh hugged me, begging me to stay.

'Listen I'm only thirteen an' feel as though I've bin fightin fer survival my whole life, which is only three years. But I feel as though I've lived ten lifetimes already. I'm nat a deserter an' I think I need ta be back in Belfast.'

'Look. We'll do a barbeque at Eoin's tonight, an' we'll talk more then, okay?' Mícheál said.

We were up in Eoin's that night and you would have thought someone had died.

'Listen up, guys,' I shouted as I set a full side of pork ribs down that were encrusted in sticky burnt sauce and spices. 'Let's enjoy ourselves an' I won't be a stranger. Like, I was a total stranger two weeks ago an' I feel as if I've known yis forever. Yer generosity is second ta none, an' I'll never forget my Keady family, who went above an' beyond their call ah duty towards a lunatic from the New Lodge Road born, bred an' buttered.'

We sang and we danced and ate our fill the rest of the evening. We laughed and we cried, and bonds were made that would last a lifetime. Morning time came soon enough, and we were all at the table in Orla's café, eating our brekkie.

Mícheál spoke first, 'I'm deliverin ya ta Belfast, just ta make sure ya don't have a detour an' ya get there in one piece.'

'There's somethin in the boot fer ya,' Eoin said, 'an' it's nat a shotgun. There's somethin fer yer Ma an' Da an' all yer brothers an' sisters.'

'Fuck's sake, ya didn't have ta.'

'I know we didn't, but we did anyway.'

We finished our food, and the two girls were crying and hugging each other as though I were going off to war and might not return.

'Fer fuck's sake, will yis girls knock it off?' Eoin said and shook me firmly by the hand, as did Mícheál. The girls pushed everyone out of the way. They dove on me, hugging and kissing me from all angles, crying their lamps out.

'Let him breathe, fer fuck's sake.' Mícheál said, pulling them off me.

I was rarely shown affection like that, and it got my big rosy cheeks to light up.

'Fuck aff, you two, I'm really embarrassed,' I said and pulled myself free.

Mícheál pulled me into the car, and they waved us off.

I slept most of the way home to Belfast and I was like a new pin when I woke up. I had all my new clobber on, and I thought I looked like a movie star, '*A monster movie star, maybe*,' the wee voice said. I burst out laughing.

Mícheál asked, 'What ya laughin at?'

'Nathin, fuck's sake, just had a wee funny thought.'

We arrived and I invited Mícheál inside for a cuppa and to meet my folks. I had a grip bag full to the brim with new clothes and I lugged it in and threw it in the hall.

Ma Lost the Plot

Ma ran to me, 'Son, son, where ta fuck have ya bin?' she was trying to scold me at the same time.

'Fer fuck's sake, Ma, control yerself an' lemme get in the fuckin door. I've bin stayin with Orla and Mícheál,' I point to Mícheál, 'in Keady, Armagh.'

'Armagh?' Ma squealed.

'Aye, Armagh an' I'll tell ya somethin fer nathin, it was a lot more enjoyable than bein stuck up the fuckin Cooley Mountains.'

'Son, son, I didn't really agree ta that, but we just didn't know what ta do, we'd already tried everythin. C'mere an' gimme a hug.' Ma threw her arms around me and then Mícheál. 'Thank ya fer takin care ah my son,' Ma said.

Mícheál laughed, 'Are ya serious? He's the one who looked after us. He's a fuckin superstar in Keady.' Mícheál lifted a large bag onto the kitchen table, removed two big long brown packages tied tight with white cord, and carefully set them on the table. He cut open the cords to reveal two full sirloins, each about two-feet-long.

'These are fer you an' yer family,' he said and placed them onto the draining board.

'These are fer Billy,' he said, as he pulled two bottles of *Black Bush* whiskey out; they were in presentation boxes.

'These are fer you, Donna,' he said and handed her a pair of plush bedroom slippers, which she put on immediately.

Next, he gave her a massive box of chocolates and a twelve-pack of hand-crafted headscarves. Ma's eyes lit up, as she examined the fine gold threads shining up at her.

Ma failed miserably at holding back the tears, as she hugged Mícheál. He took more items out of the bag, big woolly hats with fur around them and matching scarfs.

'These are for the girls.'

Ma got overwhelmed at the generosity of a total stranger and had to sit down.

'Here, Ma, take this chair, an' I'll make the Rosie Lee.'

Mícheál went out to the car and brought in a black bin bag. He plopped it down on the table and pulled out loads of t-shirts and wee light bomber jackets.

'I dunno what they're inta,' he said, 'so I just threw in a good mix ah stuff.'

The front door flew open and Da came into the kitchen. I introduced him and they shook hands.

'Is that yer car out there? Cos em wee hallions were jumpin on the roof an' I chased em aff.'

'Aye Billy, don't worry about it,' Mícheál said as if he had known my Da for years.

'Billy, Billy,' Ma said excitedly, 'look at the meat.'

'Jesus!' Da said and his eyes near popped out as he calculated how many steaks he could get out of the loins of beef.

'Billy, yer son certainly loves steaks. Don't ya, big lad?'

'Son,' my Da said to Mícheál, 'ya didn't have ta.'

Mícheál looked down at my wee Ma and Da then up to me.

Da burst out laughing, 'It'd be cheaper ta keep his picture.'

'Here, Billy, I've somethin out in the car fer ya.'

'I hope ya locked the car, or it's gone,' Da said.

'Fuck's sake Da, it's nat that bad really.'

Mícheál and I walked out to the car, and I saw the expression on his face. When he looked at the run-down area, the bricked-up houses, half-tumbled down and rubble everywhere, broken glass and barbed wire, cars lay like ghostly coffins burnt and wrecked beyond recognition.

'Yer Ma seems like a lovely woman.'

'Don't let her wee soft looks fool ya, she's worse than me but a wee dote all the same. But Da, he's a tough wee cookie an' ya wouldn't wanna get on the wrong side ah him, that's fer sure.'

I noticed a big cylindrical box, 'Is that filled with ball bearins?' I asked.

'Nah, ya head case. I'd hardly give yer Da ball bearins. It's pipe tobacco, ready-rubbed. I know yer Ma doesn't drink or smoke an' yer Da only drinks on rare occasions an' he smokes a pipe. I'd ta make a wee phone call, just ta find out what I'd ta get.'

'Oh, I understand, here, what's in that box?'

'Oh, that's a hat fer yer Da.'

'Fuck he'll love that, cos he always wears a hat.'

We went back into the kitchen and gave Da his gifts. Da got very emotional but fought to conceal that. He opened the large tube and it was full of baccy. Da stuck his face in and took a big whiff of walnut.

'I love walnut.' Da fanned out the whiff of tobacco, which filled the whole kitchen.

Mícheál gave my Da the other box, and Da opened it.

'Jeez, a hat,' Da said and put it straight onto his head.

I loved it, I thought he looked dignified in it. The hat was dark forest green with a stripped tan and brown band around it, and finished off with a green and yellow feather stuck in the band.

'Oh, Billy,' Ma cried 'that's beautiful, I'm chuffed ta bits fer ya.'

The tears streamed down her wee puffy rosy cheeks, as she went over to fix Da's collar.

'Son, don't make tea in a cup, ya heathen, ye. What d'ya think teapots are fer?' Da shouted.

'Da, it's mingin.'

'It's nat mingin, that's where all the flavour is.'

I looked inside the metal teapot at the dark brown tanning stains. So, I rinsed it and made the tea. Mícheál and I were shuffled into the living room.

'Liam, will ya set up that wee foldy out table? An nat the one with the burns on it,' Ma shouted.

Mícheál looked around at the bright luminous orange walls and the green carpet.

'Ma, have ya gat sunglasses fer Mícheál? So he doesn't go blind or get a severe headache.'

'Liam, gat me that paint an' the carpet,' she said proudly.

'Aye, Missus Kelly, yer livin room's lovely,' Mícheál said and Ma blushed.

'Ma, don't listen ta him, he's a bullshit merchant.'

Ma gave me a look that would kill and secretly waved her fist at me as she left the room.

I turned to Mícheál and said, 'Are ya fuckin havin a laugh or what? *Mrs. Kelly, yer house is lovely*,' and we laughed at my impersonation of him.

Ma came back in with a full packet of pink and white marshmallows. They were Ma's favourite, because she had no teeth, only a false set. Ma opened them and slid the tray of six towards Mícheál. I lean forward and poked my finger into one, lifting it up.

'That's the way we ate em,' I said and shoved the entire thing into my cakehole.

'I have ta apologise fer my son's fuckin bad language,' Ma said and gave me the evil eye.

She then rolled her eyes upwards and tapped her chin with her fingers, as if contemplating something.

Mícheál laughed out loud, the tea came streaming down his nose, I ran out of the living room, squealing with laughter. Ma rushed to get a box of tissues, Mícheál was so embarrassed and kept saying, 'I'm so sorry, Missus Kelly.'

Ma shouted, 'What did ya do ta him?' as if it were my fault.

'I done fuck all, Ma, its nathin ta do with me,' I looked at Mícheál and said, 'what ta fuck happened here?'

'You an' yer Ma are like fuckin twins. I'd only thought about it, an' she's standin in front ah me, tappin her chin. I near choked ta death laughin. Fer fuck's sake, I'd ta keep my mouth open, so's I could breathe, cos the tea came flyin down my nose like a beer pump.'

Da walked in, bearing a silver tray with a plate of sambos and biscuits upon it.

'Where'd ya get that silver tray, Billy?' Mícheál said.

'The fuckin altar,' Ma shouted. 'Look at Mister La-de-dah,' and Ma apologized again for forgetting herself.

'I see where Liam gets 'is sense ah humour from.'

'Don't listen ta him, Ma, he's a compulsive liar, y'know he's lyin when 'is lips are movin. Mícheál, don't fall asleep, or Ma'll have ya tied up like a chicken an' yer pockets empty, an' yu'll nat even know she done it.'

'Fuck up, you,' Ma scolded me.

Mícheál looked at Ma.

'Billy, I suppose yu'll be lookin yer leg over the night, with that fuckin hat on?' Ma shouted.

'Fer fuck's sake, Ma, is there any fuckin chance?'

Mícheál's chin was on the floor, as he stared at Ma.

Ma nudged me and said, 'Is he fuckin catchin flies or what?'

'Ma,' I shouted, 'fuckin leave him alone.'

I put my first two fingers and thumb up, as if they were a gun, and shot Ma.

'In fact, a bullet's too good fer ya. Yer head's in the clouds already. Cloud cuckoo land. Are ya listenin, Ma?'

'Son, ya sound like a fuckin train. Yakety-yak, yakety-yak, yakety-yak an' what are ya yammerin on about? I'm only havin a wee geg with Mícheál.'

'He'll nat come fuckin back, Ma,' I yelled.

'It's like a fuckin loony bin in here,' said Ma 'A fuckin hospital with swingin doors, it never staps.'

'Like you, Ma, it never stops.'

Ma took a deep breath and left but was soon back in with fresh mugs of tea.

'Look, son, I can behave,' she said and sat down, all goody-two-shoes, like. She lifted the plate of sambos and said, all prim and proper, 'Mícheál, would you care for a sandwich?'

And she stuck the plate up to his face.

Mícheál moved to take one and Ma pulled the plate away and said in a broad Belfast accent, 'FUCK AFF, I'm only slagging,' and put the plate of sambos down.

'Donna, the wee men in white coats are here fer ya,' Da shouted.

Ma started singing, 'We're comin ta take ya away, haha hehe hoho haha,' and did a silly wee walk.

'Ma, stap fuckin about.'

'Okay, son,' she then pulled her false teeth out of her overall pocket and set them on the table and said, 'Mícheál would ya like a wee bite,' and she burst out laughing at her herself.

'That's how y'know Ma likes ya, she's entertainin ya.'

Ma finally settled down and all was back to normal, well, as normal as it could be, I suppose.

'Liam, ya should show Mícheál the sights, seein as he's here,' Ma said, in all seriousness.

'What sights, Ma?'

'Well, there's a number six bus that hasn't bin set on fire yet, that's a sight,' and she started laughing for a few seconds and then farted, she laughed, and farted, laughed and farted.

Da shouted from the kitchen, 'Has she started laughin an' fartin yet?'

'Aye, Da, she's doin it nigh.'

'Nigh, that is a talent,' Da shouted with pride in his voice.

By now, Ma was farting and crying with laughter. Putt-putt—putt-putt.

'Ma, fer fuck's sake, ya sound like a fuckin motorboat.'

Ma's shoulders were bouncing up and down as she laughed and farted without a care in the world. Tears rolled down her cheeks.

I looked at Mícheál, 'That's how y'know Ma likes ya, cos she feels comfortable fartin in front ah ya.'

I couldn't think of anything to say about Ma's mental behaviour.

'Son,' Da shouted from the kitchen, where he was hiding. 'Ma will never change, Ma will always be Ma, an' I wouldn't have her any other way,' he said, chuckling to himself.

'Billy, I'm headin up ta the Felons, if ya wanna dander up?' Mícheál said.

'Sure, I'll go up an' introduce ya around.'

'Good, I'll just finish my cuppa an' we'll go.'

Mícheál spoke to Ma, 'Mrs. Kelly, I've loved bein here an' meetin y'all, I've had such a good time, honestly I have.'

He hugged me and shook my hand. 'Yu'd better stay in touch.'

'I will, I will, I promise.'

Not ten minutes later, Frank Hickey burst through the door. Frank was the chairman of the Felons club and Da was the treasurer, and they started the PDF (Prisoner Defence Fund) where single parents got help from the IRA, when their husbands were in jail.

Ma jumped, 'Frank, ya near scared me half ta death.'

'Good, good, that's the plan. Where is he?'

'Who, Mícheál? Oh, he's away up ta the Felons with Billy.'

'Donna, top brass.'

'Who? Ma said.

'Yer man, Mícheál.'

'Hey, dopey bollocks.'

'How d'ya meet him?'

'Oh, did I nat tell ya?'

'Nah, well, how'd ya meet him?'

'None ah yer fuckin beeswax,' I said.

'Ooh, Donna, did ya hear that? By the way, have ya tried ta hang anybody lately?' Frank laughed.

'Yu'll be next, if ya don't fuck up,' Ma said. 'Nigh, scoot, ya dirty wee dog.'

'Nat even a cuppa tea? Fuck's sake, I'm only down here cos she's lookin sex again.'

'In yer fuckin dreams, Frank,' Ma said and laughed uncontrollably. 'She'd knock yer block aff, if she heard ya talkin like that.'

'Ya don't have ta tell me,' Frank supped his tea and then left to go up to the club.

'Son, how did ya meet him?' Ma said.

'None ah yer business, Ma. Nosy fuckin Oliver y'are.'

'Fuck up, you. Son, there's a wee bus runnin with Artillery Youth Club ta Newcastle fer the weekend.'

'Ma are ya serious? Sure, the last time I was on a bus, I set it on fire. Don't ya remember, Ma? Yis just came outta work an' we flew past yis, Ulsterbus in flames.'

'Fuck's sake, son, yu're lucky yis all weren't killed in the flames, they were twenty foot high, we could hardly see anythin fer the thick black smoke, son. Son, d'ya think Mícheál liked the carpet?'

'Are ya serious Ma? Why would he even look at the carpet?'

'Well, nat everyone has carpet. Here, son, d'ya want the last toffee *YoYo*.'

'Ma, do fat babies fart? Well, course they do. Does a one-legged duck swim in circles? Course they does.'

The two of us had a wee laugh together.

'Y'know, yer Da means well, an' he said things I know he didn't mean.'

'Ma, I know.'

'He's only worried about ya, that's all. Like, there's eight ah yis an' yu're the only one, son…it never staps with ya.'

'I know, Ma, fer fuck's sake.'

'I love my new scarves, son. There's gold threads run through em, ya know. An' there's even wee tassels on the end, like wee gypsy scarfs, the ones the fortune tellers use.'

'Aye, Ma, I watched a program last night about how they make em.'

'Did ya, son?'

'Ma, don't be stupid, an' ya think I'm the daft one!'

'Fuck up, ya gip dog,' Ma shouted. 'I remember when ya were a cute wee baby an' I dropped y'on yer head.'

'I know, Ma, I was never the same from it. I heard that one a million times. Ma, ya need ta get some new material, fuck's sake.'

'So, bumpy nut, are ya gonna tell me or am a gonna have ta torture ya?'

'Yu're torturin me, nigh. Ma, yu're doin my nut in. Is there any chance ah ya zippin it?'

'Okay, but d'ya remember, son, the four girls playin *ring a ring o'rosie* round that big nut ah yours?' and she laughed and slapped herself on the thigh.

'That's it, I'm away, Ma.'

'How long ya gonna be this time?'

'Dunno, Ma, I might never come back fer fuck's sake.'

I banged the front door as hard as I could and nearly took it off its hinges. I could hear Ma shouting as I left.

I thought I'd call up and see Denise. I asked her out and she knocked me back.

'Where were ya? Nobody knew where ya went,' Denise was crying. 'I've bin watchin the news every night, fer fear the Shankill Butchers gat ya. Where've ya bin?'

She looked deep into my eyes.

'I can't tell ya where I ended up, but I can tell ya where I started: up the fuckin Cooley Mountains in a poky wee caravan. Da left me there, so I wouldn't get inta any trouble. I thumbed it home.'

'What, from down south?'

'Aye, an' then Da disowned me again, an' threw me out. I feel asleep in the back ah a lorry an' that's all I can tell ya.'

'Aye, right, yer Da left ya down south on yer own.'

'Aye, he fuckin did!'

'Pull the other one, there's bells on it,' Denise cried sore and was really upset.

She asked me to leave, which I did, banging the door behind me.

I could feel the anger inside me ready to explode, *'Kick her door in an' tell her ya love her an' that ya only came home fer her. Yu're the only fuckin reason I'm here'*, but this time I didn't listen to the wee voice in my head. *'Ya do love her, yu've always loved her, ya just didn't know what it was, ya fuckin eejit.'*

'GET OUTTA MY FUCKIN HEAD!' I screamed.

I had started walking back home and I noticed two men at the end of the street, and as I passed, I recognized their faces. They were two undercover cops, I noticed two-foot patrols on either side of the road.

I shouted at the top of my voice, 'Two undercover cops, yis rotten bastards! Waddaya want? Cops, cops, cops!' I screamed.

The two-foot patrols moved in to protect themselves, as I doubled back and took the long way home. I've something of a photographic memory for faces. I knew all the undercover store detectives in town, especially the ones in the big *Co-Op* on York Street, where we stole our glue. I used to wire everyone off and they would share their spoils. I arrived at the front door and head-butted it open. The door clattered. Ma came running out and took me over to the sink, as my head was bleeding, and I could feel it trickling down my face.

'Y'opened up an oul scar,' Ma said. 'Fuck's sake son that front door won't take much more punishment y'know.'

'Ma give over, it's only a wee gash.'

'Son, it won't stop bleedin, ya may need a wee stitch.'

'Fuck aff, Ma, I'm nat goin ta the hospital with a wee cut that size. They'll laugh their balls aff at me, fer fuck's sake.'

Da and Mícheál came in the front door and followed the drops of blood into the kitchen,

'Oh fuck, accident prone Annie's home.' Da said. 'What've ya done ta yerself this time!'

'Da it's only an oul previous war wound that's opened up again, that's all.'

'It's like a three-ringed circus here, ya just dunno what's comin next. He's been in the hospital that many times, people actually think he works there. People ask him fer directions an' all.'

'I'm nat surprised, cos he's no sense ah fear, he's a legend in Armagh.'

'By the way, son, Mícheál's gat ya a job behind the bar with yer Ma in the Felons. Fifty-five quid a week, fer five nights, but the catch is yu've ta work weekends.'

I was elated and so excited about starting work.

'Don't lemme down nigh,' Mícheál said.

'No fuckin way,' I stated confidently.

'Wednesday ta Sunday every week, are ya sure yu're up ta it?'

'Aye, no probs. Is it easy? Cash in hand?' I asked.

'Cash in hand, that's a cracker, yer only thirteen fer fuck's sake,' Mícheál said, and everyone laughed.

'Twenty-five ah what y'earn goes ta yer Ma fer yer keep, as everyone pays their way.'

'I'd a done somethin like that anyhow, so I would,' I said, all proud.

'Well, I gotta go an', big man, keep in touch, I'm only a phone call away. I'd hug ya but I don't want ya covered in blood,' Mícheál patted me on the back. 'Ciao,' he said and left.

We were all excited about my job news.

Da spoke to me, 'How'd ya bump inta him?'

'I'm sworn ta secrecy, so if I told ya, I'd have ta kill ya.'

'Oh, that oul chestnut,' Da said.

'Aye, Da I hear ya.'

'Yer Ma'll keep a close eye on ya, an' no backchat or slabberin.'

Shoot It and Boot It in the Felons

Wednesday couldn't come quick enough, and I was excited and nervous at the same time. Frank called to see my Da and they both went into the kitchen to carve up the steaks.

'Finger width,' Da said as he and Frank took turns carving, 'six fer Dolly, six fer Sarah Webb, six fer Lily Reeves next door, six fer wee Nellie Meekin,' and they made wee steak parcels for the neighbours.

Frank called me into the kitchen and told me to sit down.

'Y'know I'm yer real Da,' he said laughing.

'Take him home with ya, if ya want,' Da said.

'You two make a great fuckin double act,' I said, 'fuck's sake, Da, watch yer fingers.'

'Fuck's sake,' Da said as he and Frank continued to cut three two-finger thick steaks. 'We'll have ta try one, just ta be sure.'

Frank walked over to the cooker and opened up the grill and took a large frying pan out.

Ma shuffled in and shouted, 'Hair oil, put that pan down, or ill bate ya over the head with it, y'animal dog.'

Da added, 'Sure, he'll nat feel it, as it'll slide aff his head, with all that boot polish he uses.'

'I don't dye my fuckin hair,' Frank protested.

'Button it an' sit down.' Ma took the pan and put a thick slice of beef dripping in it and let it slide about the pan until it melted. Three big fat juicy steaks were sizzling in no time at all. The smell was glorious. Ma poked the steaks with her finger then flipped them, they continued to sizzle and crackle away. My mouth was watering, and I was in a trance watching the steaks all toast and crisp round the edges.

'Son, do a loada bread an' butter will ya?'

'No problem, Ma,' and I grabbed the *O'Hara's* plain loaf and started buttering the bread. Ma plopped three plates down with a sizzling steak on each of them.

'Don't touch just yet,' she said.

She grabbed a huge onion out of the cupboard and had it peeled, sliced and fried in no time. She dumped the blackened onions on top of the steaks and said, 'Bon appétit.'

All you could hear was the clatter of our eating irons, rattling the plates as we got stuck in. Da lifted a slice of buttered bread and went over to the pan and rubbed the bread, butter-side down, around the inside to soak up all the juices. He stuck the brown soggy slice of bread in his mouth.

'Aghh,' he sighed, 'this is beautiful.'

Frank said, 'Billy ya don't even need ta use yer knife. The steak's so saft, ya could break it up with yer fork. Ahh, Jesus, it just melts in yer mouth.'

Afterwards Da filled his pipe, lit it, and supped his tea, looking very contented.

'Where'd ya get that big drum ah baccy?' Frank asked.

'Mícheál brought it up fer us,' Da said and took four big handfuls of baccy and put it in a big leather pouch that looked as though it were from World War One.

'Don't smoke that yet.' I said, 'sure, I'm still atein, fuck's sake.'

'No problem, son,' Da replied.

Frank filled his pipe, 'Jesus, that was some scoop wasn't it?'

Frank and my Da sat in the kitchen, lips smacking away as they puffed and puffed at their pipes. The two of them looked so contented, just sitting and puffing in silence.

Frank leaned forward to whisper something, and then spoke out loud for all to hear, 'Who're we gonna rob this week?'

'Fuck up, Frank,' Da said. 'D'ya think my son's ears are painted on?'

'Well, he's gonna hear things up in the club.'

'Just be quiet, Frank, an' lemme enjoy this smoke.'

'Okay, Skipper, no problem. Are we even gonna shoot anyone?' Frank said and laughed.

'Donna,' Da shouted, 'come in here an' dig the fuckin face aff Frank, God fergive me fer swearin.'

Ma came rushing into the room and stuck her fist in Frank's face. He cowered into the corner.

'Liam, cover yer ears, I don't want ya ta be subjected ta his bullshit.'

'His hands won't fit over 'is fuckin ears. Sure, he's like Dumbo the Elephant,' said Frank.

'Frank, I'm warnin ya,' Ma pressed her fist into his gob.

Da was killing himself laughing. Ma put Frank into a headlock.

'Referee!' Frank shouted, as if to beg for mercy.

Ma let go of him, "Have ya no home ta go, ta Frank?'

'Aye, I have.'

'Well, why aren't ya there?'

'Donna, she's lookin fer sex again, she fuckin scares me. Donna, she has me tortured day an' night. I haven't had a full night's sleep in a fortnight, I'm wrecked. Would ya nat send him up, ta gimme a rest?' Frank pointed over to me.

'He's only a pup, an' what makes ya think he'd know what ta do?'

'That's the beauty of it, he doesn't have ta know, sure, I taughth'er everythin she knows.'

'Listen ta ya, Casanova.'

The front door rapped.

Franks shouted, 'If that's Margaret, I'm nat here.'

Ma answered the door, it was wee Dan Megran looking for bread until tomorrow.

'There's only half-a-loaf? Is that okay?' Ma said.

'Cheers, Donna, I'll give it back ta ya themarra.'

'Don't worry, Dan, an' here's a couple ah wee steaks fer ya.'

Dan said thank you and dandered up the street in a drunken stupor.

'Frank, d'ya ever stap?' Ma said.

'I'll stap when they're nailin the lid shut.'

'Jesus, Frank, that's a bit morbid.'

'Donna, she'll still be tryin ta jump me.'

'She's a wee quiet woman, wouldn't say boo ta a goose.'

'Aye, that's what everyone thinks.'

'I'll tell her, cos y'know I know her well. We used ta work in the mill together, ya dirty hallion ye.'

'Right, Skipper, that's me away, an' if ya don't see me themarra, I'll be up in the hospital waitin on a hip.'

'Get out, get out, ya hallion ye,' said Ma.

'I might just have trouble walkin,' Frank said.

Ma ran over and started beating him round the head with her hands. We were all in stitches laughing.

Ma shouted down the street after Frank, 'Yu're nathin but a dirt bird, ya tramp.'

She came back in and said, 'I duuno how Margaret sticks him, he's a dirty wee clart, she'd fuckin kill him if she'd the slightest inclination ah the way he talked about her.'

We all head off to bed and I was still sucking wee bits of meat out from my teeth. I whizzed around my chops with a wet brush as some minger had stepped on the tube of toothpaste and emptied it onto the floor. They had wiped it up but you could still see white streaks on the floor and the empty tube lay there flattened.

Wednesday came, sure enough, and Ma and I headed off to work in the Felons club. In no time at all, I was pulling pints, as Ma was a brilliant bar lady and a good teacher. It was busy enough and there was a wee diddly-dee three-piece playing away. It wasn't long before the bar was packed, loads of people shouting, 'Donna, Donna.' to get Ma's attention.

'Quick, stick on a pinta double, before that cunt Frank does!'

Frank always rushed it, and everyone knows when you're pulling a pint of double that it can't be rushed, you've to let it settle. But Frank just wanted it out to get the money in.

Ma was always shouting at him, 'Fuck's sake, Frank. Look at the state ah that.'

Ma's pints were always perfect: pure black with an inch of white creamy head that slid down the inside of the glass with each slug.

People used to say to Frank, as a pretence, 'Oh I'm already gettin served.' They didn't want Frank to serve them. Ma always got loads of tips for that reason, not to mention her very broad sense of humour. She took no crap from anyone and was a five-foot-tall workhorse who never stopped for a break while others had a feg out the back. She was very well respected, as was Da, who at five-foot-tall was tough as fuck and feared by most men.

The night flew in, and it was chuck out time, the place quickly emptied, and the empty glasses were stacked two-foot high on the bar like huge skyscrapers. I washed, rinsed and stacked the shelves with the clean glasses, while Frank and Ma changed kegs and stocked the bar for the next day. When I was all done, I pulled myself a staff pint and went over to the pool table to smash a few balls. The committee members were tidying up and stacking chairs on top of each other, they started lifting things and checking under everything for incendiary devices.

'All clear,' one of the men shouted.

There was a bit of a commotion downstairs, then four men burst in through the door dragging a guy by the scruff. He was already beaten and bloodied up.

'That's the cunt that's robbin oul folk round here,' someone said.

They tied the guy to a chair and dragged him backwards onto the dancefloor, they brought over another chair and put his legs outstretched onto it. A huge lump of a guy held the guy firmly by the ankles. One of the other men swung a big heavy iron bar and broke his two legs in two swift swings. The man screamed in agony and pleaded 'Please, no more, please, no more.'

'This is what happens ta scum like you,' a hooded man said.

The guy was dragged off, still tied to the chair.

Franks shouted over, 'Hey big lad, rack em up, yer real Da's gonna show ya how ta play pool.'

He broke the pool balls and said, 'What happens in the club stays in the club, ya do know that?'

'Fer fuck's sake, Frank, are ya serious? Cos I was gonna go down ta the *Irish News*, first pop in the mornin.'

Ma handed me a mop to do the floors. I was trying to wring out the mop, but the mechanism was jammed. So, I stomped on it and a bit of bone or cartilage flew out of the mechanism.

'Son, go easy, yu'll break that,' Ma said.

'Nah, Ma, it was stuck, an' somethin came flyin outta it.'

'What is it?' She asked and stared at my hand.

'Oh, I think it's a bitta bone.'

'Jesus Christ, son, throw it in the bin.'

I quietly slipped one of my *Beechnut* chewing gums out of my pocket and tossed it into my mouth and crunched it.

'Aye, it's definitely bone' I said.

Ma's chin almost hit the floor. She thought I had eaten the bit of bone. Her knees started to buckle.

'Ma, Ma, I'm only sleggin, I'm only sleggin,' and I showed her the piece of white bone that was in my other hand.

'Jesus, fuck, son, I thought yu'd turned cannibal.'

'Donna,' Frank shouted, 'he's a cheeky fucker, just like you.'

'Fuck up, Frank,' Ma shouted, 'or I'll come over there an' dig yer face in.'

'Frank, my Da's already filled me in. I may be green-lookin but I'm far from a fuckin cabbage.'

He laughed then slaughtered me at the game of pool.

'Pull yerself another one an' relax, an' I hope that wee incident earlier didn't unsettle ya.'

'Nat at all, it was just like a night out with the lads.'

'Donna,' Frank shouted, 'I like him, he's definitely a keeper.'

Ma shouted, 'Well, fuckin keep him then, he'll ate ya outta house an' home. Son, if he's torturin ya, I'll come over an' fix him.'

'No need, Ma, he looks as though he'd enjoy it. I'm a big-boned fucker,' I said.

Franks almost choked on his pint. 'That's a cracker. Donna, did ya tell him he's big-boned? He looks like Man Mountain Dean. Donna, what d'ya feed him.'

'Plenty,' Ma shouted.

'Yeah, yeah, two funny cunts aren't yis? I get enough abuse at home, an' I don't need it here.'

'Ya may get used ta it, son, cos it gets plenty rough in here,' said Ma.

'Donna,' Frank shouted.

'Fer fuck's sake, Frank, I'm busy, what is it?'

'Well, Donna, he's passed the test, he'll do well in here. Pretty soon, we'll have ya swing the club.'

Ma shouted, 'Fuckin sure ya won't, he's broke enough, without any more crap.'

Frank and I racked the balls up and Frank leaned in and softly said, 'Mícheál speaks very highly ah ya an' that's good enough fer me.'

'Mícheál who?' I replied.

'Oh, fuck, Donna, he's definitely a keeper.'

Big Sammy Miller came in, he was the night watchman. He was at least six foot tall and wore a big black heavy long coat and his hands and feet were twice the size of mine. He was very pale and waxy looking with a big thick black moustache. He looked as if he was just dug up and pulled from a coffin. He had a carry-out bag with Chinese takeaway food in it. Frank brought over three plates and dished it out. Chicken curry, ribs and a king prawn Chow Mein.

Ma shouted, 'I dunno how yis can ate that shite.'

I washed it down with the rest of my pint and then Ma and me walked home.

'How'd I do, Ma?'

'Just fine, son.'

'How much in tips did ya get?'

'A fiver. So, what about you Ma?'

'Twenty-two pounds.'

'Jesus, Ma, twenty-two quid?'

'Aye, big Gabe gimme a fiver an' Manilito touched fer a big bet, an' he gimme another. Jesus, my feet are killin me,' Ma said as she shuffled home.

I got into the house and went straight to bed; I was exhausted and didn't waken till midday. I came down the stairs to an empty house, all my brothers and sisters were at school and Ma had to get her shift done. She was also a dinner lady in Star of the Sea School. I made a cup of tea and sat in the kitchen listening to the radio. Ma came in with a load of jam and coconut cake and set it on the table.

'Help yerself, son.'

So, I grabbed two or three lumps and scoffed them.

'Did ya get the sausage rolls I left fer y'in the oven?'

'No, Ma,' then I saw the note on the table.

Ma bunged the hot sausage rolls onto a plate and brought them to me. I put a thick line of *HP Sauce* down both sides of the sausage-rolls and ate them. Ma cut a big yellow scone up the middle and got out ham and cheese. It went down a treat.

Ma and I went out to work again that night and Ma introduced me to some of the regulars. Manilito, he was called that because he looked like the guy out of *The High Chaparral.*

'This is Big Gabe.'

He was a construction worker, a huge lump of a man. Six-foot-something and arms like legs and his hands were massive, he looked as though he could crack your skull with his bare hands but he was a gentle giant despite the fact that he was a brick shithouse with bulging biceps and his back was near as broad as the door. So, he had to walk in sideways. He had a very deep voice but rarely spoke, whereas Manilito never fucked up. He would natter away to anyone near him, he had a friend called Danny and he drank a pint of

Bass and a biff (vodka). Manilito's order was a pint of double and a wee *Mundie's*.

Danny had an industrial accident and got a big claim from it, the only problem was he was a hypochondriac and was always worried about catching something. When Danny came up to the bar Ma would speak in a worried voice.

'Jesus Danny, ya look a bit pale.'

He would run into the bathroom to check the mirror.

Manilito would say to Ma, 'Fuck's sake, Donna, don't be windin him up, I'm tryin ta get a tap aff him till next week.'

So, Ma would wait for five minutes or so and then get someone else to say: 'Jesus, Danny, ya don't look well at all.'

Ma kept on and on at him, convincing him he was at death's door, till he went home with his money still in his pockets.

The Felons was run like a well-oiled machine, and everyone knew their part. Anyone who stepped out of line was quickly dealt with. It was hard times, and the people came in to let off steam, there were loads of characters there, some good, some bad. People looking tired and after a few drinks, they were singing and dancing. Halfway through the night two hooded men got up on stage and read a list of names out and then burned the list. Men were pulled in, and one at a time their crimes were read out in front of everyone. A man was beat with hurls for twenty minutes or so then dragged off the dance floor unconscious, or to within an inch of his life. The next guy was frogmarched in and kneecapped then whisked away. The third guy, a youngish guy around mid-twenties, was dragged in kicking and squealing. He was thrown down on the floor and four men started beating him with hurls. The place was in absolute silence, all you could hear were the moans and groans of the guys swinging the hurls as hard as they could to inflict as much pain and suffering as possible. The man lay on the floor squealing for mercy, but none was shown, he gargled his own blood as he was beat around the head and body until he soon lay lifeless. He was dragged away by the ankles nearly beat to death and trailed away as if he were roadkill or something. The eerie silence remained, then the crowd started cheering and clapping. They threw beer mats at each other, while others banged their glasses off the tables. You could actually hear the poor guy's bones breaking as he lay there like a lump of meat getting pulverised, I was exhilarated, watching the beatings.

A man was frogmarched in and was pushed down into a chair, two six-inch nails were hammered through the backs of his hands, securing him into the chair. He begged and pleaded but it fell on deaf ears, the crowd booed and jeered as he begged for sympathy. A large man then took a block hammer and broke his knees, dislocating them right out of their sockets. The crowd went *aghhh* and shrugged away at the noise of the breaking and dislocating bone. It was like no other noise I'd ever heard before and was bloodcurdling. But when all was said and done, the roof nearly came off the building as everyone cheered, they whooped and ye-hawed like cowboys in a movie. *Fuck's sake*, I thought, *are they gonna houl up score cards fer the most brutal beatin?*

Ma pushed me against the wall, 'Don't go gettin yerself involved in anythin. D'ya hear me, son?'

'Aye, Ma, fer fuck's sake. I'm nat stupid.'

The big guy with the block hammer had his hood up over his face; he looked like an executioner who had worked the gallows in a past life.

Frank shouted at Donna, 'I didn't know they were givin out punishment haircuts,' and pointed over to me.

We all started laughing and Ma said, 'Son, go round with a tin ta collect money.'

'Fuck off, Ma, I'm nat going round with a cup beggin. Stap windin me up. I nearly done that, fer fuck's sake.'

It came on the news again that a bomb went off at parliament buildings in the underground car park, killing Airey Neave, the shadow secretary for Northern Ireland. The place went ballistic, cheering.

'Arrrghh, go on, son!' someone shouted, as if his horse had come in first.

A car bomb had exploded in the underground car park of Westminster Houses of Parliament. Later it came to light that the INLA claimed responsibility for it.

Tensions were very high after that in particular. People were looking for answers around the shoot-to-kill policy, which was always vigorously denied but infuriated the nationalist community. Bloody Sunday was a bloody and most heinous crime against humanity and people wanted answers that never came. The Ballymurphy Six and countless atrocities against catholic communities had people on a knife edge. Touts were dealt with in a swift and deadly manner, leaflets were circulated. Anyone found to be giving information to the security forces would be dealt with severely. Due to some choice arrests by the security forces, and the information given to the security forces it struck a blow at the heart of Republicanism and the Felons club closed ranks. Everyone was under suspicion, especially outsiders. Paramilitary shootings and beatings were happening on a more regular basis, as fear struck into the heart of the community. The so-called Shankill Butchers were claiming more victims, and it was common knowledge by the Police force who they were, and they had a free hand with no fear of recrimination, as they roamed freely between peace divides.

In the bar, it was business as usual, and it was packed with people every evening. You could walk the full length of the New Lodge Road in ten minutes and there was McLoughlin's Pub, The Circle, The Celtic, The Felons, The Starry Plough, The Vic, The Earl Inn, all on one wee road, more or less. They were the heartbeat of the community, right or wrong.

I had staples and scars all over my head and people often made jokes about them.

'Jesus Donna, could y'imagine one a yer daughters bringin him home with her?'

Ma was always quick to come to my defence. I had lumps, bumps, scrapes, staples and bruises from fighting and being hit with baton rounds and whatnot and I could hold my own in a slagging match with anyone. The punishment haircut was my favourite and Saint Pat's Chapel looking for a bell ringer was another. The more they drank the more they slagged and the more tips you got. Ma always played along, saying things like, 'Fer fuck's sake, be quiet, he doesn't know he's ugly cos we don't allow mirrors in the house,' or, 'Shh, he doesn't know he had that bad accident, as he can't remember anythin from before the time that he came outta that coma.'

'Yo, scare the dogs, any chance ah a pint?'

The tips were flying in the jar, and I loved the whole banter thing that went on. But outside of working hours if anyone made a quip, well, they would have got a swift kick in the balls. And I didn't care if they were RA or not.

Riots seemed to go on for longer and harder as anarchy gripped the nation. The punk revolution came, and people had enough of dictatorships and the Tory government. Across the UK, demonstrations were held about the Tories and the rich getting richer, while the poor still got poorer. The army and the police beat down even harder at the community and, likewise, the punishment squads got more vindictive, they used a hand-turned drill to kneecap victims and it looked and sounded horrendous. They turned the cork-gripped handle and the drill cracked and squealed through the sinew and bone, churning up cartilage and loads of blood was spilled. The victims passed out in pain, normally. They even had the idea of tying someone to a set of railings and pulling his hip bones out of their sockets. It was to incite fear into their own people, because if that's what they do for anti-social behaviour, well what would they do to touts and police informers? Time after time, both men and women were marched in and out to take their punishment and they were brutally beaten, maimed both physically and mentally for life. Some learned a lesson, some didn't, and the so-called hit list was circulated around shops, bars, businesses and public places, naming and shaming people and if they didn't leave the country, they were dead.

When people were shot and murdered in cold blood, 'the innocents', we called them, this only added fuel to the fire around the Nationalist areas. Margaret Thatcher called these victims collateral damage, human rights protests or marches sprang up everywhere, which received little to no media coverage, because of the English parliamentarian media embargo which made the working classes shout even louder. The mainland had become the main target now and by fuck that got plenty of coverage, which only highlighted the plight in Belfast and in fact all Northern Ireland people had been stripped of their basic human rights. No one looked too far ahead into the future, yet alone, prepared for it. If you woke up in the morning it was a blessing, if you didn't you were a statistic, and it was as simple as that.

People gathered around the Holy Grotto next to Denise's house, to say the rosary and to pray for peace. Huge numbers of people came there to ask God to intervene for peace and some form of reconciliation to the troubles. The army looked down from their lookout posts, built on top of the high-rise flats and scrutinized everything and everyone. Helicopters dropped stores and supplies but never hung about long. You could see rifles pointing over the edge of the army post, scoping out all and sundry. They took photos of anyone they thought looked a bit suspicious, and that was enough to get you arrested and put in jail with no judge or jury. They kept you as long as they wanted, and you would have little to no rights whatsoever. People didn't go out of their own areas, and they drowned their sorrows in a pint, which was 43p and that made life just a little more tolerable.

Wee Bridget Reid, (Bridget the midget), Republican hero, Billy Reid's, mother, would come into the bar and shout, 'Up the Provies!' Everyone would cheer. 'They murdered my son,' she'd say every time she came in. She would say to Ma, 'Here, Donna, stick a few wee sherries in that.' and she would hand Ma a wee bottle with a screw-top lid. She was a friendly wee woman who always looked sad and weary. She wore a knee-length checkered woollen coat, and a headscarf tied tightly around her head. 'Up the provies,' she'd yell again, and the people gave her a standing ovation. Many people rushed to pay for her drink, but she always refused. She was never allowed to pay, as people already had the cost covered. She was a real wee character with her wee sad frown she would have melted anyone's heart. Her wee thin face was heavily wrinkled, and she was pale and was less than five foot tall. You could see pain in her almost burnt-out eyes, and I don't think I ever saw her smile, not even once.

Ma kept everyone at the bar going and slagged them continuously, and when Ma rang the bell for last orders, Frank Hickey shouted, 'Donna, was that the bell or was that yer knickers ringin?' The place erupted in laughter as Ma would have Frank in a headlock, slapping the bake of him.

Ma was shouting at him as she slapped him, 'Ya fuckin dirt bird.'

Frank would often have to tap out, as Ma had him pinned to the bar, beating him. After his hiding, Frank shouted, 'Has anybody else gat somethin ta say? 'And everyone looked away, then they ran up to the bar to get last orders in. Frank would dust himself off and help Ma behind the bar. Frank rubbed his shoulder, 'Donna, I think ya dislocated this.'

'Fuck up, Frank, or I'll dislocate yer neck fer ya.'

People were just randomly shouting orders and Frank would be behind Ma, letting on to cut his own throat, because he was afraid of Ma. It was mental, the laugh we had. Balance was finally restored to the bar and Ma's tip jar was full. Frank would wink over to Ma and the two of them would be in stitches laughing. They were like a double act, to get the most tips out of you. Frank and Margaret were probably Ma and Da's oldest friends and went way back, since Moby Dick was a tadpole. They were all as thick as thieves and Frank and Da were interned together.

Jim McSorley was another close friend of our family, and when they all got together it was pure dynamite. Jim, who fancied himself as a bit of a crooner, would sing a song or two, he turned to Frank and said, 'I thought ya said I was tone deaf an' sounded like a crow?'

'I never said anythin ah the sort.'

'C'mon, Frank,' Ma said, 'I think there's a bitta jealousy here.'

Ma did all the mixing, playing one off against the other, which was comical.

Jim would slide halfway out of the commotion, only to get sucked back in again and he'd carry on singing.

'Frank, I hear yu've got a problem. Y'know, keepin it up?' Jim said.

'It's all lies, fuckin lies, who told ya that shite?'

Ma interrupted, 'C'mon nigh, boys it's nat a dick swingin competition.'

Da would be in stitches and Ma shouted at Billy, 'Didn't ya tell me Frank couldn't get it up?'

'Ya lyin fucker,' Frank shouted at Da.

The tears were rolling down his face by now. If Ma wasn't slagging she was singing, a total all-rounder she was.

'Here, do yis know I've metal plate in my head,' I said, trying to butt in on the banter. 'Apparently they'd ta melt the bell down in Saint Patrick's chapel.'

'Son, it was fuckin two bells, so it was,' Jim said.

'Ma, Ma, did they have ta melt two bells? Any wonder I can't lift my head aff the pilla in the mornin.'

'Don't fuckin listen ta him, sure he's twice as stupid as you,' Ma said.

Frank called into the bakery the next day and Frank being Frank would turn on his womanly charms, so to speak.

Dolly Patterson, who worked in the bakery, came out and addressed the women who were standing in a queue, waiting to be served. 'Don't listen ta that aul lad, he can't even keep it up, or so I'm told.'

'Who told ya that? Cos they're fuckin liars.'

All the people in the queue would be killing themselves laughing.

Dolly had a great sense of humour too. 'Here, Frank, d'ya want a cream Charlie or a big French dick? Oh, sorry, did I say dick? I meant ta say stick.'

Frank flew out of there and came banging at our front door. 'Donna,' he shouted up the stairs.

'What is it, Frank?'

'Stap fuckin tellin people I can't get it up, fer fuck's sake. Ya wanna seen what I went through in that fuckin bakery with that Dolly one.'

'I never said anythin,' Ma said, 'it must be that oul cunt, Jim McSorley, y'know he's jealous ah ya.'

'I'll see him the night in the club,' Frank said.

'Donna, stap tellin lies about the man,' Da shouted, and he was holding his laughter back. 'Dolly toul Frank an' everyone else in the shop that Margaret was a sex-starved woman, an' that she caught Frank with his trousers down, lookin at dirty books. Frank said he's afraid ta leave the house, fer fuck's sake, he's in hidin.'

Jim 'Sinatra' McSurely?

When Jim McSorley called in to see Da and Ma they were all over him like a rash.

Ma said, 'That oul fucker, Frank Hickey, was in here earlier an' he admitted ta bein jealous ah yer dark wavy hair, but don't let him know I toul ya.'

'Okay, Donna, say no more.'

Later that night, me, Da, Frank and Jim were in the club and Frank went to the loo. Ma went over to Jim and ran her fingers through his hair, 'Nigh, promise me, Jim, ya can't say a word ta Frank about yer hair, cos it'll land me in trouble.'

'Relax, Donna, I won't.'

Every time Frank looked over to Jim, Jim would run his hands through his hair then flick his head back.

Frank said to Ma, 'Donna, watch Jim, is there somethin wrong with him?'

'I know what ya mean, Frank, he's gettin on kinda weird. I suppose y'know already about him comin outta the closest.'

'Who? Jim?'

'Aye, Jim, sure 'is wife is leavin him, but yu've ta be sworn ta secrecy.'

Of course, Frank told everyone in the club, and we were all in stitches laughing.

Frank said, 'Like, how'd ya think I feel? I shared a fuckin prison cell with him. Sure, Donna toul me, when

Billy's at the club, he comes down an' tries on Donna's shoes, sayin, "I'm thinkin about gettin these fer the missus. He even tried her clothes on."'

'This is serious,' I butted in, 'sure, I caught him rubbin a pair ah Ma's knickers all over 'is face.'

'The dirty oul cunt,' people were saying then waving over.

Dolly came into the club and said, 'One ah yer ones asked me ta tell ya that they need a bottle ah gas for the *Superser*.'

'Thank you, Dolly,' Ma said.

'Liam, will ya run round ta Julie's an' grab a bottle ah gas? It's the yella one,'

'Ma, I'm nat stupid, like, the yella one!'

'Y'only look stupid,' Dolly chirped in and let out a big manly laugh.

'Fuckin comedians, the two ah yis.'

'An' will ya connect it up, as well, an' put it ta one bar?'

'No probs an' do ya want me ta wait till the house warms up?'

'Get out, ya cheeky fucker,' Ma shouted.

'Is that oul cunt here? Y'know the one firin the blanks?'

'Aye, Frank was at a committee meetin an' brought it up about Jim tryin my clothes on when Billy's at work. He said it was fer security reasons. Jim went fuckin nuts, shoutin, fuckin lies, all of it! I'm happily married.' Jim said.

'Are ya still here?' Ma shouted to me.

'Aye, I was makin sure no one was listenin.'

'Except yerself, ya nosey wee cunt,' Dolly shouted.

'Fuck up, ya oul begh,' I shouted.

'Son, go an' get the gas, an' no fuckin about, okay?'

'Okay, Ma.'

I got the bottle of gas and was walking down Churchill Street just past Stephen Kelly's house. Two hooded men ran down towards the Barrick just off Lepper Street. An unmarked police car followed, it was low to the ground, because of all the armour-plating and the windows had a slight green tint, because they were bulletproof. It had a deep roar as it accelerated, I knew it was after two guys, so I stepped out in front of it and with my two hands hurled the bottle of gas through the windscreen, causing it to crash into a lamppost. I quickly ran home and changed my clothes and put a monkey hat on.

'The gas will be here soon,' I said and ran up to the club.

I took Ma to the side and told her what I'd done.

'Ya done right son,' she said and patted me on the back.

Wee Seany and Matt Campbell were standing at the bar and about to leave.

Ma said, 'here, Seany, on the way home, would ya chuck a bottle ah gas inta my house, as the kids are freezin down there?'

'It's as good as done,' wee Seany said.

A few lads came up to the bar and Ma served them, 'Here Donna, a pint fer you an' the young lad,' and he thanked me for what I'd done.

Word soon got out about the fact that it was me who threw the gas bottle but no one talked out of shop. I'd actually seen misinformation getting told to someone, just to see what and where it came out. The inner circle of the Felons was the actual committee members, and they were tight and trusted each other implicitly. I knocked off and went up to the Kel Star chippy. Two pasties, four sausages, a fish, a half a chicken and chips and two large chips. A portion of curry and a portion of gravy. Tucker Kelly was on and was in great form, singing away. He did a bit of cabaret work: weddings, Bar Mitzvahs, the usual crack. He knew my Ma and Da well and he always shovelled the chips onto the order.

'An' a soft fish fer Ma.'

'I know, son,' Tucker said, 'cos, sure, she's no teeth.'

Ma always made us say that, make sure it's a soft one and wrap it separately. I'd have to drop it into work at the bar on the way home.

'I kill myself, every time one ah yer tribe comes up with the order, an' then hands me a bitta paper. *Tucker make sure it's a soft one cos I've no teeth*, every time, that kills me. Yer Ma's an headcase, so she is.'

'I know, but we're the ones who've ta live with her,' I said and scoffed. 'Plenty ah salt an' vinegar on everythin!'

He was humming *Via Las Vegas* in his Elvis voice, followed by some makeshift karate chops.

I trotted on home after sorting Ma out and buttered a loaf of bread and made a big pot of tea. The animals came charging in, like vultures, swooping down and picking a carcass bare. The food was gone in no time at all, not one plate was used. I washed out their cups and dumped all the chippy newspapers. I was fucking shattered, and it only dawned on me then just how hard Ma worked her whole life. She had three jobs, and reared eight kids, and she never even complained once. This wee woman was a workhorse, especially when Da had been interned. The next day, twenty-four bombs went off within twenty-four hours of each other across Northern Ireland. The security forces were extra vigilant as cops, screws and soldiers were all targeted. Some innocent people died, because they were mistaken for a foot patrol in Keady. The Shankill Butchers had claimed eight kills by chopping people up with hatchets and knives, it soon rose to eleven kills and one survivor. They even murdered people within their ranks, to hold command and power. They were arrested and received two-thousand years, or something mad like that, between them. People wanted to know why it was left to go on for so long without being challenged. People breathed easy again, as the news spread of their capture.

Every time you walked out the front door, it could be your last, and I was under no illusion about that. The hunger strikers wanting to be recognized as political prisoners. All this torment rushing through my head, where death seemed to be the only answer. I watched gruesome tortures; pain was everywhere I looked. This life bombarded me, non-stop. The pain on people's faces standing at the bar, eyes dead and black like the wee grannies that grieved for their grandchildren, constantly full of heartache and sorrow. There was a void that nothing could fill, just an empty stare. Women took to the streets to keep order and Dolly Patterson was one of them.

'Get inta the house, or I'll tell yer Ma,' I always heard her shouting.

I nicknamed them the Dolly Brigade, as they broke army blockades many a time. Dolly and Ma were pretty close and went back a long time, they carried guns about in their prams from house to house.

'I can't see there ever bein an end ta the armed conflict,' Ma said. 'Well, nat in my lifetime.'

The women were like wee worker ants, carrying guns and passing messages on through the area and were very acknowledged and knowledgeable in the war against England, or the armed struggle.

Sponge Bob

I called up to Denise's house and we chilled listening to music.

'Why don't ya call up on Saturday nights, instead ah sniffin glue in the graveyard.?' She asked.

'That sounds like a plan,' I said and that was how I got off the glue.

Thirty or so years on and we were happily married with our own kids, Denise would bring it up at parties and other outings. 'D'ya remember the time I gat ya aff the glue?' and everyone would be in stitches.

But when I was young Denise saw something inside of me.

'Ya need ta let go ah somethin,' she would say.

'Like what?' I'd say.

'Anger, hatred, violence; that's nat you.'

'It sure feels like me.'

'Who d'ya know, when they were ten years oul, gettin done with attempted murder?' Denise said.

'That was all a loada balls,' I protested. 'Me an' Skol were standin outside O'Hara's bakery on Duncairn Gardens, atein a bag ah buns an' there was a foot patrol comin down an' the Peeler who was with them recognized us, an' thought we were up ta no good. Robert Cluelo 'is name was. He came chargin over ta challenge me and Skol, an' Skol threw his snowball at him and hit him right between the eyes, and nearly knocked him out. Skol an' me ran away, laughin. The Peelers then scooped us an' said that we threw some kinda incendiary device at him an' that he's in hospital, nearly blinded by the shrapnel. We were outside the bakery between two peace walls ready ta get stuck into our monster buns. We were completely taken off guard by the cop.'

'So, what are ya sayin?'

'I'm fuckin sayin it was a snowball I hit him with. Shrapnel? No fuckin way. It was bits ah coconut, probably.'

The cops nearly wet themselves laughin.

'A fuckin snowball!' Skol shouted.

'Attempted murder my hole, no fuckin way,' I shouted.

We had to wait for weeks for the court case to be dropped, and Robert never lived it down. His new nickname was Sponge Bob, years later when he was a detective inspector. So, everyone called him detective inspector Sponge Bob. Fucking class, it could only happen to me.

'Well at least he got five months out on the sick,' said Denise.

'Denise, that's exactly what happened, I swear ta God. Ya go ta school with Annmarie McArdle. That's Skol's girlfriend, just ask her, she'll tell ya.'

Forty years later, Skol and Annemarie are still very much in love and happily wrapped in each other's arms.

Skol was a bit of a legend, he could throw a petrol bomb farther than any other person except for Moorso from Unity Flats. Skol had pinpoint accuracy and often had two lit ones in his hands. It was harder to throw them, in case one would spill when chucking the other one, as it was all about momentum. He was like Spiderman, climbing up walls and over roofs. If chucking petrol bombs was an Olympic sport, Skol would be getting a gold medal. He had balls to burn and was quick as fuck, he was our very own home-grown rocket launcher, as was John Moore from Unity. John could stand at his own front door in Unity and hurl half a Belfast red brick over six to seven lanes of the motorway, clear a twenty-foot partition and still hit the houses at the bottom of the Shankhill Road. He should have been a gold medal Olympian. Like pilgrims; people regularly left bricks outside his front door, so he could lob them first thing in the morning and throughout the day.

You could rob anything from anywhere as long as it wasn't in your own area, and you didn't bring the cops into the area with the heat. Then you'd make a voluntary donation to the cause. Heartbreak, sorrow, the unanswered questions to the loss of loved ones, an innocent, the bereavement stages lasted years as vital information was always being withheld by security forces. Hatred issues and some got consumed by it as marriages fell apart, and people's lives disintegrated into alcoholism or resembled a zombie-like stage. You could see it all around you, all the different levels, alcohol, drugs, isolation; it was a fucking time bomb.

One time, the Peelers raided Skol's home and walked his parents into the square in white boiler suits, while they were looking for bombs.

Skol's Da shouted, 'I'm gonna fuckin kill that Brian one, when I get a houl ah him.'

They were a wee quiet well-respected couple, who never missed Mass.

I didn't call round to Skol's for ages after that, due to the look on Skol's Ma's wee face, as she leant over the bonnet of the cop car, and his Da leaning over the other side. All because of an O'Hara's snowball. 'A bun to die for,' it was called after that.

A few weeks later, we were being chased by the soldiers during a riot and we ran into a high-rise flat and got on top of the block. We were twelve stories high, and the winds were fierce as it rushed past you and nearly lifted you off your feet. We watched the soldiers searching for us and we lay flat on top of the roof, you could hardly open your eyes or mouth, as the wind rushed in, and you had to catch your breath. Two police Land Rovers pulled up at the bottom of the flats, we heard them whirring away, as they passed Artillery Flats and chugged up the hill to us.

'Skol, do ya think they're here fer us? I asked.

'Dunno,' he replied.

We searched around the roof and in a wee store found two big, tall, blue gas bottles. We lined them up and rolled them off, one landed right between the two Land Rovers, exploded and shot up in the air like a space rocket. The other landed on one of the Land Rovers and sprung upwards as if on a trampoline and bounced down the street like a tennis ball before exploding in the "bally-ball" pitches. It was like the scene from, *The Damn Busters,* movie with the bouncing bomb. It rotated first and then bounced until it hit the dam, exploding, and breaking the dam. Our endeavours caused the Land Rovers to race off at high speed, thinking it was an RPG attack. The block of flats shook when the bottles exploded and frightened the crap out of us, as we were on the very top of the flats.

We went down to inspect the damage and six flagstones were smashed and a small crater was left. People were all out waving the tricolour and cheering. We went round hammering metal spikes into the ground at a 30-degree angle, so that the Land Rovers or cars couldn't come in. It slowed the big six wheeled Saracens down but didn't stop them. It slowed them down just enough for someone to throw a ten-gallon drum with holes in it filled with petrol then it set alight. It would burst into flames and thirty seconds or so later, the soldiers would come flying out the back, just shooting anything that moved. It was like a game to us kids, as we fought and strategised to inflict as much pain as possible. We knew every nook and cranny, as we disappeared into the shadows, like ghosts of the revolution, swift and silent, with a furious sting in our tails. When you have nothing to lose, you've nothing to fear, everyone had crosses to bear and the only way you could lift it was through street violence. I always healed quickly and, no matter what, I was right back out there again.

We would fling each other into the side of a moving bus and then lie there motionless with everyone gathered around and when we'd hear the ambulance we'd jump up and run away laughing. My mate normally did the flinging, as I had knocked him unconscious so many times and the bus didn't even stop in case it was hijacked. 'Turn them, and burn them,' we all shouted during a riot, as if they were sausages on a barbeque. We put gas bottles in boots of cars along with nails, ball bearings, nuts and bolts, and set alight to them and blocked the road with them. When they exploded, God help anyone who was nearby. No one told us what to do, we just thought things up ourselves and we, the children of the troubles were a force to be reckoned with. We were fuelled by hatred and high on adrenaline, as the army shot at us. Because, and I'm fucking telling you this for nothing, when a foot patrol is in hot pursuit, we could nearly leap over cars because if they got you, you were almost kicked to death. After a riot, we would sit round a burning car and we were like old war dogs, showing our scars and bruises where the baton rounds had hit us. Our hands reeked of petrol, as someone would bring over a load of sandwiches wrapped in tinfoil. I've seen me with a petrol bomb in one hand and a sarnie in the other hand, as you had to eat on the hoof at times.

We fought for every street and corner of our concrete wasteland. Why? I don't fucking know why, you just did every day if you had to. We decommissioned countless six wheelers as they tried to run us over. Two of us would hang onto the grille at the front of the Saracen and at the same time you'd slip a bin lid under the front wheel, and it couldn't steer, then we would chuck drums of petrol on top and light it up. The inhabitants came out blasting and would run like fuck, you'd be standing with a lit petrol bomb waiting on them to fire at ya, you'd dodge out of the way and then lob away. Some of us would do a wee dance, some just took a bow to rapturous applause and cheering. We were a pack of fucking wild animals.

One time, I was getting chased by the snatch squad and ran straight into a lamppost, knocking myself out cold. I woke up nearly two days later on someone's sofa. Even though I had been out cold, the army had still kicked the cunt out of me, and two men had dragged me into a house, with blood pishing out of me. The last thing I remembered was hitting the lamp and Skol laughing as I fell. The expression on Skol's face when he heard the clunk of my head hitting the lamp post was priceless.

It didn't seem that long ago when I tied a snake belt around the handle of a small lump hammer and swung it round and round like Thor but I gave it up as a bad job as I'd knocked myself out a couple of times. I had lumps on top of lumps on my dome. Lumpy loaf or bumpy nut, I was called. I didn't tell anyone how I got some of them, and everyone just presumed that I'd got the bumps during battle. After the first time you'd think there wouldn't have been a second time or a third or fourth.

Ma fed everyone. It was like a fucking soup kitchen half the time but that was Ma, she wouldn't let any kid go hungry, nor leave one out. Da always produced a huge box of fireworks, the aerial kind that no one else could get. At Halloween, our wall and our neighbours' walls would be lined with kids waiting to watch the fireworks display. It was the highlight of the neighbourhood, and kids sat on roofs also. The aerial display was like something out of Disneyland. and you could see it for miles around. Kids sat open-mouthed, as the skies lit up to a thunderous clap.

Skol, forty years on, still talks about it when we meet up. Skol is lucky to be alive because he was fucking about in a lift shaft and the lift came down and scraped him along the walls, pressing all sorts of iron bars and cables through his legs. Both legs were broken in twenty-two places, as well as two broken arms. He had been holding on with one arm as the lift came down and he ended up on top of the lift, stuck between floors. They had to get a specialist hoist crew from the docks to rescue him, so he was extremely lucky that he survived. So next, what did Skol do as a dare? He went down the seven hills on a bike, he'd only got the plaster of Paris taken off both arms but still had them on his legs. He flew down the seven hills like a bat out of hell, only stopping when he hit the wall at the bottom, breaking most of his fingers. Also Skol knocked about with his cousins, Geek and Tucker O'Halloran. You could hear Geek's big deep guffaw of a laugh halfway around the barrack. And when the Peelers fired at Geek, he just laughed and gave them the fingers. He was fucking fearless, his laughter drowned out the gunfire, and he was mental in the best possible way. Tucker on the other hand, was quiet and reserved, the complete opposite of Geek and he spoke very softly. You heard Geek before you saw him, and he was a very colourful character.

We roamed the docks at night looking for warehouses to break into. They were easy pickings, as the roofs were made of white roof tiles that you could break easily. We used to throw the roof tiles about like skimmers at one another. We even broke big bits of them over each other's heads, thinking it was funny. It turned out to be asbestos, but we wouldn't find out until years later how bad that stuff was for you.

We robbed a paint shop once when it was on fire and collapsing all round us at the same time. Skol and Geek kicked the wall down into the next shop, which was a wholesaler. Gallons of ketchup, pickles, cherries, corn beef and cooked ham, 3kg tins and we actually stole a wheelbarrow from the storeroom, so that we could ferry the stuff about, which further included banjos, boxes of drumsticks, boxes of *Perri* crisps, nuts, and we would go around the streets handing out mix-up bags to all the kids. The cooked ham was cut into big chunks and handed out. A slice of ham done nice and crispy in the pan, with a heap of spuds topped with butter and brown sauce, was a meal fit for a king. When a big meat lorry got hit, Da and all his cohorts went door-to-door, dishing out free meat parcels, butter, cheese, and these were your essentials.

Kids trained themselves in the art of combat and you'd set up assault courses, fucking dangerous ones. and some initiations to get into the gangs were extreme. I saw children piss and shit themselves due to electrocution by misusing the lamppost wire which hung loose with insulating tape around it. They still did it, no matter what. Tommy Gun did it the most, as it was the only thing that stopped his stuttering for a while, then he'd go again. Fuck knows what this form of electroshock treatment did to his brain. No wonder his hair fell out when he was still at school, and he always joked about how much he owed the electric board.

Roof Rack 'robics

I recall passing Speck Reynolds on the Antrim Road at Carlisle Circus and passed six or seven Prods, one pulled my coat over my head, and they were kicking the life out of me, my ribs were ready to give in under the strain of the heavy boots and I was winded. I pulled away and flung myself out onto the road. A car screeched to a standstill, I lifted my head off the ground and the bumper of the car was six inches away. I jumped up and climbed onto his roof rack and lay face down, I stuck my head down so I could see in the top of his windscreen.

'Drive, ya bastard,' I screamed, 'or I'll kick yer cunt in.'

The man sped off with all the guys in pursuit. He went onto the Westlink motorway, doing about sixty with me on the roof rack, hanging on for my life. He had to double back and dropped me off at the bottom of the New Lodge. I got home and went straight to bed.

'Who's that?' Ma shouted.

'Me,' I whimpered as my ribs were killing me.

I fell backwards down the second flight of stairs and woke up in hospital getting x-rayed. I had four badly bruised ribs. I couldn't sneeze, cough, fart or shit without yelling out in pain. Every time I laughed, I yelled, 'Arghhhh,' as it was like taking a heart attack. I wouldn't wish busted ribs on anyone, it was fucking woeful.

Da would rap the table with his knuckles, while at the same time he would rap me on the head and say, 'Yeah, sounds hollow,' and the two of us would laugh.

I'd scream in pain, and this went on for weeks. I'd nearly pass out with the pain, screaming and laughing simultaneously, and my family found this hilarious. I had just about recovered, and I went down to the bakery for a bap and other stuff. There was a grown man digging the face of a woman.

'Yo, what ta fuck are ya playin at?' I shouted.

'Mind yer own fuckin business,' he replied.

I grabbed him by the hair and pulled him off her and was kicking the head off him, when the woman jumped up.

'Leave him alone,' she screamed.

Her reaction stunned me; she then pulled a pair of tweezers out of her bag and stuck them in my eye. I screamed out in agony. I went up to the hospital to get the tweezers removed and my eye had closed over and looked like a big purple plum. I remember screaming at the guy when I was kicking him, 'Who ta fuck hits a woman?' I'd never seen Da lift his hand to Ma, not ever.

The doctor came into the room and explained how lucky I was, 'If it had gone in two or three millimetres higher, you would have lost the eye.' He stressed how fortunate I was again, and they kept me in for a day or so.

The nurse came in early morning. 'I take it, you've learned your lesson? No more plucking your eyebrows,' she quipped.

'Hardy Har Har,' I yelled.

My eye was the size of a big red apple, and looked as if it were about to explode.

'That is a serious infection,' the doctor said. 'We are going to have to lance it, in order to alleviate the pressure.'

'Holy fuck,' I yelled as I felt the warm fluid stream down my face. The smell of pus nearly made me sick.

The nurse had long black curly hair that sat in two big lumps on her shoulders.

'C'mere,' I said.

She leaned over.

'Y'know, yu're a double for Cher.'

'Really?' she said.

'Yeah, definitely,' I yelled and the two of us laughed.

Later that night, I was lying in bed and was in agony. It felt as though I'd a tumour in my head.

The doctor came into the room, took one look at me and said, 'We have to take you to the Royal Victoria Hospital.'

I arrived at the RVH in the back of an ambulance, writhing in pain and feeling as if my head was going to explode. An Indian doctor took one look at me and told me I'd a cyst in the back of my eyeball, and that he must release the pressure. He strapped me to a gurney and took out a bunch of wee silver wires. He bent them and then inserted them under my eyeball. He put four or five threads in before the abscess burst. It was like a balloon deflating and there was instant relief. The threads crackled, like the noise you hear when you stick a fork into a pickle, as he pushed and bent the wires around to the back of my eye. The pus ran down my cheeks.

'That abscess was the size of a golf ball. If it had burst inside you, you would have lost your eye.'

'Thank God,' I said, 'it felt as though I'd a tumour on my brain, fer fuck's sake.'

'You're very lucky, I was just about to knock off.'

I'd to wear a patch over my eye for ages until it healed and of course I'd hear, 'Arghh, Liam, lad, where's yer parrot?'

'Son, you do know that yu're the biggest drain on the National Health Service, don't ya?' Da said. 'It'd be cheaper ta put ya down.'

'Are ya fuckin finished, Da?'

'Aghhh,' he replied.

'Fuck yis all,' I shouted.

I went outside and called up to see Denise. We talked for ages. Gerry Rafferty's *Baker Street* played on the radio, followed by the Commodores' *Three Times a Lady*.

Denise held my head to her chest and said, 'What am I gonna do with ya? Ya really need ta take better care ah yerself.'

She ran her hand over all the lumps and bumps and scars on my head. I squinted up with one eye and she was crying.

'C'mon, please,' I said, 'I'm as sweet as a nut.'

'Ya coulda lost an eye, fer God's sake, an' ya say yu're sweet as a nut.'

'Pio,' I addressed her by her confirmation name. 'Y'know I'll always look after ya, an' won't let no harm come ta ya.'

'I know that, Liam, but you yerself need ta survive an' nat become a statistic ta be able ta do that.'

She put her lovely soft hand on the back of my neck and pulled my head to her shoulder. It was as if I'd been touched by an angel from heaven. All the pain and anger left me, as if a warm glow emitted from my entire being. Song after song played and an hour passed by and my head still rested on her shoulder.

'I'm gonna spend the resta my life with ya, ya do know that?' I said.

'I know, an' me with you.'

She'd knew I'd broke up a row, a man beating a woman, and that I shouted at him. 'Who Da fuck bates a woman? There's never a good enough reason fer a man ta bate down on a woman, ya coward, that's all y'are, a dirty yella coward.'

One of the girls in the shop was Denise's Ma's friend and she relayed what happened word for word about what I'd said. So even though I nearly lost an eye that day, my fate would be sealed for my future with

Denise. She'd seen the protector that I was and because she'd watched her Da beat her Ma at times, she knew I'd never be that kind of person.

'Whatever ya do, Denise, don't touch my ears.'

She laughed, 'Why?'

'Well after the accident, I've a kinda imbalance in my head an' when ya grab em, I black out an' go berserk. My mates used ta run up behind me an' smack me on both ears an' run. I'd be like a bull, I'd throw people over my head an' wreck the place, especially at bus stops. My mates would do it an' I'd slam people through the glass bus shelters. It's an inner ear problem. I've even chucked people through plate-glass windows in town, an' I wouldn't remember a thing, till my mates toul me. Ma brought me ta the hospital ta see a specialist an' he tested me, then he put both hands over my ears an' I headbutted him, knockin him out stone cold. I just ran outta the place screaming. Another Doctor came in an' Ma toul him that the Doctor just fainted. The doctor rang later on that day, an' I'd ta apologise ta him. Ya could be beating me with hammers, an' I wouldn't feel a thing when I'm in a rage. Well, not until afterwards, when I'd calmed down. I'd bitten the ear aff a guy, rammed my thumb into 'is eyes an' even tried to bite the throat outta a man. I was like an animal, a fucking animal. The only way I can explain it is, if ya gat two knitting needles an' rammed em inta each ear. That's the pain I'd be in, an' I'd black out.

Electricity would be pumping through my brain an' body; my blood would be boiling.'

'Jesus Christ, don't ya worry, I'll look after ya, an' I'm glad ya knocked that glue shite on the head, cos heaven knows how many brain cells it killed.'

'I think yu've ta have some ta start with,' I jested. 'This is a fuckin cesspit with hand-me-downs an' broken children who would carry the injustices they saw an' lived through fer the resta their lives. When ya think that death is better than life, day in, an' day out, an' hatred is the only driving force ya have, it's nat long before self-loathing comes a-knocking an' ya put up with all kindsa shit. Being treated fairly was a luxury we didn't have or expect. Denise, yu're the only pure an' wholesome thing or person I have in my life. I've never cried in fronta anyone, bar you, they'd ate y'up an' spit y'out, if ya showed any kinda weakness at all.'

'Denise, love,' her mother shouted, 'will ya come inta town with me ta gimme a hand?'

'Comin, Mum,' she shouted and pressed her cool hand on the back of my neck and kissed me on the cheek.

My spine went stiff as a poker and was tingling all over.

I walked down to the house and was told, 'Ma wants ta talk ta ya, she's up the stairs.'

'I haven't done anything, Ma, I was up in Denise's all day. I wasn't anywhere else, an I know nathin,' I said. 'Ma, Denise an' I need ta go get married.'

'Jesus, son, get out, get out, an' send yer Da up.'

'Okay,' I said, 'I was only sayin.'

I went down and told Da that Ma wanted to speak to him and off he went. Ten minutes later, Da called me up to the room. I walked in and Ma was crying.

'What's up, Ma?' I asked.

'Never ya mind, son,' Da said, 'an' is Denise pregnant?'

'Nah, fuckin hell, nah, we haven't even kissed yet.'

'Then why d'ya need ta get married?'

'Cos I'm in love, Ma.'

Da burst out laughing.

Ma burst out crying, 'In love, Billy, did you hear what he said?' Ma wiped her tears, 'Jesus, son, the thought ah you two nearly gimme a heart attack.' Ma started nervous laughing, 'I know he was dropped on his head a few times, but this is a cracker.'

The two of them were in hysterics.

'Fuckin dickheads,' I mumbled and went back down to the kitchen.

My sister, Tracey, came in, 'What's goin on up there?'

'Dunno, sis, I think the two ah them are on the drink or somethin.'

Ma was squealing with devilish laughter and Da was crying now.

'Them two nut jobs belong in Purdysburn,' I said to my sister.

Da stumbled out, holding onto the bannister at the top of the stairs.

'Yo, empty head,' he shouted, 'Ma wants a word.'

'I'm havin a cuppa tea, Da,' I shouted, 'be up in five, okay?'

'Okay, son.'

I sat shaking my head in the kitchen, wondering what all the fuss was about. I finished my tea and went to see Ma.

'Son, would ya do me a big favour?'

'Aye, anythin, Ma.'

'Bounce up onta the roof an' stand beside the aerial. I don't wanna miss the end ah the movie I'm watchin, at least that metal plate ah yers helps us get RTE One an' Two. Anytime ya come inta the livin room, the radio gets louder an' clearer.'

'No bother, Ma.'

So, I bounced up on the roof and stood beside the aerial while Da shouted-out directions.

'Left a bit, nigh backwards, try houlin onta the aerial. That's it, son, perfect.'

So, I stood there for thirty minutes or so and it was only when Ma shouted, 'Come down, son, yer Da's gonna put a couple ah knobs onta the side ah yer head, ta see if we can get Radio Luxemburg.'

Everyone was laughing at me. Ma and Da were in convulsions and clattered downstairs.

'Oh, favourite son, would ya like a wee cuppa tea?' Ma asked.

That was her way of apologizing for making a cunt out of me.

'No, Ma, yis two go an' sit in the livin room an' I'll make the tea. Ma, do y'wanna wee biscuit?'

Da shouted, 'Does a bear shit in the woods?'

And the two of them started laughing again.

'Does a bear shite in the woods? Do fat babies fart?' I whispered, as I'd heard them all that many times before.

'Oh, an' has the Queen any soldiers?'

Any wonder that there's no hope fer me? I thought to myself, *cos em two are mad.*

I made the tea and balance was once again restored in the Kelly household.

Da came into the kitchen, 'Here, son, bring em biscuits inta yer Ma. I'm just gonna sit an' read the paper.'

I sat with Ma, and we supped away at our tea. I looked at Ma's fine bone China cup, thick with tanning stains. 'Oh, he thinks it adds flavour, Ma, it almost looks like brown fur.'

'I know, son. Sure, I met yer Da when he used ta go ta school in 'is bare feet, he was that poor.'

'Did ya go ta school in yer bare feet?' I shouted.

He laughed, 'Don't listen ta her son, it was the other way about.'

'Lies,' Ma shouted, 'an' what're ya doin in there?'

'I'm tryin ta read the papers.'

'More lies, yu're lookin at the deaths ta see if anyone left y'anythin, ya miserable fucker ye.'

'Here, Ma, put yer feet up,' and I grabbed a wee footstool for her.

'Oh, thank ya, favourite son.'

'Ma, that doesn't work. Sure, ya say that ta us all.'

I grabbed a wee cushion and placed it on top of the wee stool.

'Ahh,' she sighed as she wriggled her toes. I set Ma's bedroom slippers beside the chair.

'Y'know, son, we're only sleggin an' all.'

'I know, Ma, but it's continuous. Even when Skol Largey or Curly Donnelly calls fer me, ya shout after me, come you home if it's startin ta rain, cos lightnin might 'it that metal plate in yer head.'

'Well, it's true,'

'I know, Ma, but ya don't have ta say it in front of my mates.'

Da called out, 'Son, ya don't have a metal plate.'

'Fuck up, you,' Ma shouted.

'Are ya fuckin serious? Ma, that's why I thought I'm fuckin simple.'

'Son, I know yer big an' ugly enough ta take care ah yerself an' I'm just preparin ya, cos people can be so cruel, especially if they don't know ya. Why don't y'invite Denise down fer a wee bite?'

'Ma,' I screamed, 'it ain't gonna happen. Fuck's sake, I'll never see her again, by the time yu're finished with her.'

'Son, I'll be on my best behaviour.'

'No fuckin way, Ma. Y'know her family are all stickies, an' yu'll just have ta say somethin. I know how ya work, Ma, an' it's nat happenin. I'm away down ta Artillery fer a few games ah pool, if anybody's lookin me. Well, except fer the Peelers.'

'Why what've ya done, son?'

'Nathin, Ma, I'm just sayin.'

I went out the front door and got halfway down the street, when I heard Da shouting.

'Yo, numb nuts, stay outta trouble, d'ya hear me?'

People stared over at me but I ignored them and my Da as well. I played a few games of pool and was sitting chilling like a villain when I spied the cops talking to Pat Henry, one of the youth leaders. I, along with three others, headed out the fire exit door that led to the back of the wee row of shops. I ran up the steps and climbed on top of the maisonettes' roof and lay flat on my belly. I could see the cops at my house, and a foot patrol had taken up position, watching the Peelers backs. I lay frozen, wrecking my brain. What had I done? It was two in the morning, and I still lay there, and it was now raining, and I was frozen to the bone and shivering. The coast was finally clear, I dropped down the wall and went into the house, and ran into the kitchen to put the kettle on.

Ma came into the kitchen, 'What've ya done nigh, son?'

'Nathin, Ma,' I eventually got the words out, as my teeth were nearly breaking, because they were rattling so much. 'Ma, sure I was in the house fer weeks with my ribs, fuck's sake, I could hardly breathe.'

'Well, yu've definitely done somethin, cos they were goin mad lookin ya.'

'Aye, they'll have ta catch me first,' I quipped. 'Fuck it, Ma, I'm goin back down ta Keady.'

'Son, it doesn't matter where ya go, trouble just seems ta find ya.'

'Aye, Ma, an innocent victim, I am.'

'Sounds like a line from a country song,' Ma said, and we both laughed. 'An' what're ya gonna tell Denise this time?'

'Dunno, Ma. It's all about stayin alive long enough ta get outta this fuckin place.'

'Go an' get yer head down an' we'll talk themarra.' Ma said.

'Okay, Ma, night, night.'

I could barely get my legs to move, they were that cold. I slid between the damp sheets, and I lay for ages, shivering and rattling uncontrollably. I took my socks off and put them on my hands so I could rub them together for some heat, before falling asleep. My brother, Kieran, said I only put the socks on my hands to stop myself playing with my balls but what did he know?

Next morning, I came downstairs and put the kettle on and made a pot of tea. I opened the front door, and it was a real peasouper, you couldn't see your hand in front of your face. I heard the foghorn *PARRRP* from the docks. I had a mug of tea in one hand and with the other I was trying to swirl the fog in front of me. I turned to close the door and I was yanked backwards into the fog. I felt the heavy boots kicking at me until I was dragged by the neck into the back of a Peeler jeep and brought down to North Queen Street Police station.

'You're being charged with kidnapping.'

'I'm sayin nathin, nat one fuckin word, till I see my solicitor!' I shouted.

It was 11.30am, by the time my solicitor arrived. He came to where they were holding me and told me that I was getting done with disturbing the peace, hijacking and kidnapping. He said that the police had me hijacking a car then forcing the owner to drive with me on the roof rack.

'So, I kidnapped him, he was in the car, and I was on the roof? It's a fucking joke, that's what it is.'

They had video footage of me getting on the roof-rack and shouting at the driver but there was no footage of me getting my head kicked in by the Prods.

It was four-thirty before I got out of the police station.

'Ma, it's a joke,' I yelled.

Da said, 'Son, ya just disappeared an' left the front door lyin wide open.'

'It's cos I made threats ta kill the taxi driver that they're sayin it's aggravated kidnappin. Fuckin bastards, the lotta em. Anyone who helps em cunts should be taken away an' shot. Aye, sure, yer woman from one ah the backstreets who ended up fuckin aff with a British solider, they burnt her house ta the ground. Aye, pity em cunts weren't still in it. Fuck me, Ma, I thought I was gettin kidnapped by aliens this mornin, my feet didn't even touch the ground. I couldn't see a thing, just felt the boots, an' they shouted ya Fenian cunt in their English accents.'

'Oh, I dunno about aliens, son, but yu're definitely a moon cat.'

'Hardy Har Har. Da, yu're a fuckin geg. I'll never ferget the driver's face or his green Vauxhall Viva. I'll kill that cunt, if I see him again.'

'Sometimes, yu're better aff lettin sleepin dogs lie,' Da said.

Over the Top

I got the bus to Keady and strolled into Orla's café. She leapt over the counter and nearly squeezed me to death, 'Ah, we missed ya so much.'

I almost had to beat her off me with a stick.

'Oh, Liam, everyone's bin askin about ya. Ah course, we know nathin, ya sly dog, ya.'

I told her everything, why the Peelers were looking for me and the roof rack incident, where I was spitting flies out of my mouth, flying down the motorway at sixty.

'I'll get us a pot ah tea,' Orla said.

In no time, we were joking about as usual.

'An' how's yer ribs?'

'So, so, y'know what I say: if it doesn't kill ya, it'll make ya stronger.'

'I see yu've added a few more scars ta the collection.'

'Aye, just a couple.'

'Well, Liam. I think a few war wounds on a guy make him all the more attractive.'

'Honestly, Orla, do ya really mean that?'

'Nah, I'm only sleggin.'

'Ya fuckin witch, I thought y'were serious.'

'I am, I am, just pullin yer leg.'

'Well, as long as that's all yer pullin.'

'Liam Kelly, I'm shocked,' Orla screamed. 'Nah, I'm only sleggin. God, we never stop talkin about ya.'

I gave her a hand to clean up, after she closed the bakery, and we retired to the flat. Mícheál came bursting through the door with his arms outstretched. Orla jumped up instantly and ran to him, he ran past her and hugged me. He turned right away and said, 'Only sleggin,' and Orla and him hugged and kissed.

'It's all yer fault, Liam.' Orla said.

'What is?'

'Him, he gets on just like ya nigh, yu've ruined him. He says whatever he wants then says, Oops, did I say that out loud?' Just like you do. It's like livin with ya, fer fuck's sake.'

Mícheál looked at Orla and drummed his fingers on his chin, 'Lemme see, lemme see,' he said and laughed.

'Look, see what I mean? He's gat all yer foibles.'

'Oh, I don't believe in God,' I said.

'What d'ya mean?'

'I don't believe in God. Oh, foibles, I thought ya said boibles.'

We all laughed hysterically.

'Boibles, ya sound like a Dublin knacker. Oh fuck, did I say that out loud?' Mícheál said.

Orla smacked herself on the forehead, 'D'ya see? Look what I've ta put up with, twenty-four-seven.'

Mícheál and I were still laughing, the two of us now were drumming our fingers on our chins and looking up to the ceiling and saying, 'Lemme see now, lemme see.'

A car horn beeped outside. Mícheál quipped, 'Fuck, is that yer taxi already? Fuck, did I say that out loud?'

Mícheál grabbed me and nearly squeezed the shit out of me.

'How's yer wee Ma?'

'Ah, she's fine. Still as mad as ever, fuck's sake. She'd me standin on our roof, holdin onta the TV aerial, cos she toul me the metal plate in my head helps get better reception. Ahh, sure, I'm a stupid cunt. She asked Da ta screw a couple ah knobs on my metal plate ta tune in ta Radio Luxemburg. Holy fuck, is it any wonder I'm back here?'

'How's the wee smilin assassin?'

'Who, Da? Yep, he's doin okay.'

'Y'know yu're the only one who turns dickhead over there inta a bigger dickhead.' Orla said.

'Referee,' Mícheál said, 'please.'

And he showed Orla the red card, which he produced from his pocket.

'D'ya mind? Nah, but I babysit,' I quipped and high-fived Mícheál. 'Fuck. Did I say that out loud? I'm so sorry, Orla.'

'Aghh,' Orla breathed a sigh.

'I've really missed this, y'know. Ma said the lift doesn't go ta the top floor, when it comes ta me, but I love her ta bits, an' I wouldn't let anyone say a bad word against her. She's a wee fuckin workhorse.'

'We're goin on a wee road-trip, so we are,' Mícheál said. 'Eoin's just waitin on the nod. This's gonna be a geg. Big L on tour.'

'We should sell tickets, fer fuck's sake,' I said.

'No messin, this's a serious mission an' we'll be on the road till it's done. Hope we get the green light fer this one. Eoin's at the green barn, so he is, so this'll come from the very top.'

'Young Billy Boy, we'll have a laugh an' a half,' I interrupted. 'What about Billy Boy an' the Prowlers? Does that sound okay? Or Billy Boy an' the Dingbats…'

'Will ya fuck up? We're nat a band goin on the road. Discretion an' hidin in plain sight. that's what we'll be doin, an' yu'll need a strong stomach.'

'That's sweet. Sure, my Ma says my stomach's like a cesspit. Well, that's what she says when I fart. Dodododo, dodododo, yu're now enterin the Twilight Zone, please fasten yer seatbelts an' remove any sharp objects from yer pockets, as we delve into the mind of a psychopath,' I said in a deep mysterious voice.

We all looked at each other in total silence for a few seconds then laughed out loud.

'Jesus, I was shittin myself there,' Orla said.

Later that evening I was driven to a barn, where we changed cars. I was blindfolded and taken to a warehouse, where Eoin was waiting. He greeted me with open arms.

'Big man, big man, we fuckin missed ya.'

'Well, I'm here fer the beer,' I said.

Eoin raised one side of his mouth and sang, '*We're all goin on a summer holiday. No more workin fer a week or two.*'

'Ya sound fuck all like him.'

'Who?' He asked, puzzled.

'Oh, the man with the quiff. Cliff an' his three lads. Cliff Richard an' the Shads.'

'I'm sure, back in the day, when there was no TV, just radio, I'm sure he was big…'

Mícheál intervened, 'Ladies and gentlemen, we have ta stay focused, an' there's no turnin back.'

We pulled into a wee lane in the countryside and parked up. We walked behind an old deserted cottage, there was a bright yellow van with blue writing on the side which read, "British Telecom", it was bigger than a minibus and was more like a small lorry. There were ladders on the roof, and dark blue overalls and jackets on the front seat. We got changed into our uniforms and put our clothes in the car that we arrived in. A hooded man stepped out of the bushes and gave Eoin a piece of paper which he read, and then burned. The hooded man sank back into the background and disappeared.

'That's the green light, lad,' Eoin said.

Mícheál and myself got into the lorry. Eoin lifted the bonnet and checked the oil and shit before he got in.

'Jesus, Liam, did ya bring a passport? Cos we're goin ta Crossmaglen first.'

'Nah, I don't even have one.'

'Don't fuckin listen ta him,' Mícheál said.

'An' ya said no messin about. Oh, I see it nigh, ya funny cunt,' I mumbled.

We had only set off a few hours, and then we stopped and were sitting at a picnic table eating fish suppers with curry sauce on top.

'Where's the peas?'

'Yu're nat gettin any peas, ya smell bad enough, fer fuck's sake.'

'I didn't get peas anyhows.'

'I love peas an' pickles with my fish supper.'

'Just fuck up an' ate the fuckin things. *I'm just sayin*,' Mícheál mimicked me. 'Did ya bring a shovel, at least?'

'What fer?'

'Ta shovel up all the shite yer talkin,' Mícheál said.

'Don't worry there's shovels in the lorry.' Eoin said.

'Well, I'm left-handed, d'ya have a left-handed shovel?' I said.

'Nah, nah, dickhead, yu're a geg,' Eoin said.

We got back into the lorry, and I dropped one, the two of them were nearly sick, and gagging out the window.

'That's smells like Nazi nerve gas...'

ABOUT THE AUTHOR

Liam Kelly was born in Belfast in 1965 and grew up on the New Lodge Road, north Belfast. Liam was accidentally knocked down in 1973 and because of this has no early childhood memories. He woke up after a three-month coma in 1974 and the only person he recognised was his granny. When he got out of hospital, he stayed with his aunt in Glengormley for ten months. On returning home, he experienced a baptism of fire when he walked out his parents' front door and into the middle of a full-scale riot on the streets of Belfast. At nine years of age, Liam was convinced he was a giant, due to having to return to Primary One at school in order to learn to read and write again.

The troubles profoundly impacted Liam's early childhood experiences and the levels of rage seemed all-encompassing, leading him to join the Merchant Navy in 1980, another (book) major turning point in his young life. Liam married his childhood sweetheart, Denise, and they had two children, Lia-Marie and Chei. Liam credits Denise as his saving grace, she saw something inside him that nobody else could see. Denise brought these qualities to the forefront and turned him into a loving husband and father. Sadly, Denise died in 2017 from cancer and her loss profoundly affected Liam's mental health.

In July 2018 Liam was arrested and spent 20 months in custody where he began writing poetry and stories. He credits Prison Arts Foundation (PAF) with guiding him on this path as a writer and jokes about never having read a book until he went to prison. Liam is an award-winning writer and poet, receiving Koestler Arts awards for his writing, as well as prizes at the prestigious Listowel Writers Week. His *Memoirs of a Belfast Boy* won a Silver Koestler Award 2024. His writings have been published in *Time In* magazine and *Connect* Newsletter. A regular patron at PAF's community hub, Liam has recited and exhibited his poetry at PAF's yearly art exhibition in Belfast, TenX9 and the Black Box.

NVTV Mary Ann Quigley "My Parlour" interview with Liam Kelly.

Printed in Great Britain
by Amazon